African Philosophy

D0947895

African Systems of Thought

General Editors
Charles S. Bird
Ivan Karp

Contributing Editors
Thomas O. Beidelman
James Fernandez
Luc de Heusch
John Middleton
Victor Turner
Roy Willis

African Philosophy

Myth and Reality

SECOND EDITION

Paulin J. Hountondji

Translated by Henri Evans
with the collaboration of Jonathan Rée

Introduction by Abiola Irele

INDIANA UNIVERSITY PRESS
Bloomington and Indianapolis

First published in French 1976
French edition copyright 1976 by François Maspero, Paris

First published in English 1983
English edition copyright 1983 by Paulin J. Hountondji
Introduction copyright 1983 by Abiola Irele
Translation copyright Hutchinson & Co. (Publishers) Ltd
Preface to the second edition copyright © 1996 by Paulin J. Hountondji

The paper used in this publication meets the minimum
requirements of American National Standard for Information
Sciences—Permanence of Paper for Printed Library
Materials, ANSI Z39.48-1984.

Manufactured in the United States of America

Library of Congress Cataloging-in-Publication Data

Hountondji, Paulin J., date
    [Sur la philosophie africaine. English]
    African philosophy : myth and reality / Paulin J. Hountondji ;
translated by Henri Evans with the collaboration of Jonathan Rée ;
introduction by Abiola Irele. — 2nd ed.
       p.   cm. — (African systems of thought)
    Includes bibliographical references and index.
    ISBN 0-253-33229-X (cl : alk. paper). — ISBN 0-253-21096-8
(pa : alk. paper)
    1. Philosophy, African. I. Title. II. Series.
B5305.H6813   1996
199'.6—dc20   96-12249

1 2 3 4 5 01 00 99 98 97 96

Contents

Preface to the second edition   vii

Introduction by Abiola Irele   7

Part One: Arguments

1   An alienated literature   33

2   History of a myth   47

3   African philosophy, myth and reality   55

4   Philosophy and its revolutions   71

Part Two: Analyses

5   An African philosopher in Germany in the eighteenth
    century: Anton-Wilhelm Amo   111

6   The end of 'Nkrumaism' and the (re)birth of Nkrumah   131

7   The idea of philosophy in Nkrumah's *Consciencism*   141

8   True and false pluralism   156

Postscript   170

Notes and references   184

Index   219

Preface to the second edition

To the memory of Odera Oruka

African Philosophy: Myth and Reality originally appeared in French twenty years ago; the earliest essay in the collection—the first chapter of this book—dates from 1969. The intellectual environment has changed greatly in the ensuing years, during which *African Philosophy* has provoked lively debate.

Within the limits of this preface it would be impossible to respond to all the comments and criticisms it has occasioned. I will therefore save for a future occasion a full explication of how I understand the ideas which I defended at that time and why I still defend them in their essentials. On such an occasion, I will attempt to clarify the premises, tacit or explicit, the demands, and the expectations that, directly or indirectly, motivated the critique of ethnophilosophy presented in *African Philosophy.*

I will also elaborate on what this critique owes to my own philosophical background, especially to my long acquaintance with philosophies of consciousness. In this connection I will explain my attachment to a certain idea of philosophy which, since Plato, demands that it be *episteme* rather than *doxa,* science rather than opinion; to Husserl, who identifies in a very technical manner some of the intellectual devices and methods that allow philosophy to become "a rigorous science"; to Descartes's *cogito;* and to all doctrines that value intellectual responsibility and demand that each affirmation be sustained by a proof or a rational justification.

I will discuss what idea of Africa and her destiny, what ambition, what vision of the continent's future, led me to reject the theoretical model of ethnophilosophy as a facile and unacceptable solution. I will explain the role played by the works of Césaire and Fanon, by a certain understanding of Marx (highly influenced, it is true, by Althusser's approach), and by the militant commitment within the democratic movement in Dahomey and in Africa as a whole in shaping this vision. I will need to explain how this criticism of ethnophilosophy broadened into a critique of intellectual self-imprisonment in general, a critique of the scientific and technological relations of production on a world scale, and finally, a sociology of knowledge in countries of the periphery, entailing an increasing interest in the anthropology of knowledge and issues in the politics of science.[1]

In this preface, however, I will limit myself to an effort at clearing up some of the most common misunderstandings regarding the questions raised in the book and its overall conceptual framework.

That *African Philosophy* stimulated such a heated debate was probably due to the highly sensitive nature of the topic. The themes of the book did not concern professional philosophers alone: they also related to ideological and political questions and to cultural issues in the broadest sense. By identifying ethnophilosophy as a defined thought-pattern and a permanent temptation of Africanist discourse, *African Philosophy* was a warning, an invitation to exorcise demons too often ignored or hidden. As the Senegalese philosopher Mamoussé Diagne put it, it was, therefore, a sort of psychoanalysis (Diagne 1976). Readers may have welcomed the book's firm stand against intellectual self-imprisonment and unanimism, its insistence on the right to the universal, and its assertion that all cultures, based on their own preoccupations and concerns, have a vocation to invent not only locally viable solutions but also concepts whose validity transcends regional boundaries.

Such an agenda was bound to provoke widespread criticism. Yet I am grateful to most of my critics for prompting me to clarify certain ambiguities, refine some notions, and occasionally, deepen the analysis. Remarkably, even when these criticisms appeared to be purely theoretical, they generally carried political implications. Conversely, even when political criticisms resorted to amalgam and denigration instead of honest refutation, they inevitably referred back to theoretical questions that needed to be identified and examined.

The very first sentence of the first essay in *African Philosophy* has given rise to sharp controversy: "By 'African philosophy' I mean a set of texts, specifically the set of texts written by Africans and described as philosophical by their authors themselves."

At least three points have been made against what was perceived by many readers as a "definition" of African philosophy. First, the nationality or geographic origin of the authors is not a sufficient condition for Africanness. It has been suggested that something more is needed: dedication to "the African cause" (Yai 1977). Second, an author's own intention and self-assessment is not sufficient reason for any work to be labeled as philosophical. Third, and this is the strongest objection, the mention of writing amounts to restricting, quite arbitrarily, the forms of philosophical expression and overlooks the extraordinary richness of oral literature.

Some years ago, in reply to this triple criticism, I pointed out the polemical thrust of the incriminating sentence. Though it had the formal structure of a definition, this prefatory declaration was not meant as a definition. It should be read as a counterassertion that was far more important for what it rejected than for its positive content. It aimed at establishing, against the dominant ethnological conception, this very simple equation: African philosophy equals African philosophical literature. That is, the whole of philosophical texts produced by Africans. Rather than a definition, this is "still an external characterization of the object to be defined," with a view to indicating the only possible place where it is likely to be found (Hountondji 1981, 49).

By completely putting aside the idea of an implicit, silent, latent philosophy, I meant to value discourse and the history of discourse as being the only possible place where philosophy appears. Writing, at this stage, did not really matter. Writing was still to me a modality of the explicit. The possibility of an oral philosophical literature (a philosophical "orature") was not excluded. It is for this reason that I cited Griaule's *Conversations with Ogotemmeli,* a few pages later, as a more valuable contribution than Tempels's *Bantu Philosophy.* The French anthropologist had chosen to transcribe the words of *one* sage among many. He showed the possibility of a long-term project which would consist of a systematic transcription of such speeches, at least as a starting point of a critical discussion—what my Kenyan colleague the late Odera Oruka[2] would later call "philosophical sagacity"—rather than as a reconstruction of implicit philosophy behind the habits and customs of the host society through a lot of non-verifiable hypotheses which always amount to overinterpreting the facts (Hountondji 1976, 31; Griaule 1965; Oruka 1983, 1990).

I returned to this question in the fourth essay and, after comparing the effects of the written and the spoken word, I finally admitted the privilege of writing and its absolute necessity for the development of critical philosophy and scientific culture as a whole. By the same token, I came to qualify my appreciation of Griaule's approach.

The problem, indeed, was no longer the same. The perspective in chapter four is not merely descriptive. The preoccupation is practical: What does one do today? Should we, in order to remain ourselves, renounce writing and pretend to ignore what we have long known, deceive ourselves and others as we continue to proclaim the superiority of our oral cultures, write lengthy indictments against writing, in articles which, by their very existence refute in practice what they pretend to say? Or should we take note of the real process of our thinking today, and the role of writing in the development of all research, including research on oral cultures?

I totally agree with Anthony Appiah when he states, "Oral traditions have a habit of transmitting only consensus, the accepted view: those who are in intellectual rebellion (and European anthropologists and missionaries have met plenty of these) often have to begin in each generation all over again" (Appiah 1992, 92). *African Philosophy* did not say otherwise. For all that, it did not deny the importance of oral literature, as some critics understood; neither did it attempt to minimize the heritage of traditional beliefs. The Postscript was, in this regard, quite clear, and I am grateful to Lansana Keita for pointing it out (Keita 1985, 113).

One can imagine, however, the ideological context, the extraordinary climate of suspicion, that for many years sustained such debate. A Beninese critic even found the word to describe what he, following many others, considered an unforgivable transgression: "the fetishism of writing" (Dossou 1994). One should have realized by now, nevertheless, that nowhere in *African Philosophy* is writing valued for its own sake; neither is "orature" considered intrinsically inferior.

Having said this, what is it to be an African? Is it belonging to a race, in this case the black race, if we decide to restrict ourselves to black Africa? Should one, to be an African, share in a common culture and adhere to the value system or systems conveyed by this culture? Must one profess a given religious or political credo?

Mudimbe and Appiah, as is well known, brilliantly dealt with such questions not long ago (Mudimbe 1988, Appiah 1992). My point of view was similar. One had to free the horizon, reject any definition of an African that would, by implication, restrict or confine him or her in a conceptual, ideological, religious, or political stranglehold and reinforce the illusory belief that some inexorable fate weighs him or her down forever. Frantz Fanon made a strong statement in this regard: "Il ne faut pas essayer de fixer l'homme, puisque son destin est d'être lâché"/"One should not try to restrict a human being, since his fate is to be set loose" (Fanon 1952, 187).

To acknowledge Africans' freedom of thought, one had to get rid of all sorts of essentialist and particularist doctrines born of a hundred years of

Africanism. This is the meaning of the famous "geographical criterion" which, according to one of my harshest critics, would allow me to "escape the debate on the content of African philosophy" and "lead to deception" (Yai 1977).

I addressed this criticism in the book itself, as Appiah quite rightly pointed out (Appiah 1992, 90). My purpose was to demythologize the concept of Africa by bringing it back to its primary meaning, to the minimal significance that had been, for years, overloaded by gluttonous ideological speculation. I am not bothered, therefore, by seeing my remarks caricatured in the following way: "Hountondji's definition is inadequate in that [. . .] anyone who has specialized in Spinoza, Kant, or Wittgenstein, provided he was born in Africa, is a great African philosopher" (Yai 1977).

I have never assumed that such a person should necessarily be a *great* African philosopher, but on the other hand, I see no reason why she or he should *a priori* be denied being a philosopher and being an African. The realm of the thinkable is immense. Why should we exclude the works of Western philosophers or forbid Africans to appropriate them while Westerners still have the right to extend their curiosity to all continents and cultures without renouncing or losing their identity?

"Is Africa [. . .] nothing but a geographical concept, or is it rather a political and cultural reality?" (Yai 1977). The question is disturbing as long as we continue to confuse concept and reality. As if the concept of dog could bark! As if it were not always necessary to distinguish between denotation and connotation, between what a concept designates and what it means, as if there were not, within connotation itself, different levels of meaning that allow multiple determinations, from the most simple to the most complex!

I have no difficulty admitting that the concept of Africa is first of all a geographic concept in that it designates a continent. Second, it lends itself to other determinations as a political, cultural, or even anthropological and religious concept, among a thousand other possible determinations. We should know what words primarily mean and not confuse levels of discourse.

I subsequently returned to this issue in a number of articles. Today the concept of Africa is overdetermined. It needs to be reduced—relieved of all those adventitious connotations that confuse it—and restored to its primal simplicity in order to reveal, by contrast, the extreme complexity of the intellectual, cultural, political, economic, and social life of the continent. Then we can truly appreciate the internal dynamisms, imbalances, and tensions, and assess the issues at stake:

There was, therefore, need to start by *demystifying* Africanity, by reducing it to a *fact*—simply the *fact* and, in itself, perfectly neutral, of belonging to Africa—by removing the mystic halo of values arbitrarily grafted upon this fact by ideologists of African identity. There was need, in order to deal with the complexity of our history, to bring back the scene of that history to its original simplicity; in order to deal with the richness of African traditions, there was need to *impoverish* resolutely the concept of Africa, to *free* it from all connotations, ethical, religious, philosophical, political, etc., loaded on it by a long anthropological tradition, the most evident effect of which was to close the horizon, to close history prematurely. (Hountondji 1987, 7)

I now come to the third difficulty: the African philosopher would be a self-proclaimed philosopher! My inaugural statement, I must confess, amounted, strictly speaking, to begging the question: How can one admit, in fact, that to be a philosopher it is enough to believe or say that one is so? I would probably *not* use the same words today. Much controversy would have been spared if I had written more cautiously, "By 'African philosophy' I mean the set of philosophical texts produced (whether orally or in writing) by Africans."

My opening sentence did not, in fact, have a deeper meaning. It was not intended to settle the question: On what conditions is a text philosophical? I intended only to pose, for reasons of clarity, two unavoidable questions before testing the solidity of the proposed answer:

1 What is the mode of existence of philosophy? *Answer:* That of a text or set of texts, that of a piece or pieces of explicit discourse.
2 What does "African" mean in the phrase "African philosophy"? *Answer:* Something African is something made by Africans.

One had to start somewhere. Why not from here? I did not try to escape, as a critic wrote, the debate on the content, but I had to postpone it. D. A. Masolo understood the point: the nature of philosophy as a specific kind of discourse is not dealt with until chapter four of the book. Here, I examined the real history of what is commonly known as philosophy in the international university tradition, and confronted philosophy in this sense with other disciplines and forms of discourse to assess their relations (Masolo 1994, 200–202).

Such an assessment is always a risk. Following the teaching of Althusser, I ventured to consider the theory of science the hard core, the heart, the moving wheel of philosophy. No doubt this view of philosophy somehow restricted the subject and amounted, as some colleagues said, to a sort of "epistemologism." Moreover, by the time I decided to make a book out of a selection of these articles, Althusser had published his *Elements of Self-Criticism,* where, among other things, he renounced what he considered an error in his own previous work—theoreticism—and suggested a new definition of philosophy: though still superficially a theory of science, philosophy would be, in the last analysis, "class struggle within theory" (Althusser 1974)!

I was not distressed that Althusser changed his mind. I just mentioned the fact in a note, while postponing the necessary revisiting of my own views on philosophy. I knew that this self-criticism was in part an outgrowth of the political upheaval caused by the May 1968 student riots in France and the bitter feeling among some of Althusser's followers that his thought had left them totally unprepared (e.g., Rancière 1974). I took the matter seriously and was conscious that, whether in France or elsewhere, one definitely cannot overlook the demand that philosophy should, directly or indirectly, enable its practitioners to understand better the issues at stake on the political, economic, and social battlefields, and thereby contribute to changing the world. However, I could not admit that philosophy should, on these grounds, be reduced to a web of slogans or a mere duplication of ideology. Althusser's new views on philosophy therefore raised at least one question: What is the specificity of philosophy, understood as "class struggle within theory," compared to other forms or manifestations of class struggle?

Despite Althusser's self-criticism, I insisted in *African Philosophy* on the necessity of conceptual rigor, and the importance of the theory of science as a core discipline or sub-discipline of philosophy. According to some critics, this entailed a form of scientism. However, scientism, strictly speaking, makes science an absolute, overestimates its power, and restricts itself to scientific data without taking into account the influence of the paradigms defining the current state of knowledge or the complex links which tie knowledge to the conditions of its production. Nothing of the kind takes place in *African Philosophy.* Instead, the book develops a critique of intellectual and scientific dependence. It acknowledges the "immense movement towards the acquisition of scientific knowledge that is now developing on the continent" (107). It shows "how this process of acquiring the international scientific heritage conditions the actualization and, as it were, the reappropriation of our pre-colonial knowledge" (107). That is quite different from overestimating science, let alone the existing science, which is entirely managed and controlled by the West. Instead, *African Philosophy* pleads for renewed autonomy and Africa's own effort to take up its intellectual destiny. I am grateful to Abiola Irele for his sharp perception of this point: the real concern, in the book, is "for the improvement of the quality of life on our continent [. . .], a concern of a very practical order," which makes "the technical and theoretical debate about African philosophy [. . .] turn, in reality, most essentially upon the question of what intellectual direction to give, in this day and age, to a continent beset by a multitude of problems" (30).

My reluctance to treat philosophy as a duplication of politics was unacceptable to many, especially those of a certain leftist orientation. I took exception, in the book, to the theoretical inconsistencies and dead-locks of Nkrumah's *Consciencism;* I rejected the conception of philoso-phy as an ideological comment on politics. The only possible effect of such a redundant discourse would be, I argued, to confuse the issues and obscure the political goals themselves. As a consequence, people who could have fought for these goals would be reluctant to accept the ideological credo associated with them. This would shrink the social basis for action at a time that required the widest possible alliances.

I therefore resisted attempts to absorb philosophy into politics. I denounced ideologism, which to my eyes was based on the "metaphysi-cal illusion," the idea of a "metaphysical depth of the political." I refused "the total politicization of philosophical discourse." I advocated, instead, "the autonomy of the political" and, by implication, the autonomy and specificity of philosophy. In my view, this liberation of philosophy was a pre-condition for the development of a critical "theory of politics" as part and parcel of philosophy—a theory devoted, though not exclusively, to "analyzing the real functioning of ideologies and identifying the forms, the modalities and the multiple sources of political mystification" (see Postscript, in this volume).

Readers may find it curious that these views were subject to strong attack by the Communist Party of Dahomey (PCD), an underground group of activists who, it must be said, fought with conviction against General Kerekou's Marxist military dictatorship. In the *Introduction to Economic and Social Realities in Dahomey,* a booklet meant to be the first of a series of studies, the Central Committee of the PCD, after quoting extensively from Marx, Engels, Lenin, and Stalin, comes down to the political and social situation in Benin, and in this context, submits a number of writings by local "careerist intellectuals" [*sic*] to sharp criticism in order to "protect the purity of the Marxist-Leninist science, whose flag [the Party] intends to raise high in the country" (PCD 1979,

60). In this connection, *African Philosophy* receives special treatment. First, the book is favorably mentioned as a good refutation of all missionaries and ideologists who, "while denouncing the cruelties and atrocities of colonization, in fact tried to theorize and promote imperialist domination in Africa" (PCD 1979, 47). On the other hand, *African Philosophy* is severely reproached for eclecticism, idealism, lack of proletarian conscience, lack of party spirit, underestimation of the Marxist materialist philosophy which (nowhere in the book) is acknowledged to represent "a big jump forward in the history of human thought." The book is criticized for not dealing with economic and social realities in Africa or Benin. The author, it is said, "vilifies the great Stalin and still pretends to be Marxist. He invites an anarchist and petty-bourgeois debate from which would emerge 'constantly fleeting truths'. [. . .] P. Hountondji's philosophy, insofar as it makes no room for the proletarian ideology, is, in the last analysis, idealistic and reactionary. There is so much to say about the bewildering character of this book [. . .]. Paulin Hountondji's philosophical thought [. . .] is the synthesis of the ideology of the radical petty-bourgeoisie which dominated the democratic movement in our country from 1967 to 1976" (PCD 1979, 60–63).

Given its dogmatic—not to say catechistic—flavor, this criticism would not be worth mentioning if it were not the barest, the most simplistic and straightforward expression of a type of argument which, in various guises, occurred often in other criticisms. My only surprise was to read that I pretended to be Marxist. I do not remember ever having made such a claim. What I said was that instead of swallowing Marxism in little pills, instead of consuming Marxist ideology as a dogma, as a closed system responding to all imaginable questions, it was better to promote full intellectual responsibility in a Marxist theoretical tradition in Africa. In light of the heuristic principles forged by Marx, and insofar as these principles help to clarify the issues, we should proceed to "the concrete analysis of concrete situations" and avoid walling ourselves up in a given system. This was definitely an anti-dogmatic position and another way of calling for a critical appropriation of existing theoretical traditions by Africans. It was unacceptable to both dogmatic Marxists and dogmatic anti-Marxists.[3]

This should be kept in mind when one considers some of the politically oriented criticisms leveled against *African Philosophy*. For instance, some commentators viewed the distinction between a broader and a narrower sense, a debased and a more rigorous use of the word "philosophy"—in fact an elementary, even commonplace distinction—

as a subtle means to defend the social status of professional philosophers as opposed to traditional sages. These critics interpreted the demand for conceptual accuracy as an expression of social and political elitism. Instead, they expected professional philosophers in Africa to pay attention and give full expression to "the spontaneous philosophy of the masses." To this effect, these critics advocated the authority of Gramsci (Niamkey 1976a, 1976b, 1977; Yai 1977).

The same critics questioned the assumption that philosophy should be a personal effort by the individual to think independently. They viewed this as a commonplace prejudice of bourgeois ideology. Philosophy as a private intellectual production was seen as a myth which develops in a social context dominated by the rule of capital. In fact, this so-called private production derives from a "private appropriation of knowledge collectively produced [...]. Signing a text or a thought is but an effect of the publishing contract which, in turn, is but a form of employment contract." The idea of philosophy as a written tradition refers, it is said, to "a banker's conception of philosophy"/"une conception bancaire de la philosophie" (Niamkey 1977).

I responded to these criticisms in several articles, two of which subsequently appeared in English in the Zambian-Dutch journal *Quest* (Hountondji 1977, 1981, 1982a). Here I wish only to clarify a basic misunderstanding. What mattered most to me was not so much the ownership of ideas—whether philosophy belonged to the individual or to the group—as the responsibility for asserting or denying those ideas. I quote here from an article of mine that that has not been published in English:

The philosopher does not own his ideas, true. He just finds them in his path, they "come to his mind," as is usually said, suggested by circumstances and drawn from a common fund inherited from tradition. But for this very reason, given the extreme richness of this fund, which contains all possible ideas, including the most contradictory ones, the individual thinker remains responsible for choosing one idea instead of the other and for valuing one element of the cultural heritage in preference to the other [...]. Ideas are not mere merchandise: they are also meanings, even in the capitalist world, and therefore protocols of possible actions and experiments. Beyond the practical (i.e., moral, political, etc.) responsibility generally attributed to all human beings, we must also conceive of a theoretical, intellectual responsibility. (Hountondji 1977)

On the other hand, one of the most insistent charges against my work is that of Eurocentrism (in the widest sense of "Europe"), or occidentalism. To some commentators, *African Philosophy* does not only question ethnophilosophy—that is, a certain interpretation and use of African traditions—it expresses displeasure about African cultures themselves. The author, they say, uses Western norms to deprecate African ways of life. He invites total rejection by Africans of their ancestors' thoughts and values, and calls for frantic westernization. In the same current, he makes a "case against African studies and students of Africa," he "expresses opposition to the study of African traditional thought," while "he [. . .] at the same time insists on the philosopher's freedom to study non-African ideas"; he "dismisses the notion of cultural pluralism as 'a pretext for a conservative cultural practice,' and advocates, instead, 'the irreversible advent of a world civilization' [. . .], the dissolution of African particularities (real or imaginary) in the emergent world civilization, meaning, of course, a cultural *pax Europeana*" (Owomoyela 1987, 84–85, 92).

Only a ·cursory reading of *African Philosophy* could lead to such misinterpretation. See, for example, chapter eight, on "True and False Pluralism"; not only do I *not* dismiss cultural pluralism, I positively advocate it. Moreover, I aim to deepen perception beyond the mere plurality of cultures into the internal pluralism, the inner tensions and dynamism, and the capacity for change of *each* culture. Unfortunately, quotation marks do not guarantee valid interpretations, since phrases are often quoted out of context. That is obviously the case here. *African Philosophy* is definitely *not* a return to Lévy-Bruhl's theory of primitive mentality or to ideologies of Western superiority. It does *not* assume that "all that is African is barbarous." Nor does it deny the urgent need in Africa for self-rediscovery and self-rehabilitation. It does exactly the opposite. It warns against wrong ways, against illusory paths and intellectual dead ends which, in the long run, can never lead us where we want to go.

It seemed to me that a certain understanding and practice of anthropology was one of these wrong ways. I did not accept the notion of "primitive society," meant to identify the specific object of ethnology, as opposed to sociology. I doubted the adequacy of the many alternative notions designed for the same use, such as *archaic, illiterate, small scale,* or *simple societies, societies without history,* etc. I questioned the basic presupposition that the communities studied by ethnographers were basically different from other human communities. This presupposition was, to me, a retrospective justification of imperialist domination. It allowed a sort of scientific marginalization or, so to speak, bantustanization of these communities.

Tempels's *Bantu Philosophy* seemed to me an eloquent example of this process of exclusion. The white scholar's discourse is based here on the black man's silence, and this, in turn, is the outcome of a long historical process which remains unquestioned. As a result, the ethnographer does not meet any resistance while submitting the Bantu people to all sorts of conceptual manipulation. Ethnophilosophy performed such a manipulation. It was based on oversimplification and a reductionist view of the societies under study. It was certainly more respectful of the so-called primitive's humanity to refer to a coherent system of ideas as the ultimate explanation for his or her deeds, instead of attributing them to an irrational mentality, as Lévy-Bruhl did. Yet, the assumption that one could freely construct such a system without the subjects' participation, and then expect them to approve of it, seemed to me unacceptable. The consequence was unanimism[4]—the illusion that all men and women in such societies speak with one voice and share the same opinion about all fundamental issues. This implies the rejection of pluralism, the sweeping away of all internal contradictions and tensions, the denial of the intense intellectual life, and the extreme cultural richness associated with these societies.

One question remained to be addressed: What happens when the Third World, say, in the persona of an African scholar, undertakes to do anthropology? What happens when an African does ethnophilosophy? I was distressed most of all that while taking over this exogenous discourse, African scholars could not help but continue to address the Western public primarily. African ethnophilosophy seemed to me, therefore, an extroverted discourse and, strictly speaking, an "alienated literature." In addition to ethnophilosophy, I tended to dismiss African anthropology as a whole, on the grounds that its very contents could not avoid being biased by its external destination. My critique of exclusion was specified, therefore, as a criticism of extroversion.

I would admit today that I probably overstated my case. Later publications of mine were to give the proper correctives. Among other things, they take note of the important theoretical developments within anthropology and African studies. These developments include a greater awareness of the antiquity and historical depth, the inner complexity and dynamism of indigenous cultures, the nature and modes of the settlement of conflicts, the impact of integration into the world market through the slave trade and colonization, the articulation of modes of production, the factors of change, the multiple autochthonous traditions and schools of thought. Anthropology today is not what it used to be. The French anthropologist Claude Rivière may have been right to state, as he did in 1978, that the philosopher was at least one decade late (Rivière 1979). I would say, more simply, that anthropology's original sin, that of being a discourse by Westerners for Westerners, seems to have been dissolved by history even more quickly and efficiently than one might have expected. However, this does not render meaningless epistemological concerns about its status and methods.

In any case, however serious this original sin, it may have been excessively pessimistic to assume that African scholars doing African studies could not avoid treading the same paths as the first Western Africanists. I fully agree that today we, in Africa, still have an urgent need for self-rediscovery: "Even if Europeans had not invented African studies, Africans would have had to invent it" (Owomoyela 1987, 92).

Let me just add that, given the fact that African studies *were* invented by Europeans, Africans today should not merely carry on these disciplines as shaped in Europe. Africans must reinvent them. Such reinvention implies a sharply critical awareness of the ideological limits and the theoretical and methodological shortcomings of former practices. Some time ago I wrote the following play on words: "Une fausse science n'est pas toujours, ni forcément, une science fausse"/"A fake science is not always, or necessarily, a false science" (Hountondji 1990b). It may contain useful information or reveal objective facts. These should, however, be reinterpreted outside the theoretical and ideological framework of the original doctrine. We can learn even from the most biased works by anthropologists from Europe and the West; we can learn from Lévy-Bruhl and from others whose biases are greater, as well as from the most scrupulous, rigorous, and self-demanding Western Africanists. The real point, here again, is about the ways and means of a critical appropriation of the existing knowledge (Hountondji 1988). We must be particularly careful and demanding when the knowledge at stake is about ourselves and when the appropriation takes the form of repatriation.

For decades, African scholars have done important work. The evolution of African scholarship on Africa is encouraging and should be accelerated. However, it should by no means be considered an end in itself. It is not enough to have Africans doing African studies. The real question is how the scientific achievements of African as well as non-African scholars can be made to serve African countries, and through what channels the knowledge accumulated can be mastered, capitalized, developed, and occasionally applied by African societies to the solution of their problems and the improvement of their quality of life.

There is much more to say about Tempels than was said in *African Philosophy*. The criticisms leveled here at *Bantu Philosophy* were and still are justified in their own way. They question not only the methodology but also the basic assumptions and the ideological setting of the Belgian missionary's approach. They do not, however, fully place *Bantu Philosophy* in the socio-political context of the former Belgian Congo; neither do they relate it to Father Tempels's personal development as a priest and scholar.

The new materials brought forth, in this regard, by Father Smet's and Willy de Craemer's investigations are of prime importance. They allow us to see, besides the abstract image of the ethnophilosopher, a man of flesh and blood,[5] a field researcher patiently transcribing folksongs and other products of oral tradition among the Balubas of Katanga and Kasai, a white militant whose political activism got him into trouble with the colonial administration in Leopoldville, a progressive Franciscan concerned with the basic problems of missiology, a man whose ideas about catechesis got him into trouble with the Vatican, and a priest who was best known in Zaire as the founding prophet of a charismatic movement known as the Jamaa (De Craemer 1977; Smet 1977a, 1977b, 1978; Tempels 1945, 1948, 1949a, 1979).

Although I would not change a word of *African Philosophy* in view of this new research, my critique of *Bantu Philosophy* needs to be placed in this wider setting. I developed this theme in a lecture I gave in 1987 in Paris at the invitation of the French Society for Philosophy (Hountondji 1987, 1989a). In this connection, I would raise three points, on three concerns that Tempels himself addresses. First, I would qualify Aimé Césaire's strong criticism (which I not only accepted but tried to extend) that Tempels had prescribed an imaginary medicine for the sufferings of the Bantu people at a time when they were struggling for better salaries and housing through repeated strikes and riots. The "polemical and political writings" published by Smet testify to Tempels's awareness of the social and economic problems in the colony. Nevertheless, both these writings and *Bantu Philosophy* reflect Tempels's contempt for the social group known as *les évolués,* the educated Congolese, whom he considered inauthentic blacks and traitors to their own culture. In fact, the leaders of the social agitation in the Belgian Congo were *évolués.* This was not a coincidence. In that regard, *Bantu Philosophy* is inseparable from the "progressive" colonizer's attempt to join the rank and file of the colonized people and to cut them off from the "subversive" influence of the educated elite. Ethnophilosophy in Tempels's work can be seen as associated with political bantuism—a political stand that was considered highly subversive by the colonial administration and yet, at the same time, was regarded as bluntly conservative and even reactionary by progressive Africans.

The second concern expressed in Tempels's study is about the language of evangelization, or the way to adapt the Christian message and make it more intelligible to the Bantu's mental habits and concepts. This kind of preoccupation is at the core of missiology, the theory of missionary practice, as it was developed at the time by such theologians as Father P. Charles, professor at the Catholic University of Louvain and member of the Royal Academy of the Colonial Sciences in Brussels. In fact, all of Tempels's work after *Bantu Philosophy* (1945) turns most essentially upon this issue. It includes, among other titles, the two-volume work *Notre rencontre* (Tempels 1948, 1949a, 1962a, 1962b). This fact invites us to pay greater attention to the missiologic component of Tempels's most celebrated book.

There is, of course, a third concern: the theoretical or "scientific" one, in the wider meaning of "science." Beyond the political and religious motivations, *Bantu Philosophy* is based on the assumption that only a philosophical synthesis of Bantu thought will give all Bantu studies, including "ethnology, linguistics, psychoanalysis, the science of law, sociology, and religious studies," their ultimate coherence and intelligibility (Tempels 1949a, 16).

As practiced by Tempels, ethnophilosophy is marked by these three preceding concerns. Better knowledge of the context in which Tempels developed his ideas causes me to modify and in some instances to qualify the critique I developed in *African Philosophy*. By and large, however, the new information confirms and reinforces this critique.

Ethnophilosophy did not begin with Tempels. Significant examples are cited herein of earlier works based on similar assumptions and approaches. In this respect, chapter four corrects, to some extent, the somewhat hasty assertions of chapter one. Later articles went further in this direction. The word "ethnophilosophy" itself, which I thought should be coined to mean "an ethnological work with philosophical pretensions," was much older than I believed.[6]

I realized this when, soon after my article was published in *Diogenes,* I read (or re-read) the *Autobiography of Kwame Nkrumah,* where the Ghanaian leader tells how, shortly after getting his M.A. degree in philosophy at the University of Pennsylvania in 1943, he registered for a

Ph.D. thesis on ethnophilosophy (Nkrumah 1957). This suggests that ethnophilosophy was, in the early 1940s, an acknowledged academic discipline, at least in the university milieu where Nkrumah moved (unless, of course, he introduced the term in retrospect when he wrote his *Autobiography*). Nevertheless, I did not correct the misleading statement about "coining" the word in the late 1960s, though two of the articles gathered into *African Philosophy* were specifically about Nkrumah. I did, however, make the correction much later on (Hountondji 1987).

It can be conjectured that ethnophilosophy as a discipline appeared in the wake of what was known as ethnoscience. If this is so, ethnophilosophy should be understood as a subspecies of ethnoscience—among other subspecies such as ethnobotany, ethnozoology, ethnomedicine, ethno-musicology—unless it is conceived as the mother discipline and logically presupposed by all other ethnosciences. The International African Institute in London was probably conscious of doing ethnophilosophy when it organized its third international seminar in Salisbury in 1960 on African systems of thought, though the word "ethnophilosophy" was not used in the papers presented (Fortes and Dieterlen 1965).

On the other hand, the critique of the ethnophilosophical approach was not new in the late 1960s or early 1970s when Towa and I began to publish. Here again, Father Smet's careful investigation brought to light the intellectual excitement which followed the publication of *Bantu Philosophy* and the sharp criticisms leveled at Tempels in the Congo and in Belgium by such scholars as Boelart and de Sousberghe, among others (Smet 1975). What was new was "neither the word nor the thing, but the conjunction of the word and the thing, the use of 'ethnophilosophy' to mean, instead of an intellectual project and forthcoming science, rather a discipline already in the making, whose first attempts, however, stirred up such doubts about its viability and consistency, that the word could no longer be used otherwise than now, i.e. in a critical and polemical sense" (Hountondji 1987).

Questioning ethnophilosophy did not amount to denying the existence and importance of endogenous thought. Only a cursory reading could give the impression that Africa was treated as an intellectual and cultural *tabula rasa* in *African Philosophy*. For not only is oral literature acknowledged in its own right—requiring only that attention be paid to its internal pluralism and dialectics—but beyond the realm of discourse, it was recognized that a whole domain of silent, implicit, and unformulated thought continually informs, orients, and influences our deeds and conscious thoughts. I wrote the Postscript at a time when I was re-reading

Lévi-Strauss's *Savage Mind.* I have never been sure, until now, that I really understood what the founder of structuralism called "the science of the concrete" or "the logic of totemic classifications." This was, however, the background for my pleading that one should grasp the residual, odds-and-ends logic that gives implicit thoughts their specific kind of coherence and not hastily interpret them as components of *one* conceptual system.

I returned to this issue in at least two articles. In one of them, I compared A. Kagamé's linguistic relativism, which he unduly modeled on Aristotle's doctrine of categories, with Kwasi Wiredu's warning against "tongue-relative" metaphysical problems as opposed to "tongue-neutral" ones, and his appeal to African philosophers to think in their own languages. There is room, I concluded, for a systematic exploration of the unthought thoughts, the unconscious assumptions imposed on our conceptual procedures by the languages we speak, but instead of boasting about these constraints and proudly presenting them as our philosophy, we must treat them as our counter-philosophy, an inner obstacle that must be permanently fought against, in order to free our thinking, as far as possible, from all kinds of bias, and thereby to come as close as possible to the universal (Wiredu 1980, 1984; Hountondji 1982b).

My reading of Marc Augé's outstanding monograph on the lagoon societies of Côte d'Ivoire led me to the same conclusion. While identifying "the persecutive conception of misfortune" at the root of so many behaviors and cultural manifestations, the French anthropologist suggests that one should look for such an "ideo-logic," that is, the logic of collective representations, in every lineage society (Augé 1975). This was an important and exciting investigation. It provided the philosopher with valuable material for meditation and critical reflection. By no means, however, should it be considered philosophy.

In a more recent article I pleaded for the "sociology of collective representations" to be conceived as an independent discipline. Philosophers may occasionally have to engage in this kind of investigation. They may even reach important, epoch-making results, as was the case with a celebrated, though controversial article by Robin Horton. Philosophers must not forget, however, that philosophy begins at the very moment they undertake to appreciate critically the material discovered (Horton 1967, Hountondji 1990a).

Finally, unless one wants to reduce the whole debate to a quarrel about words, there is nothing shocking in deciding, like Wiredu, to call this material "African traditional philosophy," as opposed to "African modern philosophy." The qualifier avoids absolutizing and locking oneself into the given legacy. It leaves room for invention and personal intellectual responsibility.

It should be noted, however, that so-called traditional philosophy is itself plural. As I have said, the adjective "traditional" may be misleading because it flattens the cultural legacy and favors the illusion that all its components are both contemporary to and convergent with one another. It would be better to retain the noun and, instead of "African traditional thought," consider "African traditions of thought." I am still reluctant to accept any formulation that could lead to the oversimplification of Africa's cultural past. I still maintain, as I did in the Postscript below, that what appears at first sight as the "practical ideology" of a given society is but its *dominant* practical ideology; there must be additional investigations into the wide range of non-dominant, marginal, and even adverse ideologies.

Conversely, so-called modern African philosophy is also a tradition of its own, or a set of texts, as I have said. What matters, therefore, is not the mere fact that it exists, but what we make of it today. What matters is intellectual creativity and freedom.

In the wake of Cheikh Anta Diop's writing, scholars such as Pathé Diagne and Théophile Obenga drew attention to the antiquity and historical depth of African philosophy. This direction of research seems to me particularly exciting. It allows us to put the colonial and late pre-colonial period into perspective and to probe more deeply into Africa's past. It encourages us to look beyond the era of the slave trade. Still, special efforts must be made to find the missing links if we are to establish historical continuity between ancient Egypt and today's Africa. Whatever the outcome, however, we need to disenclose Africa's history and to consider the last four or five centuries, that is, the whole period of integration into the world-market, the period of subjection, and the development of underdevelopment as a parenthesis within the whole history of Africa (Diop 1981, Diagne 1981, Obenga 1990).

From this perspective, ethnophilosophy appears as a by-product of underdevelopment, a consequence, among many others, of cultural amnesia. Questioning ethnophilosophy is therefore a first step on the long road toward self-recovery and self-confidence. It is a pre-condition for the rediscovery of Africa's age-old civilization and history.[7]

Notes

1 Most of my recent publications deal with these questions. The overall concern is this: How can Africa appropriate the international legacy of knowledge and know-how and reappropriate its own knowledge traditions in a way that allows mastery of the whole process of knowledge production for the benefit of the majority, not just some? (See Hountondji 1988, 1989b, 1990b, 1992, 1994, 1995.) On the other hand, questions about my own intellectual development are fully dealt with in my forthcoming *Enjeux d'une critique: philosophie, anthropologie des savoirs et politique en Afrique* (Paris, 1996).

2 I heard about Oruka's death while editing this preface in Groningen, the Netherlands, in February, 1996. The Kenyan philosopher, it is reported, was "hit by a vehicle" on December 9, 1995, in Nairobi. Let this preface be read as a friend's homage, in memory of the work done together for more than twenty years.

3 In contrast to the PCD's criticism, an example of dogmatic anti-Marxism may be found in a booklet by my colleague from Côte d'Ivoire: Abdou Touré, *Le Marxisme-Léninisme comme idéologie: Critique de trois théoriciens africains: A. A. Dieng, P. Hountondji et M. Towa* (Abidjan, 1980).

4 I took the word from Jules Romains, a French novelist of the early twentieth century, who meant something quite positive: the feeling of solidarity with human beings, the doctrine which advocates "unanimous life" as a means to break free from individual loneliness and create communion within human groups (see Romains 1908, 1932–1946). When I borrowed the word, I completely inverted its original meaning and gave it a pejorative sense.

5 Franz Tempels was born in Berlaar, near Antwerp, Belgium, on February 18, 1906, and died in 1977. He took the name Placide at his Franciscan noviciate in 1924. See biographies by A. J. Smet in *Revue africaine de théologie* 1 (1977): 77–128 and *Documentation et information africaines* 17 octobre 1977: 959–61.

6 See chapter one, "An Alienated Literature," p. 34. This chapter was first published in 1970, a year before Marcien Towa's exciting booklet, where the word "ethnophilosophy" was used with the same pejorative and critical meaning (Hountondji 1970, Towa 1971).

7 I am indebted to Flora Wilson Hazoume, supervisory librarian of the Kennedy-King Library, American Cultural Center in Cotonou, for helping me formulate this preface in a readable English. I alone am responsible for whatever gallicisms remain in the text.

References

Althusser, Louis. 1974. *Eléments d'autocritique.* Paris: Hachette.

Appiah, Kwame Anthony. 1992. *In My Father's House: Africa in the Philosophy of Culture.* New York: Oxford University Press.

Augé, Marc. 1975. *Théorie des pouvoirs et idéologie: étude de cas en Côte d'Ivoire.* Paris: Hermann.

De Craemer, Willy. 1977. *The Jamaa and the Church: A Bantu Catholic Movement in Zaire.* Oxford: Clarendon Press.

Diagne, Mamoussé. 1976. "Paulin J. Hountondji ou la 'psychanalyse' de la conscience ethnophilosophique." *Psychopathologie africaine* 12,3: 443–49.

Diagne, Pathé. 1981. *L'europhilosophie face à la pensée du négro-africain* and *Problématique néo-pharaonique et épistémologie du réel.* Dakar: Sankoré.

Diop, Cheikh Anta. 1981. *Civilisation ou barbarie.* Paris: Présence Africaine.

Dossou, François C. 1994. "Ecriture et oralité dans la transmission du savoir." In *Les savoirs endogènes: pistes pour une recherche,* edited by P. Hountondji, 257–82. Dakar: CODESRIA.

Fanon, Frantz. 1952. *Peau noire, masques blancs.* Paris: Seuil. Translated as *Black Skin, White Masks.* New York: Grove, 1967.

Fortes, Meyer, and Germaine Dieterlen, eds. 1965. *African Systems of Thought.* London: Oxford University Press.

Griaule, Marcel. 1948. *Dieu d'eau: entretiens avec Ogotemmêli.* Paris. Translated as *Conversations with Ogotemmeli: An Introduction to Dogon Religious Ideas.* London: Oxford University Press, 1965.

Horton, Robin. 1967. "African Traditional Thought and Western Science." *Africa* (London) 37,1: 50–71 and 2: 155–87.

Hountondji, Paulin, J. 1970. "Comments on Contemporary African Philosophy." *Diogenes* 71: 109–30.

———. 1976. *Sur la "philosophie africaine": critique de l'ethnophilosophie.* Paris: Maspero. Translated as *African Philosophy: Myth and Reality.* Bloomington: Indiana University Press, 1983.

———. 1977. "Sens du mot 'philosophie' dans l'expression 'philosophie africaine'." *Le Korè* 5–8. Also published in Claude Sumner, ed., *African Philosophy/La philosophie africaine.* Addis Ababa, 1980.

———. 1981. "Que peut la philosophie?" *Présence Africaine* 119: 47–71. Translated as "What Philosophy Can Do." *Quest: Philosophical Discussions* 1,2 (1987): 2–28.

———. 1982a. "Occidentalisme, élitisme: réponse à deux critiques." *Recherche, pédagogie et culture* 56: 58–67. Translated as "Occidentalism, Elitism: Answer to Two Critiques." *Quest: Philosophical Discussions* 3,2 (1989): 3–29.

———. 1982b. "Langues africaines et philosophie: l'hypothèse relativiste." *Les études philosophiques* 4: 393–406.

———. 1987. "Le particulier et l'universel." *Bulletin de la société française de philosophie* 81,4: 145–89. Translated as "The Particular and the Universal."

SAPINA Newsletter: A Bulletin of the Society for African Philosophy in North America 2,2–3 (1989): 1–66.

————. 1988. "L'appropriation collective du savoir: tâches nouvelles pour une politique scientifique." *Genève-Afrique* 26,1: 49–66.

————. 1989a. "L'effet Tempels." In *Encyclopédie philosophique universelle. Vol. 1: L'univers philosophique,* edited by André Jacob, 1472–80. Paris: Presses Universitaires de France.

————. 1989b. "L'espérance têtue: la vie quotidienne dans un pays de la périphérie." *L'événement européen* 8: 119–38.

————. 1990a. "Pour une sociologie des représentations collectives." In *La pensée métisse: croyances africaines et rationalité occidentale en questions.* Paris: Presses Universitaires de France.

————. 1990b. "Scientific Dependence in Africa Today." *Research in African Literatures* 21,3: 5–15.

————. 1992. "Recapturing." In *The Surreptitious Speech: "Présence Africaine" and the Politics of Otherness: 1947–1987,* edited by V. Y. Mudimbe, 238–48. Chicago: University of Chicago Press.

————. 1994. "Démarginaliser." In *Les savoirs endogènes: pistes pour une recherche,* edited by Paulin Hountondji, 1–34. Dakar: CODESRIA.

————. 1995. "Producing Knowledge in Africa Today." *African Studies Review* Fall.

Keita, Lansana. 1985. "Contemporary African Philosophy: The Search for a Method." *Diogenes* 130: 105–28.

Masolo, D. A. 1994. *African Philosophy in Search of Identity.* Bloomington: Indiana University Press.

Mudimbe, V. Y. 1988. *The Invention of Africa: Gnosis, Philosophy, and the Order of Knowledge.* Bloomington: Indiana University Press.

Niamkey, Koffi Robert. 1976a. "L'impensé de Towa et de Hountondji." *Le Korè* 1.

————. 1976b. "Controverse sur l'existence d'une philosophie africaine." *Le Korè* 3–4.

Niamkey, Koffi. 1977. "Les modes d'existence matérielle de la philosophie et la question de la philosophie africaine." *Le Korè* 5–8.

Nkrumah, Kwame. 1957. *Ghana: Autobiography of Kwame Nkrumah.* London: Thomas Nelson.

Obenga, Théophile. 1990. *La philosophie africaine de la période pharaonique: 2780–330 avant notre ère.* Paris: L'harmattan.

Oruka, Odera. 1983. "Sagacity in African Philosophy." *International Philosophical Quarterly* 23,4: 383–93.

————. 1990. *Sage Philosophy: Indigenous Thinkers and Modern Debate on African Philosophy.* Leiden: Brill.

Owomoyela, Oyekan. 1987. "Africa and the Imperative of Philosophy: A Skeptical Consideration." *African Studies Review* 30,1: 79–99.

Parti Communiste du Dahomey (PCD). 1979. *Introduction aux réalités économiques et sociales au Dahomey.* Paris: Nouveau Bureau d'Edition.

Rancière, Jacques. 1974. *La leçon d'Althusser.* Paris: Gallimard.

Rivière, Claude. 1979. "Les destins associés de la philosophie et des sciences sociales en Afrique." *Ethnopsychologie* 34,1: 89–105.

Romains, Jules. 1908. *La vie unanime.* Paris: Gallimard.

———. 1932–1946. *Les hommes de bonne volonté.* Paris: Flammarion. 27 vols.

Smet, A. J. 1975. *Philosophie africaine, II: Textes choisis et bibliographie sélective.* Kinshasa: Presses Universitaires du Zaïre.

———. 1977a. "Le Père Placide Tempels et son oeuvre publiée." *Revue africaine de théologie* 1: 77–128.

———. 1977b. "In memoriam: le Père Placide Tempels." *Documentation et information africaines* 17 octobre: 959–61.

———. 1978. "L'oeuvre inédite du père Placide Tempels." In *Philosophie et libération.* Kinshasa: Faculté de Théologie Catholique.

Tempels, Placide. 1945. *La Philosophie bantoue.* Elisabethville: Lovania. Translated as *Bantu Philosophy.* Paris: Présence Africaine, 1959.

———. 1948. "Catéchèse bantoue." *Bulletin des missions* 22: 258–79.

———. 1949a. "La christianisation des philosophies païennes." In *Trait d'union.* Antwerp: Centre d'Action Missionnaire.

———. 1949b. *La philosophie bantoue.* Enlarged ed. Paris: Présence Africaine.

———. 1962a. *Notre rencontre.* Léopoldville: Centre d'Etudes Pastorales.

———. 1962b. *Notre rencontre, II.* Léopoldville: Centre d'Etudes Pastorales.

———. 1979. *Ecrits polémiques et politiques.* Edited by A. J. Smet. Kinshasa: Faculté de Théologie Catholique.

Touré, Abdou. 1980. *Le Marxisme-Léninisme comme idéologie: Critique de trois théoriciens africains: A. A. Dieng, P. Hountondji et M. Towa.* Abidjan.

Towa, Marcien. 1971. *Essai sur la problématique philosophique dans l'Afrique actuelle.* Yaoundé: Clé.

Wiredu, Kwasi. 1980. *Philosophy and an African Culture.* Cambridge: Cambridge University Press.

———. 1984. "Philosophical Research and Teaching in Africa: Some Suggestions." In *Teaching and Research in Philosophy: Africa.* Paris: UNESCO.

Yai, Olabiyi Babalola. 1977. "Theory and Practice in African Philosophy: The Poverty of Speculative Philosophy. A Review of the Work of P. Hountondji, M. Towa, et al." *Second Order* 2,2.

African Philosophy

Introduction

Philosophy can be regarded as the most self-conscious of disciplines. It is the one discipline that involves by its very nature a constant process of reflection upon itself. This process of self-reflection, inherent in the nature and practice of philosophy, bears not only upon its purposes, objectives and methods, upon its relation to the world and to human experience in its multiple expressions, upon its status among other disciplines and forms of intellectual pursuit and discourse, but also, most radically, upon its very nature as an activity and as an enterprise.

This view of philosophy as a critical activity whose function embraces an interrogation of its own nature and meaning is undoubtedly a legacy of the Greek philosophers. There is a significant sense, indeed, in which it can be said that the history of Western philosophy has been shaped largely by a long and sustained reflection upon the nature of philosophy as a thing in itself. Beginning with Plato's often made distinction between *doxa* (opinion) and *sophia* (wisdom), the meaning of philosophy and its area of concern have formed a central question of philosophical reflection in the Western world. Thus, the development of Western philosophy has proceeded in such a way as to determine not simply the problems that have been examined but also the manner in which they have been handled, the principles which command thought and discourse about them and ultimately the ways in which they can be considered possible objects of thought and discourse at all. This has had the consequence of leading philosophical thought back to itself, as it were, so that philosophy has come to be concerned not only with the content of thought (and even with formal modes of thought) but also with its own self-definition as an activity engaged with both. A significant part of the business of philosophy has thus been committed to the effort to apprehend its own being.

The effect of this distinguishing feature of philosophy has been to render extremely thin the line of demarcation between philosophy as an immediate activity and *metaphilosophy* as a mode of conceptualizing that activity. By a curious turn of events related to the special circumstances in which the discipline finds itself in Africa today, the concept of philosophy has become the object of attention focused not only on its relevance to the contemporary situation in Africa but also, indeed, on its meaning and nature as a universal concept. Over the past decade or so the central question that has dominated discussion among professional philosophers in the academic departments of African universities has been that of the philosophical status of the world-views and value systems of traditional African societies. From this central question have flowed a number of related issues which have provoked an intense debate as to the meaning of philosophy itself.

The course of this debate has run along a line of development marked by questions such as the following. Can we talk of 'African philosophy' in the same sense that we are accustomed to speak of Western philosophy, Indian philosophy, Chinese philosophy – in the sense, that is, of an established tradition of speculative and/or conceptual thought? Do the various cosmologies and thought systems generated within the framework of pre-colonial African societies and cultures, as reconstituted by anthropology especially, constitute a philosophical tradition in this sense, apart from the evidence that they offer of the once-denied capacity of African people for reflection upon the world and upon experience? Do these world-views demonstrate a systematic coherence and a fundamental unity from which we can deduce a distinctive African mode of thought, even a form of rationality? If so, what is the relation between this African mode of thought and other traditions of philosophy, in particular that associated with Western civilization with which one is most familiar? Are the categories of African thought, considered as a distinctive system, translatable into those of Western philosophy? If a relation can be found between the two, how can we define the common ground on which they meet and which is covered by the meaning of philosophy? In other words, and in more general terms, what is philosophy? Is it wholly and sufficiently defined by the Western tradition of logical discourse, the ordering of the processes of thought and the elements of discourse into an articulated system? Is philosophy concerned simply with theoretical matters and second-order questions, or does a definition of philosophy admit of other possibilities that take account of the universal human disposition to apply both mind and imagination to the facts of experience?

Such are the issues that have been raised in the debate on the question of African philosophy which have led our philosophers to undertake both a critical examination of the traditional systems of thought in Africa, to which they stand in a cultural and sometimes avowedly affective relation, as well as a reassessment of the tenets and assumptions which they have inherited from their training in Western philosophy, from which their practice of philosophy derives.

It ought to be remarked that the question of African philosophy, as it presents itself to the professional philosopher in Africa at the present time, arises directly from what is recognizably his peculiar situation, both as regards the context of his life and values and his mode of insertion within the social order in contemporary Africa. It is now a commonplace to observe that the encounter between Africa and Europe has brought about a conflict of cultures, a situation that, in the specific historical context of colonization, has produced a tension at the heart of the African system of values. This situation has provided a constant subject of reflection for the intelligentsia which has emerged as a result of the social forces set in motion by the incursion of Europe into the historical process in Africa. The attempt of this intellectual élite to take the measure of the impact of Western civilization upon the African world defines the path along which, since the eighteenth century at least, the development of modern African thought has run,[1] and the area of its concern has been determined primarily by political and social questions and interests. The present focus of African reflection, as dictated by the realities of the post-colonial era, has been the immediate and practical issues of 'development', understood as a process of the accommodation of African lives to the demands of modernity. It is especially in this connection that the observed divergence between traditional values in Africa and the Western paradigm that governs the very idea of modernity has come to assume a practical importance and to represent something of a dilemma.

For the professional philosopher this dilemma involves primarily a consideration of the relationship between the modes of thought which inform the traditional values and cultural expression of African life on one hand and, on the other, those enshrined in

Western philosophy, which historically have shaped the course of Western civilization and are held to underlie its contemporary manifestations. The fact that Western civilization has everywhere acquired a hold upon human life in our time gives the theoretical consideration an urgent practical significance in Africa, whether that significance is explictly recognized by the philosopher or simply lies in the rear of the field of his theoretical activity.

Seen from the point of view of their global import, the circumstances in which philosophical reflection is proceeding in Africa today present some important parallels to those that presided over the early phase of the elaboration of Western philosophy itself. The most striking parallel concerns the effort of the ancient Greek philosophers to define the exact scope of their theoretical activity in relation to an existing body of myths and belief systems according to which the civilization of their own day actively functioned. That effort was commanded by their concern to formulate a mode of rationality which offered a more adequate account of the world and of human life and experience in its fullest range. Moreover, their preoccupation with the practical engagement of philosophy with the concrete facts of existence appears to us today to have been an immediate function of their social situation and class interests. It is not too much to say that Western philosophy was born into conditions of cultural and social crisis.

In a similar way, the professional philosopher in Africa today operates in a situation of cultural and social tension. For although his mind has been moulded by the principles of Western philosophy, he too is confronted by the vast body of world-views and thought systems which continue to inhabit the consciousness of the majority of Africans and to determine a fundamental attachment on their part to a traditional way of life, a situation that commands his attention and makes demands of his philosophical loyalties. Faced with a dualism both of modes of thought and of modes of existence, the philosopher in Africa is compelled to undertake an examination of the implications of this dualism for his discipline and for his practice of that discipline with specific reference to the African situation.

It is apparent from these considerations that there can be no form of reflection in Africa today that does not bear a direct relation to history and culture. In this broad perspective of the conditions of thought and discourse on our continent, the present debate on the question of African philosophy, for all its academic and technical character, can be seen to form part of a comprehensive process of reflection by the African intelligentsia upon our total historical being: it represents a significant moment in the intellectual response of Africans to the challenge of Western civilization.

The larger historical and ideological background to this process of African self-reflection is provided, of course, by the colonial experience, and an essential dimension of that experience was represented by the effects of the colonial ideology upon the minds and sensibilities of the Westernized African élite. The basic proposition of the colonial ideology and the challenge it contained have been summed up in this observation by a prominent African philosopher, Peter Bodunrin: 'For too long, the Western conception of Africa has been that of a continent that has contributed little or nothing to human ideas and civilization.'[2]

The whole movement of African self-reflection takes its source from this proposition. We may go even further and say that both the ideological expression of African nationalism and its specific effect upon the current debate on the question of African philosophy derive from a pre-existing European discourse, dating back to the Enlightenment, upon non-Western peoples in general and Africa in particular. The ideological and philosophical issues that this discourse has presented to us in Africa arose initially as a European preoccupation – from the attempt of the European mind to understand itself through the mirror of other races and cultures, from its perception of the humanity of non-Western peoples, which afforded a justification for their domination. This ideological significance of Europe's contemplation of a world in which it was master by reason of the quality of its collective mind emerges most clearly from Hegel's philosophy of history, which, when all is said and done, is nothing but a celebration of the European spirit. The way in which Africa features in Hegel's speculations serves further to underline this direction of his philosophy, for by excluding Africa totally from the historical process through which, according to him, the human spirit fulfils itself, Hegel places Africa at the opposite pole to Europe, as its ideal and spiritual antithesis. The logic of Hegel's philosophy of history owes as much to his attachment to the dialectic as to a naïve symbolism suggested by the opposition of the white race to the black.

Hegel's philosophy of history remains the most exalted statement of European self-affirmation in opposition to other races, the most elaborate rationalization of European ethnocentrism. It provided a powerful philosophical base for the chorus of denigration of the non-white races which accompanied and buoyed up the European colonial adventure all through the nineteenth and well into the twentieth century. If much of the literature that provided the parts for this chorus of denigration was manifestly inferior, if not downright feeble-minded, it was left to the new discipline of anthropology to sustain the main theme under the guise of science. For it was no accident that it was precisely the period of greatest European colonial expansion that saw the development of anthropology as a constituted discipline devoted exclusively to the study of non-Western peoples, to whom were attached the labels 'savage', 'inferior', 'primitive' as qualifications to their full participation in a human essence. The theoretical grounding of the new discipline in the social Darwinism of Herbert Spencer during its formative years attests to the ethnocentric emphasis which Hegel's philosophy of history had imparted to the European mind in its consideration of itself and the world upon which it gazed.

The high point of this ethnocentrism in anthropology was attained in the work of Lucien Lévy-Bruhl, who devoted his entire life and career to the demonstration of the radical disparity between the nature and quality of mind of the European and what he called 'primitive mentality', which he attributed essentially to non-Western peoples and cultures. There is a certain irony in the fact that Lévy-Bruhl's enterprise in this direction was undertaken as a deliberate reaction against the work of the founding fathers of anthropology – Frazer, Tylor and Morgan. For although their evolutionist perspective placed the white man and Western civilization at the summit of the human scale, it did not preclude a universalist conception of man, considered from the viewpoint of his development through the entire range of history. Indeed, Tylor's organic conception of culture, despite his Hobbesian view of 'primitive' societies, tended to maintain a theoretical and residual, if not a real and practical, connection between the humanity of the white race and that of the non-white. It was this connection that Lévy-Bruhl undertook to eliminate at the very level of mind itself. Hence his opposition of two forms of mental operations which defined not simply two types of society and culture but two types of man: on one hand, Western societies that had emerged from the Mediterranean civilization within which developed rationalist philosophy and positive science and, on the other hand, 'primitive' societies ruled by a mentality to which the Western mode of thought was not merely foreign but wholly inaccessible. On the assumption that mental operations are sociologically determined and culturally bound, that 'collective representations' exercise constraint and impose their grid upon the individual mind, Lévy-Bruhl proceeded in several works to develop his notion of 'primitive mentality', which he characterized as a mode of apprehension in which the principle of identity, the notions of causality and the conception of time – ordinary features of Western logic – did not operate. It was for this reason that he proposed the well-known term 'pre-logical' to describe it in its most general aspect.[3]

For Lévy-Bruhl, the collective representations and value systems of so-called primitive societies have little or no intellectual content or character, for the mentality from which they proceed relies on a mystical form of participation for its experience of objective phenomena and in its attitude to the universe. At their highest level the mental functions of individuals within these societies are regulated by the mythical archetypes proposed by these representations, in which concepts have no place, since concepts are the fruits of philosophical reflection, in which primitive man does not indulge.[4] His mentality is thus of a wholly different character from that of the European; it stands, indeed, as its negative image:

The two mentalities which are face to face are so foreign to each other, so divergent in their habits, so different in their means of expression! The European employs abstractions almost without thinking, and the simple logical operations have been rendered so easy for him by his language that they cost him no effort. With the primitives, thought and language are of a character almost exclusively concrete. . . . In a word, our mentality is above all 'conceptual', the other barely so.[5]

It is plain that the whole purport of Lévy-Bruhl's characterization of primitive mentality was to establish rationality as a prerogative of Western civilization and as a defining quality of the white man which set him above the rest of humanity. His enterprise consisted in working out in the realm of epistemology, and to its furthest limits, the antithesis between Western and non-Western man that is inherent in Hegel's philosophy of history. More generally speaking, his contribution to anthropology and to European ideas is posited on an explicit hierarchy of values for which the Western serve as an absolute reference.

The varied fortunes of Lévy-Bruhl's notion of a primitive pre-logical mentality, both within scholarly circles and in the general intellectual and moral perception of so-called primitive man in Europe, culminated in the attempt by its originator in his last work, *Carnets*, published posthumously,[6] to attenuate its meaning. None the less, the notion had acquired so tenacious a hold upon the European consciousness that it formed a major plank in the system of colonial ideology and thus represented an outstanding issue with which African thought was later to contend.

Lévy-Bruhl's work may be said to mark the ultimate phase of classical anthropology. In the years between the two world wars the discipline underwent a major transformation in method and in spirit which came to reverse its ideological thrust with regard to the colonial situation. It is one of the ironies of the development of anthropology that it came in this new phase to provide both inspiration and ideas for a challenge to the colonial ideology with which it was bound up during an earlier phase. The assumption of the cultural superiority of Europe on which its classical practitioners had based their consideration of other societies and cultures began to give way to a new attitude towards non-Western forms of cultural expression, no doubt as a consequence of the empirical emphasis of the new anthropology in field work. The idea of Western culture as a universal norm began to be abandoned by those anthropologists whose direct experience of other cultures had impressed them with the range of possibilities of human adaptation to the natural environment and of human potential for cultural creation. From this revelation emerged the position of cultural pluralism and cultural relativity which began to mark anthropology in the inter-war years and finally came to dominate it after the second world war. The implications of this new position were pressed to their ideological and political conclusions in the avowed anti-imperialism of the American culturalist school of anthropology, led notably in this respect by Melville Herskovits,[7] but even where national loyalties and, in many cases, the administrative status of European anthropologists within the colonial system prevented such a stance, anthropology now offered a new and positive evaluation of non-Western cultures, whose effects were to be far-reaching.

Of particular interest for the development of African thought in its confrontation with the colonial ideology is the contribution of French anthropology. The tradition of sociology which the work of Durkheim and Mauss had established (a tradition to which, incidentally, Lévy-Bruhl belonged and whose most illustrious representative today is Claude Lévi-Strauss) seems to have defined for French anthropology as a major area of interest the value systems of non-Western cultures. As regards Africa, the pioneering work of Marcel Griaule in this direction complemented the studies of Delafosse and Delavignette in respect of material culture and social institutions and culminated in the celebrated presentation, in his *Dieu d'eau*, of a Dogon world-view whose symbolic and conceptual organization revealed an evident architecture. Griaule's prestige and influence helped to promote a school of French Africanists based at the Musée de l'Homme in Paris which counted among its members Germaine Dieterlen; her *Essai sur la religion bambara*[8] confirmed the preoccupation of this school with the systematic reconstruction of collective world-views and thought systems in Africa.[9]

However, from the point of view of its ideological impact and of its immediate relevance to the present debate on African philosophy, the most important work to emerge from the new orientation in anthropology was produced by a Belgian missionary, Placide Tempels, whose work *Bantu Philosophy*, published in French in 1945, was the first to attribute a developed philosophical system to an African people, the Baluba of present-day Zaïre. Its demonstration of the new spirit of accommodation for other cultures went so far as to represent a total retreat from the positions of classical anthropology. In particular, his insistence on the need for a recognition of the rationality of so-called primitive man carried a pointed refutation of the theories of Lévy-Bruhl on 'primitive mentality':

To declare on *a priori* grounds that primitive peoples have no ideas on the nature of beings, that they have no ontology and that they are completely lacking in logic, is simply to turn one's back on reality. Every day we are able to note that primitive peoples are by no means just children afflicted with a bizarre imagination. It is as Men that we have learned to know them in their homes. Folklore alone and superficial descriptions of strange customs cannot enable us to discover and understand primitive man. Ethnology, linguistics, psychoanalysis, jurisprudence, sociology and the study of religions are able to yield definitive results only after the philosophy and the ontology of a primitive people have been thoroughly studied and written up.[10]

Tempels proceeded further along this line of argument to claim for the Bantu an elevated system of thought which, though particular to them, with its own 'local colour' as he put it, deserved to be honoured by the term 'philosophy':

What has been called magic, animism, ancestor-worship, or dynamism – in short, all the customs of the Bantu – depend upon a single principle, knowledge of the Inmost Nature of beings, that is to say, upon their Ontological Principle. For is it not by means of this philosophical term that we must express their knowledge of being, of the existence of things?[11]

Beyond its declared attitude of sympathetic understanding of the Bantu as a people and its vindication of the African claim to an elevated system of thought, Tempels' work has acquired a permanent interest as the immediate source of the issues thrown up in the present debate on African philosophy. As is well known, the crux of the philosophy he attributes to the Bantu is an ontology in which being is conceived as 'vital force'; the universe is experienced as an interrelation of forces within the whole realm of existence. The crucial passage in his work requires to be quoted:

I believe that we should most faithfully render Bantu thought in the European language by saying that the Bantu speak, act, live as if, for them, beings were forces. Force is not for them an adventitious accidental reality. Force is even more than a necessary attribute of beings: Force is the nature of being, force is being, being is force.[12]

This ontology, which is held by Tempels to underlie Bantu consciousness and action, finds expression in the social institutions and the moral and religious life of the people. The interrelation of forces is ordained in a felt hierarchy running down from God, the supreme incarnation of vital force, through man (the dead ancestors, the living community of humans), to the animal and the inanimate world. We have thus in this philosophy something like an African version of what Lovejoy has called the 'great chain of being', characterized in this case by a pulsating life of interacting essences, of forces – in short, a universal vitalism.

Tempels' avowed purpose in undertaking the study of Bantu philosophy was to arrive at an understanding of the profound workings of the Bantu mind in order to facilitate the integration of Christian principles within its scheme of values. His conceptual approach to this evangelical mission was to establish a relation of identity between Bantu philosophy and Christian theology, which for him embodied the most living aspects of European thought, the most authentic values of Western civilization. If the terms of this procedure stop short of an open advocacy of the Bantu mode of thought, they amount in effect to an effort at a reconciliation between Africa and Europe at the level of spirituality and, indeed, of mind. As he puts it: 'We arrive, therefore, at the unheard-of conclusion, that Bantu paganism, the ancient wisdom of the Bantu reaches out from the depths of its Bantu soul towards the very soul of Christian spirituality.'[13]

The importance of Tempels' work in the intellectual history of Africa is difficult to overestimate. It is true that his *Bantu Philosophy* remains within the stream of European discourse upon the non-Western world and, in the particular instance, upon Africa. Moreover, it was conceived as part of a strategy for the spiritual conquest of Africa. But the concessions which Tempels had to make were on such a scale as to imply the total recognition of the African mind in its own individuality. Hence Tempels' work registers, despite the paternalistic tone of its expression, a decisive break with the ethnocentric emphasis of classical anthropology.

But quite apart from this ideological significance which it assumed in the colonial context, *Bantu Philosophy* provided a conceptual framework and reference for all future attempts to formulate the constitutive elements of a distinctive African mode of thought, to construct an original African philosophical system. It is in this respect that Tempels bequeathed to the present generation of African philosophers a problematic question.

The French sociologist Gérard Leclerc has remarked that 'decolonization signals, at the very least for Africa as for the rest of the Third World, the achievement of the sovereign right to language within a history henceforth worldwide, the substitution of a dialogue for the centuries-long narcissistic monologue of the West'.[14] The observation underlines the fact that the process of African self-reflection leading to this conquest of the right to language could not proceed in any way other than through polemics. The intellectual presuppositions of colonialism represented a formulation in negative terms of African identity; its racism was a large statement about the nature of the African which called for a refutation. In the intellectual confrontation with imperialism, it was necessary to enforce this refutation by elaborating a new set of valuations which reversed the terms of the colonial ideology. In the event, it can be observed that the terms of reference of modern African thought came to be defined largely by the colonial ideology and its vicissitudes within the discipline of anthropology.

This fact is most evident in the way in which Léopold Sédar Senghor has formulated his theory of negritude, which represents the extreme point of the racial and cultural consciousness of the African. The very terms he employs reflect his motivation, for they amount, in fact, to an elucidation of African difference and its passionate justification. Senghor's theory of negritude rests upon a theory of culture which postulates a reciprocity between the collective character of each race, as conditioned by an original formative environment, and the different cultural forms and civilizations to be found in the world.[15] This point of view fits properly into the perspective of cultural pluralism, which is a development of modern anthropology. It is not for nothing that Senghor's formulation of negritude takes the form largely of elaborate explications of African life and values, of what one might call a synthetic anthropology of the African world.

But perhaps the most significant aspect of Senghor's theory of negritude is that it contains within it a theory of knowledge, indeed an epistemology. The key notion in Senghor's theory is that of *emotion*, which he virtually erects into a function of knowledge and attributes to the African as a cardinal principle of his racial disposition. The considerable attention he has devoted in his writings to what he calls the 'physio-psychology of the Negro' is intended to clarify those elements in an original organic constitution of the African, and of the black race in general, which make for a distinct manner in his perception of the world and, ultimately, in his mode of being. In identifying those elements as constitutive of a particular quality of emotion, Senghor postulates a distinctive African mode of apprehension, one of the 'affective participation' of the black subject in the object of his experience. Since for Senghor each race, each civilization, has its characteristic manner of envisaging the world, this African manner, founded upon the values of emotion rather than upon the logical categories signposted by Western philosophy, is as valid in its own terms as the Western one inherited from ancient Greece, hence his celebrated and controversial assertion: 'Emotion is African, as Reason is Hellenic.'[16]

Thus Senghor assumes on his own account the dichotomy between the nature of the mind of the European and of the African (of so-called primitive man in general) made explicit by Lévy-Bruhl and, paradoxically, presses into the service of his negritude the notion of 'primitive mentality', which formerly carried a pejorative connotation, in order to give it a new and positive meaning. In the intellectual climate of Bergson's philosophy, which sought to promote the recognition of an inner life of things which simple intellection is unable to grasp, and of Surrealism, which sought to penetrate the depths of human consciousness beyond the reach of discursive reason, Senghor was emboldened to propose, as a valid approach to experience, those mental processes which had been attributed to so-called primitive man, and had therefore been considered inferior, but which now began to appear in a new light.[17]

What is more, Senghor finds a specific vindication of the cognitive value of emotion as a function of knowledge in the richness of those mental projections which he claims it determines in the collective representations of African peoples, in those mythical and symbolic schemes of thought and expression which define a structure of being and consciousness within the traditional culture. In this way, Senghor gives to his formulation of negritude the dimension of a cosmology.

Senghor's formulation goes well beyond the requirements of a refutation of the colonial ideology to take on the character of an autonomous system, of a personal philosophy in the sense of a whole vision of the world. His negritude is a compound of various influences drawn from the intellectual stock of his time, an eclectic system which finds its unity in an individual intelligence informed by a singular passion. It is in this respect that Tempels' *Bantu Philosophy* features prominently in Senghor's negritude. The vitalist emphasis of Bantu philosophy, as expounded by Tempels, is integrated into Senghor's theory in such a way as to demonstrate a distinctive African spirituality and world-view, an 'objective negritude' which serves as validation for the new conception of man, for the African humanism, which his theory seeks to promote.

For all its grounding in the ethnographic literature devoted to Africa, Senghor's negritude presents itself less as an empirical statement of the social facts and values that make up African cultural expression than as an all-encompassing concept of African identity, in its most abstract and undifferentiated aspect. It proposes a vision of a common cultural and spiritual inheritance of all Africans which is the expression of an original mode of being. This philosophical bent of negritude inspired a movement among several French-speaking African scholars towards the investigation of traditional thought systems, in an attempt to derive from them a distinctive African philosophy both as an empirical fact and in the technical terms of the discipline.

The work of Alexis Kagamé stands out in this respect. In his book *La Philosophie bantou–rwandaise de l'être* he sought to follow up and verify the ideas of Tempels regarding Bantu ontology. Kagamé reconstructs a philosophical system of the Rwanda through an analysis of their language and the terms which it employs to designate the notion of being and its modalities, terms which, according to him, prescribe an order of concepts and determine a conception of the world given explicit expression in the oral tradition.

The details of Kagamé's exposition of Bantu–Rwanda philosophy are now familiar to scholars of African culture.[18] It may be remarked here that Kagamé's main point, that the ontology of the Rwanda is given in the grammatical structure of their language and the semantic field that it proposes to its users, is specifically designed to deny the universal application of the categories handed down to Western philosophy by Aristotle. Whatever the merits of the case he presents, which is contested by Hountondji in the present book, the association he makes between thought processes and their symbolization in language recalls the Whorfian hypothesis in sociolinguistics and introduces into the field of philosophy the same order of relativity in culture that is now recognized by modern anthropology. The fact too that his exploration of the Bantu world-view takes him well beyond Tempels, whose theory of 'vital force' he finds inadequate, has raised the question of the possibilities for developing a distinctive approach to philosophical activity in an African register, if not in African languages.

Kagamé's work is the most prominent in the body of monographs and studies devoted to the traditional thought systems of various African societies by scholars of what may be called the philosophical school of the negritude movement. The work of Tempels and Kagamé became for this school not only models but, taken together, a fundamental reference, in such a way that Bantu philosophy became a specific problem for these scholars in their general attempt to construct an authentic African system equivalent to that of Western philosophy. It is against this trend of philosophical activity in Africa, which has now received the name of 'ethnophilosophy', that a reaction has set in today among a significant section of the younger generation of African philosophers.

Two explanations can be advanced for the development of the present reaction against ethnophilosophy. The first has to do with its intimate association with cultural nationalism and, in the franco-phone African context in particular, with the negritude movement, which has come under ceaseless attack from a section of the French-speaking black intelligentsia that may be described as its radical wing. The second explanation is partly a consequence of the first but is directly related to the growth of philosophy as an academic discipline in the new African universities created after independence, which saw the emergence of a new generation of academic philosophers anxious to remove their discipline from the shadow of the ideological preoccupations of African nationalism in order to affirm its independent, scientific character. The way in which these two factors have combined to make the question of African philosophy a lively one today can be said to signify changing African attitudes to the general issue of African identity as posed by the ideologues of African nationalism, which is now being given a redefinition in the post-colonial area: a development that is most evident in the way the movement of ideas has been proceeding in recent years among French-speaking African intellectuals.

It is not often realized in the English-speaking world that Senghor's theory of negritude has stirred up a controversy in francophone Africa which is, if anything, even more intense than the generally hostile reception it has met with from English-speaking African intellectuals. While Senghor's francophone critics accept the historical necessity for the rehabilitation of the black man and the revaluation of African culture, they have advanced strong theoretical objections to his formulation of negritude as a unified conception of the black race. Negritude is presented in these objections as not only too static to account for the diversified forms of concrete life in African societies but also, because of its 'biologism', as a form of acquiescence in the ideological presuppositions of European racism. Senghor's theory has been felt to be too thoroughly implicated in the system of imperialist ideas to be considered an effective challenge to its practical applications. The question of African identity required, from this point of view, a different approach which could not play into the hands of imperialism, which offered no form of compromise with its theory or practice.

It is essential in this connection to mention the work of Cheik Anta Diop, who attempts to define African identity in strictly sociological and materialist terms, to give the sense of African being a proper historical depth rather than a 'metaphysical' dimension, as with Senghor. Diop has achieved prominence today for his first work, *Nations Nègres et culture*, published in 1954, which has attained the status of a classic in black intellectual circles.[19] As is now well known, the primary objective of the book is to demonstrate the Negro origin of ancient Egyptian civilization and thus to refute the argument that the black race had produced no great world civilization. Diop argues further from the fact that historians have fully accepted the decisive influence of Egypt upon the early formation of Western civilization in classical Greece: Europe itself owes an immense cultural debt to Africa.

Diop's theory extends beyond the thesis put forward in his first work to his attempt in subsequent works to demonstrate the continuity of ancient Egyptian civilization in the traditional cultures of contemporary Africa. His examination of ancient Egyptian institutions and thought provides him with a cultural argument for postulating an essential affinity between the forms of social organization and the cosmology of the ancient Egyptians and those that appear to him to characterize the traditional world in black Africa. In this respect, despite Diop's declared antagonism towards Senghor's theory, there appears to be a remarkable convergence of their thinking. For not only do their ideas flow from a unified vision of Africa, but Diop also draws upon Tempels' *Bantu Philosophy* and its vitalist conception of the universe to characterize the African world-view. The historical and cultural connection between ancient Egypt and black Africa which Diop postulates leads him to affirm the existence of a distinctive African philosophy which originates in ancient Egypt and is perpetuated in the cosmologies of the various African societies today.[20]

The interest of Diop's work lies, then, in two directions. In the first place, the specific form which his historical approach to the question of African identity takes is intended to counter the evolutionist view of classical anthropology which contrives to place the white race and Western civilization at the apex of human development. As against the unilateral and ethnocentric conception of Hegel and Western scholars who have derived their view of history from him, Diop proposes a wider perspective from which to view the course of human development, a perspective that throws a new light upon Africa; his ideological project consists in projecting a vision of universal history in which Africa is profoundly involved.

Secondly, that vision implies not merely the attribution of a distinctive historical personality to Africa, but also the claim, through the connection with ancient Egyptian civilization, to an original heritage of philosophical thought.

Although Diop's work diverges in general method and in certain important details from Senghor's, it appears in retrospect to share a common spirit of cultural nationalism with negritude. Diop's ideas may even be said to complement those of Senghor by putting the weight of scholarly erudition behind the general proposition of negritude. History may be for Diop a primordial and determining factor of Africa's cultural unity, but the upshot of its course has been to effect a singular differentiation of the African in terms of his cultural expression and attitude to the world; it is this that Senghor has conceptualized as a structure and mode of being. The difference between Senghor and Diop reduces itself ultimately to one of perspective upon the African problematic created by the colonial experience – that of defining the African identity.

In the work of writers who have risen to prominence after them, this issue has been superseded by a new perspective upon African problems related to the post-colonial situation. The social and political realities of independent Africa have modified the climate of African opinion to such an extent that the ideological confrontation with imperialism has lost much of its earlier force and significance. The ideological cleavages on the continent which independence brought in its wake reflect a concern with new social problems in the African states which have to do with the creation of a new internal order consequent upon the formal end of colonial rule. This concern now exerts a far greater pressure upon African minds than the question of identity. The steady accumulation of opposition to negritude culminating in a general climate of disaffection towards the theory, thus indicates not only a different point of view with respect to the issues raised by the movement as a whole but also a totally new orientation of thought in French-speaking Africa.

It is impossible to doubt the influence of Frantz Fanon's writings in securing a clear ideological base for this new orientation and in imparting to it a radical spirit. Fanon's views of the African situation were shaped by the revolutionary idea of the total transformation of society. For him the struggle against colonialism had meaning not simply as a means to an objective purpose, signified by the attainment of political independence, but as a process through which colonized man would remake his humanity, diminished and distorted by the experience of domination. Fanon attached a psychological and moral value to violence which is inseparable from his vision of man creating his own identity in the effervescence of a progressive movement in history. His critique of Senghor's theory of negritude springs immediately from this revolutionary spirit. It is directed not only against the idea of a collective personality of the race objectified in the forms of articulation of the traditional culture but also against the implications of this idea in the post-colonial context. As he says: 'African culture will take concrete shape around the struggle of the people, not around songs, poems or folklore.'[21] Cultural expression for Fanon thus refers not to a predetermined model offered by the past but to a reality that lies in the future as a perpetual creation: for him culture is not a *state* but a *becoming*.

The political argument of Fanon's dismissal of negritude is developed more fully by Stanislas Adotevi in his book *Négritude et négrologues*, which contains the most comprehensive critique of the ideas of Senghor so far published.[22] Adotevi directs a fierce attack not only against the theory, especially as regards its biological underpinnings, but also against what he regards as its political uses in the post-colonial period. He argues that negritude was essentially a form of acquiescence with the colonial ideology, made more evident in recent times by the collaboration of its propagators with neo-colonialism. Negritude appears in the light which Adotevi projects upon it as a form of alienation in the Marxist sense of the term – as an ideological veil thrown over the interests of the new African bourgeoisie. The close association which is invoked between Senghor's theory and his options and policies as the head of an independent African state for twenty years provides a ready foundation for this kind of political interpretation.

Thus in the climate of opinion which now prevails in francophone Africa negritude can be said to have been compromised by the character of an official ideology which it came to assume. But beyond the political question, the reaction against negritude has had the effect of giving to the debate on African problems a new direction which does away with the question of racial and cultural identity in order to focus upon issues deemed more appropriate to the changed historical situation of the continent.

The radical tone introduced by Fanon into the debate on African problems, and especially on the cultural issue, has become evident in the writings of some of the younger professional philosophers who have turned their attention to the question of African philosophy against the background of the contemporary situation in Africa. The most prominent among these are Marcien Towa, a professor of philosophy at the University of Yaoundé, and Paulin Hountondji, the author of the present book, who stand together in the forefront of the reaction against ethnophilosophy in franco-phone Africa. Although there are important differences between their views, taken together they answer to a common position and a common objective – to lay finally to rest the issue of African identity so as to clear the path for a new direction of thought.

The way in which the progression from the critique of negritude towards a new ideological stance which transcends the issues it raises has come to affect the position represented by ethno-philosophy is clearly marked in this observation by Towa:

Senghorian negritude, and ethnophilosophy which seeks to perpetuate it, foster the illusion that Africa can offer to Europe a heightening of its soul (*un supplément d'âme*) before the complete liquidation of European imperialism in Africa. In reality, no cultural development of any import-ance will be possible in Africa until she has built up a material strength capable of guaranteeing her sovereignty and her power of decision not only in the political and economic field but also in the cultural. Our inferiority in material terms places our culture at the mercy of the great powers in our time.[23]

In his *Essai sur la problématique philosophique dans l'Afrique actuelle*, from which this quotation is taken, Towa develops argu-ments against ethnophilosophy which rest for the most part on methodological and technical grounds, but the final emphasis of the essay rests upon the political and social implications of philo-sophical activity, which for Towa must have a revolutionary function. It is for this reason that in a crucial passage of the essay he rejects the notion of a unique and immutable quality of African being: 'The transformation of one's present condition signifies at the same time the transformation of one's essence, of what is particular to the self, of what is original and unique about it; it is to enter into a negative relationship with the self.'[24] The hallowed idea of a fidelity to one's profound self, the reverence for the accumu-lated heritage of the past felt to be somehow compacted within the deep places of the individual being – all this is swept aside by Towa as no longer corresponding to the concrete facts of African existence. It is not only that the triumphs of cultural nationalism are discounted; they are presented by Towa as disabling, if not downright reactionary, in the post-colonial situation.

The complementary aspect of Towa's negative appraisal of ethnophilosophy and his call for a renunciation of the self as constituted by the African past is an opening out to new perspectives of thought and action, self-alienation in the positive Hegelian sense. This aspect of Towa's thinking is given direct expression in his advocacy of Western philosophy as the only intellectual method capable of leading to the transformation of Africa. For Towa the explanation of the historical development of Europe lies in its adoption of a rational approach to the world, of the logical tools developed within philosophy and applied to the objective universe of human life and expression. An immediate connection exists, therefore, between Western philosophy and the development of science and technology which recommends Western thought to Africa and which gives it a practical function as a means of our salvation in the modern world.

The fact that Towa is a professor of philosophy is not without interest for an appreciation of his ideas, for his essay reflects not only his concern for a rigorous definition of the area of his discipline but indeed a passionate faith in the effective significance of philosophy within the context of real life. Towa's preoccupation with the problem of philosophy and its function in Africa is dictated by immediate concerns of a political and ideological order. As he says in a subsequent work, 'philosophy is essentially a relation between a theory and the demands of social life'.[25]

Towa's thinking is obviously tributary to Fanon's, and his manner consists in carrying to their logical limits the ideas of the latter, in giving explicit conceptual form to their implications. The marked ideological orientation of this effort makes for certain theoretical weaknesses in the development of his arguments, for Towa is not far from equating philosophy with political radicalism. His critique of ethnophilosophy thus ends with the substitution of one form of ideological affiliation of philosophy for another.

In contrast to Towa, Hountondji does not claim an explicit social and political function for philosophy. The primary objective of his work, as reflected by the essays collected in this book, is to hold the African philosopher to a more rigorous conception of the discipline than is apparent in the work of the ethnophilosophers. His position on the question of African philosophy thus makes no concession to ideology, as is the case with Towa. Although their ideas coincide on many points, Hountondji's assessment of ethnophilosophy is much more severe and uncompromising in its approach. Indeed, in its comprehensiveness this assessment amounts, in fact, to what one might call a 'critique of ethnophilosophical reason', caught at the very roots of its conceptual foundation.

It will perhaps not surprise the reader to learn that this book stirred up a lively controversy within French-speaking African intellectual circles almost immediately upon its first publication in 1977, a controversy that shows no signs of subsiding even now. It is not difficult to understand why this is so, for besides presenting an emphatic challenge to the powerful intellectual establishment in French-speaking Africa represented by the ethnophilosophers, it raises at the same time a number of problems of a character likely to sustain a long debate both on the question of African philosophy and on the whole subject of intellectual life and activity in Africa.

It is, I believe, fair to observe that Hountondji's concern for rigour leads him to so restricted a definition of the scope of philosophy that it cannot be expected to command anything like wide assent. His emphasis on the strictly critical function of philosophy, which turns out to be in reality an endorsement of the current in Western philosophy that derives from Kant, is not likely to win the adherence to his position of those who propose a larger human significance for philosophical reflection. In this particular respect the categorical stand he takes against the notion of a collective philosophy derived from a reconstruction of the world-views and systems of thought of traditional cultures has drawn from his critics the charge of élitism. For although the critics do not subscribe to the procedures of ethnophilosophy, they have argued that Hountondji's conception of philosophy – that of a conscious and explicit mode of discourse which involves the individual responsibility of whoever engages in such a discourse – limits the possibility of an intelligent and coherent formulation of the facts of experience to the activity of a class of professionals who assume for themselves the sole charge of thinking for the rest of society. Moreover, it excludes from the purview of philosophy those other areas of mental activity in which are engaged the deepest responses of mankind to experience and which cannot but add a vital dimension to the theory and practice of philosophy. Such an area is indicated precisely by myth, which by its very nature is collective and which, besides its effective function in providing a normative reference for social life in pre-industrial societies, also affords an insight into the processes of the human mind, as demonstrated notably by Claude Lévi-Strauss.[26] From this perspective Hountondji's refusal to grant a philosophical significance to the productions of the oral tradition in which these mental processes are given signal expression is held to betray an insufficient awareness of the formal import of these productions because of their character as mental constructs. For if philosophy cannot be defined by the properties of song, it may well employ the formal modes of the latter for expression; the philosopher can thus legitimately burst into song to enforce his apprehension.

The charge of élitism is often linked to what is also perceived as the 'theoricism' of Hountondji, ascribed to the influence of his former teacher, Louis Althusser. The claim that Hountondji frequently makes that philosophy is, by its historical constitution and ultimately by its essential nature, a second order of science in its empirical practice, nothing other than the form of its reflection, gives rise to this charge. This claim clearly reflects a double preoccupation. On the one hand, it represents a concern for the application of a rigorous method in the conduct of philosophy in Africa, a reaction against the conceptual naïveté and perhaps mediocrity of much of what passes today for African philosophy. On the other hand, it betrays an anxiety to preserve the discipline from the incursions of ideology. This latter aspect of his preoccupation has been interpreted as a curious limitation to his intellectual commitment to Marxist philosophy, which entails a social application of thought.[27]

There is often a tendentious character to the criticisms levelled against Hountondji's ideas, which tend to be disengaged by his antagonists from the technical framework of their development in order that they may be related to ideological considerations. None the less, it is possible to consider that Hountondji's emphatic tone betrays him into the occasional simplification or overstatement of his case; to discern a peremptoriness which, while it corresponds to the strength of his conviction, obscures the finer points of his argument and therefore leaves room for its misrepresentation.

The English-speaking reader of these essays may well sense more than a hint of the polemical in their author's conduct of his argument, which is not habitual in a debate of this kind within his own intellectual milieu. Their general tone certainly contrasts with the manner in which professional philosophers in English-speaking

Africa – such as Peter Bodunrin, Henry Oruka, Kwasi Wiredu – have gone about canvassing a point of view similar in many ways to that of Hountondji on the same question. The sharp polarization which he often suggests between ethnophilosophy and traditional philosophy in the Western sense is absent from the contributions of the English-speaking writers to the debate on African philosophy. The latter have tended rather to consider the entire field of mental productions accessible to the African through his total cultural experience as a legitimate province of activity for the African philosopher. Their efforts have been bent towards making clear the discriminations that need to be established so as to ensure a proper methodological relationship between the different areas which may be thought to constitute this general field. Wiredu's position in particular seeks a fine mediation between the African and Western traditions of thought in what he calls an 'African practice of philosophy' which would integrate individual reflections upon African material, upon themes contained in traditional African systems of thought, into a comprehensive philosophical enterprise informed in its spirit and methods by the canons of Western philosophy. In this way the modern African philosopher would be able to take charge, in an all-inclusive approach to philosophy, of the heritage of thought provided by his particular background while bringing it into a meaningful relation with the more formalized system of thought of international philosophy.[28]

It is significant that the force of the controversy which, along with Towa, Hountondji has provoked on the question of African philosophy has obliged him in a recent article to restate his case more scrupulously, in such a way as to bring his position close to that of Wiredu, summarized above.[29] More important, his reply introduces a clearer ideological element into his point of view than hitherto by deliberately drawing attention to the political implications of his conception of philosophy – and, by implication, all forms of intellectual activity – in the present African context. He rejects what he considers the populist tendency of his critics, who equate the cause of the African 'masses' with an undiscriminating defence of the traditional culture in which for the most part they are still bound and who therefore promote the illusion of a uniformity of thought within that culture which takes institutional form in a collective philosophy. Against this unanimist view of the traditional culture projected on to philosophical activity in the modern context Hountondji emphasizes once again the role of argument and debate in philosophy, which give it a critical function, and concludes that this function needs to be placed at the service of a democratic ideal that has become especially relevant in the present atmosphere of political life in Africa.

The modification of stance implied by his reply to his critics and its explicit political conclusion seem to me to confirm the spirit of Hountondji's work as revealed in this book. From the purely technical point of view, his critique of ethnophilosophy is intended to put in order the house of African philosophy. Even the minimal definition he gives of African philosophy ('texts written by Africans'), which wears the air of a tautology, has a value equivalent to Descartes' systematic doubt: it is designed to clear the decks, so to speak, for new and serious beginnings. In its polemical thrust his whole work assumes the character of a manifesto, comparable with Ayer's *Language, Truth and Logic* in its uncompromising stand upon the nature of philosophy. Furthermore, his insistence upon the need for a concerted organization of scientific activity as a condition for philosophy in Africa corresponds to a concern for the improvement of the quality of life on our continent. Thus what has been taken to be his theoricism turns out, in this perspective, to be rooted in a concern of a very practical order.

In this light Hountondji's contribution to the technical and theoretical debate about African philosophy can be seen to turn, in reality, most essentially upon the question of what intellectual direction to give, in this day and age, to a continent beset by a multitude of problems. His work belongs in the last resort not to the limited circle of professional philosophy but to the wider context of social thought in contemporary Africa.

ABIOLA IRELE

Part One
Arguments

1 An alienated literature*

To Nunayon-Hervé
There are two ways of losing oneself: through fragmentation in the particular or dilution in the 'universal'.

AIMÉ CÉSAIRE, *Lettre à Maurice Thorez* (1956)

By 'African philosophy' I mean a set of texts, specifically the set of texts written by Africans and described as philosophical by their authors themselves.

Let us note that this definition begs no question, since the meaning of the qualifier 'philosophical' is irrelevant – as is, indeed, the cogency of the qualification. All that matters is the *fact* of the qualification itself, the deliberate recourse to the word *philosophy*, and whatever meaning that *word* may have. In other words, we are concerned solely with the philosophical intention of the authors, not with the degree of its effective realization, which cannot easily be assessed.

So for us African philosophy is a body of literature whose existence is undeniable, a bibliography which has grown constantly over the last thirty years or so. The limited aims of these few remarks are to circumscribe this literature, to define its main themes, to show what its problematic has been so far and to call it into question. These aims will have been achieved if we succeed in convincing our African readers that African philosophy does not lie where we have long been seeking it, in some mysterious corner of our supposedly immutable soul, a collective and unconscious world-view which it is incumbent on us to study and revive, but that our philosophy consists essentially in the process of analysis itself, in that very discourse through which we have been doggedly attempting to define ourselves – a discourse, therefore, which we must recognize as ideological and which it is now up to us to *liberate*, in the most *political* sense of the word, in order to equip ourselves with a truly theoretical discourse which will be indissolubly philosophical and scientific.[1]

---

* An article written for UNESCO in 1969 and published in *Diogène*, no. 71 (1970), under the title 'Remarques sur la philosophie africaine contemporaine'. The original text has not been significantly modified.

Archeology: Western 'ethnophilosophy'

A forerunner of 'African philosophy': Tempels. This Belgian missionary's *Bantu Philosophy* still passes today, in the eyes of some,
for a classic of 'African philosophy'.[2] In fact, it is an ethnological
work with philosophical pretensions, or more simply, if I may coin
the word, a work of 'ethnophilosophy'. It need concern us here only
inasmuch as some African philosophers have themselves made
reference to it in their efforts to reconstruct, in the wake of the
Belgian writer, a specifically African philosophy.

Indeed, *Bantu Philosophy* did open the floodgates to a deluge of
essays which aimed to reconstruct a particular *Weltanschauung*, a
specific world-view commonly attributed to all Africans, abstracted
from history and change and, moreover, *philosophical*, through an
interpretation of the customs and traditions, proverbs and institutions – in short, various data – concerning the cultural life of African
peoples.

One can readily discern Tempels' motives. At first sight they
appear to be generous, since he had set out to correct a certain
image of the black man disseminated by Lévy-Bruhl and his school,
to show that the African *Weltanschauung* could not be reduced to
that celebrated 'primitive mentality' which was supposed to be
insensitive to contradiction, indifferent to the elementary laws of
logic, proof against the laws of experience and so forth, but that it
rested, in fact, on a systematic conception of the universe which,
however different it might be from the Western system of thought,
equally deserved the name of 'philosophy'. At first sight, then,
Tempels' object appeared to be to rehabilitate the black man and
his culture and to redeem them from the contempt from which they
had suffered until then.

But on closer scrutiny the ambiguity of the enterprise is obvious.
It is clear that it is not addressed to Africans but to Europeans, and
particularly to two categories of Europeans: colonials and missionaries.[3] In this respect the seventh and last chapter bears an eloquent
title: 'Bantu philosophy and our mission to civilize'. In effect, we
are back to square one: Africans are, as usual, excluded from the
discussion, and Bantu philosophy is a mere pretext for learned
disquisitions among Europeans. The black man continues to be the
very opposite of an interlocutor; he remains a topic, a voiceless face
under private investigation, an object to be defined and not the
subject of a possible discourse.[4]

What, then, is the content of this Bantu 'philosophy'? I shall not try to analyse the whole book but will content myself with a brief review of its main findings in order to confront them with the real discourse of African philosophers themselves.

According to Tempels, Bantu ontology is essentially a theory of forces: Bantus have a dynamic conception of being, while the Western conception is static. For the black man, then, being is power, not only inasmuch as it possesses power, for that would merely mean that power is an attribute of being, but in the sense that its very essence is to *be* power:

For the Bantu [says Tempels] power is not an accident: it is more even than a necessary accident; it is the very essence of being. . . . Being is power, power is being. Our notion of being is 'that which is', theirs is 'the power that is'. Where we think the concept 'to be', they make use (*sic*) of the concept 'power'. Where we see concrete beings, they see concrete forces. Where we would say that *beings* are distinguished by their essence or nature, Bantus would say that *forces* differ by their essence or nature.[5]

However, power so defined is not only a reality; it is also a value. The Bantu's entire effort is devoted to increasing his 'vital power', for all power can increase or diminish. This again, Tempels tells us, is opposed to the Western conception. As far as the European is concerned, one either possesses human nature or one does not. By acquiring knowledge, by exercising his will, by developing in various ways, man does not become more human. On the contrary, when a Bantu says, for instance: 'I am becoming strong' or when he says compassionately to a friend who has been struck with misfortune: 'Your vital strength is reduced, your life has been eroded' these statements are to be taken literally as implying an essential modification of human nature itself.

Another principle of this Bantu 'philosophy' is the interaction of forces. This interaction, says Tempels, is not merely mechanical, chemical or psychic, but, more fundamentally, it is akin to the metaphysical dependence which links the creature to the creator (in this sense that 'the creature is, by its very nature, permanently dependent on its creator for its existence and subsistence').

Yet another principle is the hierarchy of forces. An important one, this, since it is the foundation of social order and, so to speak, its metaphysical bedrock.

At the top of the scale, we are told, there is God, both spirit and creator.

Then come the forefathers, the founders of the various clans, the archpatriarchs to whom God first communicated the vital force.

Then there are the dead of the tribe, in order of seniority; these are the intermediaries through whom the elder forces exert their influence over the living generation.

The living themselves, who come next, are stratified 'not only by law but in accordance with their very being, with primogeniture and their organic degree of life, in other words with their vital power'.

Right at the bottom of the scale the lower forces, animal, vegetable or mineral, are also said to be stratified according to vital power, rank or primogeniture. Thus, analogies are possible between a human group and a lower animal group, for instance: 'He who is the chief in the human order "demonstrates" his superior rank by the use of a royal animal's skin.' (This is the key to totemism, according to Tempels.)

Stress is laid on the internal hierarchy within the living group, a hierarchy founded, according to Tempels, on a metaphysical order of subordination. This order was in jeopardy every time the colonial administration imposed on a black population a chief who did not fit the norms of tradition. Hence the protests of the natives: 'So-and-so cannot be the chief. It is not possible. Henceforth nothing will grow on our soil, women will no longer give birth and everything will be stricken with sterility.'

Finally, as the ultimate crown of this theoretical edifice, Bantu 'philosophy' emerges as humanism; 'creation is centred on man', and especially on the living generation, for 'the living, earthly, human generation is the centre of all mankind, including the world of the dead'.

If it be added that the interaction of all these forces, far from being haphazard, takes place according to strict and immutable laws (of which Tempels formulates the three most general), one is immediately aware of the miraculous coherence of this ontological 'system' – and of its great simplicity. However, its author assures us that it is the ultimate foundation of the entire social practice of the Bantus, of all Africans and of all 'primitives' and 'clan societies'.

Political criticism

This is all very fine, but perhaps too good to be true. One is reminded of Césaire's massive criticism, grave in content, global in scope. While accepting some of Tempels' points, Césaire views his exposition as a politically oriented project and highlights its practical implications.

Césaire's criticism may be summed up in a sentence: Bantu 'philosophy' is an attempt to create a *diversion*. It diverts attention from the fundamental political problems of the Bantu peoples by fixing it on the level of fantasy, remote from the burning reality of colonial exploitation. The respect shown for the 'philosophy' and the spiritual values of the Bantu peoples, which Tempels turns into a universal remedy for all the ills of the then Belgian Congo, is astonishingly abstract (albeit perfectly understandable in view of the author's political lineage), compared with the concrete historical situation of that country. Further, when it is considered that 'the white man, a new phenomenon in the Bantu world, could be apprehended only in terms of the categories of traditional Bantu philosophy', that he was therefore 'incorporated into the world of forces, in the position that was his by right according to the rationale of the Bantu ontological system', that is to say, as 'an elder, a superior human force greater than the vital force of any black man',[6] then the real function of Tempels' much vaunted respect for Bantu 'philosophy', and at the same time the relevance of Césaire's criticism becomes apparent. The humanist thinker throws off his mask and reveals himself as the guardian of the colonial order, and his hazy abstractions can be seen for what they are, concrete devices in the service of a very concrete policy which is nothing less than the preservation of imperialist domination. Césaire's irony can now be fully appreciated:

Bantu thought being ontological, Bantus are interested only in ontological satisfaction. Decent wages? Good housing and food? I tell you these Bantus are pure spirits: 'What they want above all is not an improvement in their material or economic situation, but recognition by the white man and respect for their human dignity, for their full human value.' In short, one or two cheers for Bantu vital force, a wink for the Bantu immortal soul, and that's that. A bit too easy, perhaps?[7]

Yet Césaire's criticism left the theoretical problem untouched, since, in his own words, his target was 'not Bantu philosophy itself, but the political use some people want to make of it'. The idea that there might exist a hidden philosophy to which all Bantus unconsciously and collectively adhered was not at issue, and Césaire's criticism left it unbroached. The theory has therefore remained very much alive; in fact, it has provided the motivation for all our subsequent philosophical literature. The history of our philosophy since then has been largely the history of our succeeding interpretations of this collective 'philosophy', this world-view which was assumed to be pre-determined, and to underpin all our traditions and behaviour, and which analysis must now modestly set out to unravel.

As a result, most African philosophers have misunderstood themselves. While they were actually creating new philosophemes, they thought they were merely reproducing those which already existed. While they were producing, they thought they were simply recounting. Commendable modesty, no doubt, but also betrayal, since the philosopher's self-denial in the face of his own discourse was the inevitable consequence of a projection which made him arbitrarily ascribe to his people his own theoretical choices and ideological options. Until now African philosophy has been little more than an ethnophilosophy, the imaginary search for an immutable, collective philosophy, common to all Africans, although in an unconscious form.[8]

From Tempels to Kagamé: continuity and discontinuity

Such is the mainstream of African philosophy, which I must now endeavour to describe. Reference to Tempels enables us from the outset to see its essential weakness, to which I shall return. But fortunately there is more to African philosophy, even in its ethnophilosophical vagaries, than the mere reiteration of *Bantu Philosophy*.

In the first place, its motivations are more complex. The aim is no longer to furnish European settlers and missionaries with an easy access to the black man's soul, raised to the status of unwitting candidate for 'civilization' and Christianization. African philosophers aim to *define* themselves and their peoples, in the face of Europe, without allowing anybody else to do it for them, to *fix* and *petrify* them at leisure.

Moreover, even if this attempt at self-definition maintains the fiction of a collective philosophy among our authors, they nevertheless show genuine philosophical qualities in the *manner* in which they claim to justify this fiction. The severe rigour of some of their deductions, the accuracy of some of their analyses, the skill which some of them display in debate, leave us in no doubt as to their status. They are certainly philosophers, and their only weakness is that the *philosophical form* of their own discourse has been created in terms of a myth disguised as a collective philosophy.

One example will suffice to illustrate this point: Kagamé. *La Philosophie bantou–rwandaise de l'être*, expressly and from the outset, establishes its point of view in relation to Tempels' work as an attempt by an autochthonous Bantu African to 'verify the validity of the theory advanced by this excellent missionary'.[9] Nor can it be denied that the Rwandais priest is often in accord with the Belgian missionary, particularly where we are concerned here.

1   The idea of an immutable, collective philosophy conceived as the ultimate basis of Bantu institutions and culture, recognized more or less consciously by every Bantu. 'Philosophical principles', writes Kagamé, '. . . are invariable: since the nature of beings must always remain what it is, their profoundest explanation is inevitably immutable.' And again, concerning his 'sources' of information: 'We shall have to resort to a kind of institutionalized record. . . . Even if the formal structure of these "institutions" is not the expression of a philosophical entity, it may be shown to be a direct consequence of a mode of formulating problems which lies within the purview of philosophy.'[10]

Let us note, however, that Kagamé is here much more subtle than Tempels. Unlike the Belgian missionary, he is duly wary of attributing to his fellow countrymen a philosophical *system* in the full sense of the word, with clearly and logically defined articulations and contours. All he admits to is a number of invariable 'philosophical principles' that give no indication of forming a system; and he willingly speaks of 'intuitive philosophy', as opposed to academic, systematic philosophy.

2   The idea that European philosophy itself can be reduced, in spite of its eventful and variegated history, to a lowest common denominator, namely, the Aristotelian–Scholastic philosophy. In fact, this second idea explains the first, since it underlay and triggered off the strategy of *differentiating* African 'philosophy' from European philosophy.

On the other hand, as far as the *content* of this Bantu 'philosophy' is concerned, there are undeniable convergences between Kagamé and Tempels, especially as regards the Bantu conception of man.

3   The idea that man is indivisible, a simple unit, and not, as the Europeans believe, a compound of body and soul. Thus, Kagamé tells us that there is no word in Kinyarwanda to denote the soul, at least as long as the individual is alive.

4   The idea that God, and not the natural parents, is the real begetter and author of individual destinies.

5   The idea that people's names indicate their destiny.

6   Above all, the idea that humanity is at the centre of the Bantus' thoughts and preoccupations, to such an extent that other beings are conceived solely in opposition to it, as negations or inverted images of their own natures as thinking beings: things (*ibintu* in Kinyarwanda) are by definition beings deprived of intelligence, as opposed to humans (*umuntu*, pl. *abantu*), which are defined as the intelligent being.

As against these similarities, Kagamé does part company with Tempels (without expressly saying so) on a number of very important points.

In the first place, his method, which is founded on direct linguistic analysis, differs from Tempels'. Among all the 'institutionalized records' of Bantu culture, Kagamé deliberately emphasizes language and its grammatical structure.[11] Hence perhaps the exceptional value of his book. Kagamé nags us – and in doing so renders us signal service – with the disturbing reminder that we might think very differently if we made systematic use of our mother tongues in our theoretical work. Indeed, the Rwandais philosopher is much more sensitive than was his Belgian predecessor to the contingency of language and the inevitable rooting of even the most abstract human thought in a world of pre-existing meanings.

More rigorous in method, Kagamé's analysis is also less ambitious in aim. It is offered to us expressly as a 'monograph', valid only for a specific geographical and linguistic area: Rwanda and its close neighbours. This is a far cry from Tempels' rash generalizations, with their claim not only to open wide the doors of Bantu philosophy but also to hold the key of all 'primitive' thought.

Moreover, it is obvious that Kagamé, while he joins with Tempels in asserting the existence of a collective Bantu philosophy, carefully avoids confining it within a narrow particularism. On the contrary, he more than once emphasizes its universal aspects, by which it is linked with, among others, European 'philosophy'. For instance, he tells us that 'formal logic is the same in all cultures' and that concept, judgement and reasoning have no Bantu, Eastern or Western specificity: 'What is expressed on this subject, in any language of Europe or Asia, America or Africa, can always be transposed into any other language belonging to a different culture.'[12]

Kagamé is also peculiarly sensitive to those transformations of Bantu 'philosophy' which result from its contacts with European culture. To him these transformations appear profound and significant, whereas Tempels believed that 'acculturation' could never impart more than a superficial veneer. Thus, the Rwandais philosopher warns us: 'You will not find, in our country at the present time, more than a few people who have not corrected their traditional views on the world and on the heroic style of the past.'[13] In particular, he insists at length on the innovations introduced by the missionaries into the vocabulary and even the grammatical structure of Kinyarwanda.[14] In this he shows himself sensitive to the internal dynamism and capacity for assimilation of his own culture – so much so that he himself gives us the facts with which to refute his own initial methodological assumption, posing the immutability of philosophical principles.

Such divergences are important and would suffice to differentiate Kagamé's work clearly from Tempels'. But beyond these formal differences even more striking is the fact that the two authors, while both postulating the existence of a constituted Bantu philosophy, give different interpretations of its content. Thus (although his criticism remains general and is not directed overtly at Tempels) Kagamé in fact rejects the fundamental thesis of the Belgian missionary, according to which the equivalence of the concepts of being and power is the essential characteristic of Bantu thought. It is true that the Rwandais priest also recognizes a difference between the Aristotelian concept of substance and kindred concepts in Bantu thought. This difference is that the 'philosophy of European culture' tends to conceive being in its static aspect, while the philosophy of Bantu culture prefers to consider its dynamic aspect. But he states that this is only 'a slight nuance', for the two aspects remain complementary and inseparable in any mode of thought:

In both systems, indeed, there are inevitably a static and a dynamic aspect at the same time.
1.   Any structure, considered apart from its finality, must appear static.
2.   If you then consider a structure as having an end, as being structurally oriented to action or being used for an end, that structure will present its dynamic aspect.

It therefore follows that if the philosophy of Bantu culture is called dynamic, it must be remembered that it is in the first place static. If the philosophy of European culture is described as static, it must not be forgotten that it is in the second place dynamic. Let me summarize these two correlative aspects in a double axiom:

1.   Operational predisposition presupposes essence.
2.   Essence is structured in terms of its finality.[15]

While Tempels is not mentioned, the target of this critique is clear. But this is far from being the only divergence between Kagamé and Tempels. Many others occur in their interpretations of Bantu 'philosophy', even though they both suppose this 'philosophy' to be constituted and pre-existing, confined once and for all in the African's eternally immutable soul (Tempels) or at least in the permanent essence of his culture (Kagamé). Who is right? Which is the better interpretation? The choice is the reader's. Perhaps he will wish, in order to form his own opinion and close the debate, to return to the evidence itself and take cognizance of the original text of African 'philosophy', that secret text so differently interpreted by Tempels and Kagamé? This is what one usually does in Europe (and even Asia) when, in the name of intellectual integrity, one studies an author or a doctrine with a view to arriving at one's own conclusion in the face of the 'conflict of interpretations'.[16] Only a return to sources can enlighten us. It alone can enable us to discriminate between interpretations and assess their reliability or simply their pertinence.

Unfortunately, in the case of African 'philosophy' there are no sources; or at least, if they exist, they are not philosophical *texts* or *discourses*. Kagamé's 'institutionalized records', or those which Tempels had earlier subjected to 'ethnophilosophical' treatment, are wholly distinct from philosophy. They are in no way comparable with the sources which for an interpreter of, say, Hegelianism, or dialectical materialism, or Freudian theory, or even Confucianism are extant in the explicit texts of Hegel, Marx, Freud or Confucius, in their discursive development as permanently available products of language.

I can foresee an objection. Of course I know that among Kagamé's 'institutionalized records' the products of language occupy a large place (proverbs, tales, dynastic poems and the whole of Africa's *oral literature*). I shall even add that Kagamé's work is so exceptionally interesting precisely because of his extraordinary knowledge of the traditions, language and oral literature of Rwanda.[17] But the point is that this literature – at least as it is presented by Kagamé – is *not* philosophical. Now, scientific method demands that a sociological document is interpreted *first* in terms of sociology, a botanical text (written or oral) first in terms of botany, histories first in terms of historiography, etc. Well then, the same scientific rigour should prevent us from arbitrarily projecting a *philosophical discourse* on to products of language which expressly offer themselves as something other than philosophy. In effecting this projection, Kagamé – and Tempels before him, along with those African ethnophilosophers who followed suit (we are less interested in the European variety)[18] – committed what Aristotle called (and Kagamé himself is rather fond of invoking Aristotle) a *metabasis eis allo genos*, i.e. a confusion of categories.[19] This leaves readers with no means of checking their interpretations. As the evidence derived from the 'institutionalized' – but not philosophical – 'records' is inadequate, readers are brutally thrown back upon themselves and compelled to recognize that the whole construct rests on sand. Indeed, Kagamé, in spite of the very attractive qualities of his analysis and the relative accuracy of some of his sequences, has remained *on the whole* the prisoner of an ideological myth, that of a collective African 'philosophy' which is nothing but a revamped version of Lévy-Bruhl's 'primitive mentality', the imaginary subject of a scholarly discourse which one may regret Kagamé did not apply to something else.

Kagamé himself seems to have been aware of the difficulty, for he felt compelled, in order to render the idea of a collective philosophy plausible, to assume, at the beginnings of Rwandais culture, the existence and deliberate action of 'great initiators', intuitive philosophers who are supposed expressly to have formulated the principles of Bantu philosophy at the same time as they founded the institutions of that society.[20] But it is easy to see (and Kagamé himself can hardly have been taken in) that this assumption is gratuitous, even mythological. Moreover – and this is more serious – it does not even solve the problem but rather encloses us in a vicious circle. The alternatives are as follows. Either Bantu ontology is strictly immanent in the Bantu languages as such and contemporaneous with them (which Kagamé expressly recognizes, since he infers this ontology from the grammatical structures of Kinyarwanda), in which case it cannot have been taught by 'initiators', who would have had to express themselves in these

Bantu languages; or this philosophy really was taught at a particular point in time, and in this case it is not coeval with the Bantu languages but is a historical stage in Bantu culture, destined to be overtaken by history.

Either way, Bantu 'philosophy'[21] is shown to be a myth. To destroy this myth once and for all, and to clear our conceptual ground for a genuine theoretical discourse – these are the tasks now awaiting African philosophers and scientists. I will now seek to show briefly that these tasks are in fact inseparable from political effort – namely, the anti-imperialist struggle in the strictest sense of the term.

The unshackling of discourse

I have quoted Kagamé only as an example. Despite his undeniable talent and his powerful theoretical temperament (which so brilliantly distinguishes him from some ethnophilosophers), it seems to me that his work simply perpetuates an ideological myth which is itself of non-African origin.

Unfortunately, Kagamé is not alone. A quick look at the bibliography suggested in note 1 is enough to show how much energy African philosophers have devoted to the definition of an original, specifically African 'philosophy'. In varying degrees, Makarakiza, Lufuluabo, Mulago, Bahoken, Fouda and, to a lesser extent, William Abraham remain caught in this myth, however scientific and productive their research (remarkable in some cases), sincere their patriotism and intense their commitment may have been.[22]

Theirs is clearly a rearguard action. The quest for originality is always bound up with a desire to show off. It has meaning only in relation to the Other, from whom one wishes to distinguish oneself at all costs. This is an ambiguous relationship, inasmuch as the assertion of one's difference goes hand in hand with a passionate urge to have it recognized by the Other. As this recognition is usually long in coming, the desire of the subject, caught in his own trap, grows increasingly hollow until it is completely alienated in a restless craving for the slightest gesture, the most cursory glance from the Other.

For his part, the Other (in this case the European, the former colonizer) didn't mind a bit. From the outset he himself had instinctively created a gap between himself and the Other (the colonized), as between the master and his slave, as the paradigmatic subject of absolute difference.[23] But eventually, as a gesture of repentance, or rather, to help allay his own spiritual crisis, he began to celebrate this difference, and so the mysterious primitive 'mentality' was metamorphosed into primitive 'philosophy' in the hard-pressed master's mystified and mystifying consciousness. The difference was maintained but reinterpreted, or, if one prefers, inverted; and although the advertised primitive 'philosophy' did not correspond to that which the colonized wished to see recognized, at least it made dialogue and basic solidarity possible.

It was a case, says Eboussi aptly, quoting Jankelevitch, of 'doubly interpreted misinterpretation', in which the victim makes itself the executioner's secret accomplice, in order to commune with him in an artificial world of falsehood.[24]

What does that mean in this context? Simply that contemporary African philosophy, inasmuch as it remains an ethnophilosophy, has been built up essentially *for a European public*. The African ethnophilosopher's discourse is not intended for Africans. It has not been produced for their benefit, and its authors understood that it would be challenged, if at all, not by Africans but by Europe alone. Unless, of course, the West expressed itself through Africans, as it knows so well how to do. In short, the African ethnophilosopher made himself the spokesman of All-Africa facing All-Europe at the imaginary rendezvous of give and take – from which we observe that 'Africanist' particularism goes hand in glove, *objectively*, with an abstract universalism, since the African intellectual who adopts it thereby expounds it, over the heads of his own people, in a mythical dialogue with his European colleagues, for the constitution of a 'civilization of the universal'.[25]

So it is no surprise, then, if this literature, like the whole of African literature in French (and to a lesser extent, in English), is much better known outside than inside Africa. This is due not to chance or to material circumstances only but to fundamental reasons which proceed from the original destination of this literature.

Now the time has come to put an end to this scandalous extra-version. Theoretical discourse is undoubtedly a good thing; but in present-day Africa we must at all costs address it first and foremost to our fellow countrymen and offer it for the appreciation and discussion of Africans themselves.[26] Only in this way shall we be able to promote a genuine scientific movement in Africa and put an end to the appalling theoretical void which grows deeper every day within a population now weary and indifferent to theoretical problems that are seen as pointless.

Science is generated by discussion and thrives on it.[27] If we want science in Africa, we must create in the continent a human environment in which and by which the most diverse problems can be freely debated and in which these discussions can be no less freely recorded and disseminated, thanks to the written word, to be submitted to the appreciation of all and transmitted to future generations. These, I am sure, will do much better than we have.

This, obviously, presupposes the existence of freedom of expression, which in varying degrees so many of our present-day political regimes are endeavouring to stifle. But this means that the responsibility of African philosophers (and of all African scientists) extends far beyond the narrow limits of their discipline and that they cannot afford the luxury of self-satisfied apoliticism or quiescent complacency about the established disorder unless they deny themselves both as philosophers and as people. In other words, the theoretical liberation of philosophical discourse presupposes political liberation. We are today at the centre of a tangle of problems. The need for a political struggle makes itself felt at all levels, on all planes. I shall simply add that this struggle will not be simple and that clarity as well as resolve are needed if we are to succeed. The future is at stake.

2 History of a myth*

African philosophical literature rests, it hardly needs saying, on a confusion: the confusion between the popular (ideological) use and the strict (theoretical) use of the word 'philosophy'. According to the first meaning, philosophy is any kind of wisdom, individual or collective, any set of principles presenting some degree of coherence and intended to govern the daily practice of a man or a people. In this vulgar sense of the word, everyone is naturally a philosopher, and so is every society. But in the stricter sense of the word, one is no more spontaneously a philosopher than one is spontaneously a chemist, a physicist or a mathematician, since philosophy, like chemistry, physics or mathematics, is a specific theoretical discipline with its own exigencies and methodological rules.

In this kinship between philosophy and the sciences we have the touchstone, the infallible criterion by which to judge the absurdity or relevance of any proposition on philosophy, however general. Indeed, whatever scope is assigned to philosophy to distinguish it from other disciplines, one thing is certain: philosophy is a theoretical discipline and therefore belongs to the same genus as algebra, geometry, mechanics, linguistics, etc. Now, if we pose that it is absurd to speak of *unconscious* algebra, geometry, linguistics, etc., and if we accept that no science can exist historically without an explicit discourse, then by the same token we must regard the very idea of an unconscious philosophy as absurd. Conversely, if we believe that it is of the essence of any science to be constituted by free discussion, by the confrontation of hypotheses and theories created by the thought of individuals (or at least assumed by them) and reaching total convergence through reciprocal amendment, then we must also find absurd the idea of a collective, immutable and definitive 'philosophy', abstracted from history and progress.

* A recast version of an article written in 1970, published in *Daho-Express*, no. 1411 (10 May 1974), and in *Présence Africaine*, no. 91, 3rd Quarter (1974).

But this is precisely what 'African philosophy' is, as understood by our Africanists. Why such a flagrant misconception? There is every indication that our ethnophilosophers were perfectly aware of the equivocation. It is true that Tempels seems to resort most naturally to the ideological use of the word; but one can detect in certain of his colleagues and disciples something like a scruple or at least an embarrassment. Kagamé warns us, right at the beginning of his great work, that he is using the word in the sense of 'intuitive philosophy' and not in its proper sense, and in *Un Visage africain du christianisme*, Vincent Mulago contrasts 'formal' and 'material' philosophy. But in both, this distinction functions as a theoretical assumption preceding their analysis, as a preliminary justification. And this is precisely what is so surprising. The distinction between the two ideas of philosophy should lead not to the consecration of the vulgar meaning but to its destruction. It should compel a philosopher to reject as null and void the pseudo-philosophy of world-views and make him see clearly that philosophy in the strictest sense, far from being a continuation of spontaneous thought systems, is constituted by making a clean break from them; whereas here it serves our authors as a pretext for undertaking in all sincerity, a conjectural reconstruction of African wisdom, decked out for the occasion as a philosophy.

Why this failure? Why does the conceptual distinction remain without effect? Why does the promised clarification come to nothing? The failure cannot be ascribed to igorance. It is clearly deliberate, the effect of a wish. African ethnophilosophers (like their predecessor Tempels, in spite of his apparent naïveté) knew full well that 'African philosophy', in the sense in which they under-stood it, belonged to a very different genus from European philo-sophy, taken in the usual and exact sense of the term. The two were wholly distinct and therefore incomparable, incommensurable. And yet they insisted on this comparison, setting their conceptual understanding on one side while drowning the language of science in a welter of desire.

We have already identified this desire: African intellectuals wanted at all costs to rehabilitate themselves in their own eyes and in the eyes of Europe. To do so, they were prepared to leave no stone unturned, and they were only too happy to discover, through Tempels' notorious *Bantu Philosophy*, a type of argumentation that could, despite its ambiguities (or, rather, thanks to them), serve as one way of ensuring this rehabilitation. This explains why so many

African authors, in various tones and moods, struck up the Tempelsian theme, whereas they should have been mindful of the massive and blinding fact that the Belgian missionary, by his own admission, was addressing not them but the European public.

We shall not so much insist here on this *fact* as on the way in which it determines the content of Tempels' work. Being a European's discourse addressed to other Europeans, an exhibit in a debate in which the Bantus have no part to play and appear only as an object or pretext, *Bantu Philosophy* is cut to its public's size. In a dual motion that is contradictory only in appearance, it aims on the one hand at facilitating what it calls Europe's 'mission to civilize' (by which we understand: practical mastery by the colonizer of the black man's psychological wellsprings) and, on the other hand, at warning Europe itself against the abuses of its own technocratic and ultra-materialistic civilization, by offering her, at the cost of a few rash generalizations, an image of the fine spirituality of the primitive Bantu. It is a double problematic, that of the 'mission to civilize' and the 'heightening of the soul';[1] neither can be separated from the other. The colonizers 'civilize', but only on condition that they rehumanize themselves and recover their soul. The theoretical objective of *Bantu Philosophy* is entirely contained in this double problematic, which itself finds its meaning solely in the ideological problematic of triumphant imperialism. This one has to accept: every such theoretical project, every attempt at systematizing the world-view of a dominated people is necessarily destined for a foreign public and intended to fuel an ideological debate which is centred *elsewhere* – in the ruling classes of the dominant society.

Why did the African public allow itself to be taken in? It perceived only the second aspect of the project, without linking it with the first. The problematic of the 'heightening of the soul' flattered its pride at little cost and so concealed from it the link with the first problematic (the 'civilizing mission') which was, in fact, the dominant one. The African public 'spontaneously'[2] inverted the priorities, making the secondary problematic primary and paying little or no attention to the dominant problematic which itself was inseparable from the fact of the non-African destination of the book.

This misunderstanding explains why so many of our fellow countrymen should have appropriated the 'heightening of the soul' problematic, the theoretical project of the reconstruction of Bantu 'philosophy', Rwandais 'philosophy', Dogon 'philosophy', Yoruba 'philosophy', Wolof 'philosophy', etc., or more generally of African 'philosophy', collective and spontaneous world-views which were being called upon to regenerate European philosophy; and why they did so without worrying about the political implications of such a project. This disastrous inconsistency has made us waste our time, for the last twenty years at least,[3] in trying to define ourselves, to codify a supposedly given, ready-constituted thought, instead of wading in, throwing ourselves into the fray and thinking new thoughts on the basis of today's and tomorrow's problems. We thus remain unwittingly prisoners of Europe, trying, as ever, to force her to respect us and deriving naïve pleasure from declaring for her benefit what we are naïve enough to regard as our philosophical identity. In a completely sterile withdrawal we go on vindicating our cultures, or rather, apologizing for them to the white man, instead of living fully their actual splendour and poverty, instead of *transforming* them.

We are reminded here of the Gospel truth: he who would gain his soul must lose it. By dint of trying to defend our civilizations at all costs, we have petrified, mummified them. We have betrayed our original cultures by showing them off, offering them as topics of myths for external consumption. In doing so we have unwittingly played Europe's game – the Europe against which we first claimed we were setting out to defend ourselves. And what do we find at the end of the road? The same subservience, the same display of wretchedness, the same tragic abandonment of thinking by ourselves and for ourselves: slavery.[4]

Tempels' African successors, whatever the distance – which may be important – that separates them from the Belgian missionary, have this in common with him: that they have chosen to address themselves primarily to a European public. This choice largely explains the content of their discourses. Their objective has been to describe the main features of African civilization for the benefit of their European counterparts, to secure their respect for African cultural originality – but on Europe's own terms. In the circumstances it was inevitable that they should have ended up by inventing, as a foil to European philosophy, an African 'philosophy' concocted from extra-philosophical material consisting of tales, legends, dynastic poems, etc., by aggressively interpreting these cultural data, grinding them down to extract their supposedly 'substantive marrow', turning them over, again and again, in order to derive from them what they could not, cannot and will never yield: a genuine philosophy.

As a result, the systems of thought reconstructed by our authors at the conclusion of this over-interpretation are the expression of their personal philosophical choices rather than of some collective thought of the Africans. Proof of this lies in the fact that attentive reading often reveals significant differences in the apparent monotony of these monolithic interpretations. The most important of these, as we have seen, is that which contrasts Alexis Kagamé with the author of *Bantu Philosophy*. For Tempels the main difference between European philosophy and Bantu 'philosophy' lay in their respective conceptions of being: static in the first case, dynamic in the second. For the Bantu being is supposed to be synonymous with power, so that ontology becomes a general theory of forces, of their natural hierarchy and interaction. But according to the Rwandais priest, it is artificial to contrast *being* at rest and *being* in motion, for in each case we are confronted with the same being, only considered under two different aspects: 'Operational predisposition presupposes the essence; essence is structured in terms of its finality.' This is the double axiom with which Kagamé refuted his illustrious predecessor, without naming him.

His critique, however, is not a radical one. He should have renounced Tempels' whole project instead of accepting its dogmatic naïveté and carrying it out slightly differently. Kagamé should not have been content to confute Tempels, he should have asked himself what the reasons were for his error. Then he might have noticed that Tempels' insistence on emphasizing the differences was part and parcel of the whole scheme, the reconstruction of the Bantu *Weltanschauung*, inasmuch as the scheme was not inscribed in the *Weltanschauung* itself but was external to it. Kagamé should have seen that this theoretical undertaking took its meaning only from a desire, the desire to differentiate African from European civilization at any cost, and that in these conditions the author of *Bantu Philosophy* would inevitably regard all as grist to his mill and would massively project on to the Bantu soul his own metaphysical reveries, reinforced for the occasion by a few delusive fragments of ethnography.

Because he failed to drive home his critique, Kagamé has remained a prisoner of the same myth. Enmeshed with him are all those authors, some remarkable, and all those African intellectuals who have taken it into their heads to define a specific African philosophy, a world-view common to all Africans, past, present and future, a collective, immutable system of thought in eternal opposition to that of Europe.

Such is the theoretical impasse into which we have been blind enough to stumble. Since then all our philosophical thinking has been marking time. The only prospect it has offered itself has been the systematic reconstruction of the world-view of African peoples: a mad and hopeless enterprise. Each and every African philosopher now feels duty-bound to reconstruct the thought of his forefathers, the collective *Weltanschauung* of his people. To do so, he feels obliged to make himself an ethnological expert on African customs. Anything he may produce in another vein, say on Plato or Marx, Confucius or Mao Tse-tung, or in any general philosophical area unconnected with Africa, he regards as a sort of parenthesis in his thought, of which he must feel almost ashamed. And if he is shameless enough not to go blue in the face (some would prefer him to blush), so much the worse for him! His critics are watching. They will soon drag him back to the straight and narrow path . . . of Africanism.

That is how two entirely different discourses come, eventually, to be confused: the ethnographic discourse (whose scientific status, incidentally, might itself bear investigation, especially in relation to sociology) and the philosophical discourse. That is how our philosophical literature has gradually managed, in the last thirty years, to get itself bogged down in the muddy paths of a dubious ethno-philosophy, a hybrid, ideological discipline without recognizable status in the world of theory. In treading these paths our authors have genuinely believed that their work is original, whereas in fact they have merely been following in the footsteps of Western ethnocentrism. For Europe has never expected anything from us, in cultural terms, except that we should offer her our civilizations as showpieces and alienate ourselves in a fictitious dialogue with her, over the heads of our own peoples. This is what we are invited to do whenever we are asked to develop African Studies and preserve our cultural authenticity. We forget too easily that African Studies were invented by Europe and that the ethnographic sciences are an integral part of the heritage of Europe, amounting to no more than a passing episode in the theoretical tradition of the Western peoples.

So what is to be done? Apart from a nationalistic withdrawal into ourselves, a painstaking, unending inventory of our cultural values, a collective narcissism induced by colonization, we must relearn how to think. True, we must grant African ethnophilosophers the merit of having tried, with the means at their disposal, to defend their cultural identity against the avowed or cryptic assimilationist designs of imperialism. But we must add that this ethnophilosophical argument, which they have used as a means of cultural resistance, is one of the most ambiguous ever to have been invented and that, having failed to perceive its ambiguity, they have unwittingly played their opponent's game. Motivated by the genuine need for an African philosophy, they have wrongly believed that this philosophy lies in our past, needing only to be exhumed and then brandished like a miraculous weapon in the astonished face of colonialist Europe. They have not seen that African philosophy, like African science or African culture in general, is before us, not behind us, and must be created today by decisive action. Nobody would deny that this creation will not be effected *ex nihilo*, that it will necessarily embrace the heritage of the past and will therefore rather be a recreation. But this and simple withdrawal into the past are worlds apart.

Admit, then, that our philosophy is yet to come. Take the word 'philosophy' in the active, not passive, sense. We do not need a closed system to which all of us can adhere and which we can exhibit to the outside world. No, we want the restless questioning, the untiring dialectic that accidentally produces systems and then projects them towards a horizon of fresh truths. African philosophy, like any other philosophy, cannot possibly be a collective world-view. It can exist as a philosophy only in the form of a confrontation between individual thoughts, a discussion, a debate.

That is why our first task today is to organize such a debate: an autonomous debate, not a far-flung appendix to European debates but one that will bring African philosophers together, thus creating within Africa a human ambience in which it will be possible to ask the thorniest theoretical questions. The Africanness of our philosophy will not necessarily reside in its themes but will depend above all on the geographical origin of those who produce it and their intellectual coming together. The best European Africanists remain Europeans, even (and above all) if they invent a Bantu 'philosophy', whereas the African philosophers who think in terms of Plato or Marx and confidently take over the theoretical heritage of Western philosophy, assimilating and transcending it, are producing authentic African work. And they are even more authentically African if instead of merely sharing that heritage with their European counterparts, instead of drowning their own discourse in the tumultuous streams of European debate, they decide to subject that heritage first and foremost to the appreciation and criticism of their own fellow countrymen. The real problem is not to talk about Africa but to talk among Africans. Europe is what she is today because she assumed and transformed the cultural heritage of other peoples, in the first rank of which were a people of our own continent: the ancient Egyptians. Nothing must prevent us today from taking the opposite path. We must at all costs liberate our thought from the Africanist ghetto to which it has been confined, get out of our intellectual prison, open up a breach in the closed space of our collective fantasies, so that theoretical issues may surge in, to be shared first of all with our immediate brothers.

In other words, today's African philosophers must reorient their discourse. They must write first and foremost for an African public, no longer a non-African public. That will be enough to stop them purring on about Luba ontology, Dogon metaphysics, the conception of old age among the Fulbe, etc., simply because such themes do not interest their fellow countrymen but were aimed formerly at satisfying the Western craving for exoticism. As for the African public, what it wants most is to be widely informed about what is going on elsewhere, about current scientific problems in other countries and continents, out of curiosity in the first place (a legitimate curiosity), but also in order to confront those problems with its own preoccupations, to reformulate them freely in its own terms and thus to steep them in the melting-pot of African science.

The real problem, then, is to liberate the theoretical creativity of our peoples by affording it the means of exerting itself effectively, on the basis of boundless information and through a free discussion in which the most diverse theories may be generated and refuted. In the last resort philosophy, in the active sense of the word, is, before anything else, just that: a huge public debate in which every participant's intellectual responsibility is at stake. Everything else, including science, will come afterwards, in its train.

3 African philosophy, myth and reality*

I must emphasize that my theme is African philosophy, myth *and* reality, whereas one might have expected the conventional formula, myth *or* reality? I am not asking whether it exists, whether it is a myth *or* a reality. I observe that it does exist, by the same right and in the same mode as all the philosophies of the world: in the form of a *literature*. I shall try to account for this misunderstood reality, deliberately ignored or suppressed even by those who produce it and who, in producing it, believe that they are merely reproducing a pre-existing thought through it: through the insubstantiality of a transparent discourse, of a fluid, compliant ether whose only function is to transmit light. My working hypothesis is that such suppression cannot be innocent: this discursive self-deception serves to conceal something else, and this apparent self-obliteration of the subject aims at camouflaging its massive omnipresence, its convulsive effort to root in reality this fiction filled with itself. Tremendous censorship of a shameful text, which presents itself as impossibly transparent and almost non-existent but which also claims for its object (African pseudo-philosophy) the privilege of having always existed, outside any explicit formulation.

I therefore invert the relation: that which exists, that which is incontrovertibly given is that literature. As for the object it claims to restore, it is at most a way of speaking, a verbal invention, a *muthos*. When I speak of African philosophy I mean that literature, and I try to understand why it has so far made such strenuous efforts to hide behind the screen, all the more opaque for being imaginary, of an implicit 'philosophy' conceived as an unthinking, spontaneous, collective system of thought, common to all Africans or at least to

---

* This is a rewritten and updated version of a lecture 'stammered' at the University of Nairobi on 5 November 1973, at the invitation of the Philosophical Association of Kenya, under the title 'African philosophy, myth and reality' (cf. *Thought and Practice*, vol. I, no. 2, Nairobi, 1974, pp. 1–16). The same lecture was delivered at Cotonou on 20 December 1973 and at Porto-Novo on 10 January 1974, under the sponsorship of the National Commission for Philosophy of Dahomey.

all members severally, past, present and future, of such-and-such an African ethnic group. I try to understand why most African authors, when trying to engage with philosophy, have so far thought it necessary to project the misunderstood reality of their own discourse on to such palpable fiction.

Let us therefore tackle the problem at a higher level. What is in question here, substantially, is the idea of *philosophy*, or rather, of *African philosophy*. More accurately, the problem is whether the word 'philosophy', when qualified by the word 'African', must retain its habitual meaning, or whether the simple addition of an adjective necessarily changes the meaning of the substantive. What is in question, then, is the universality of the word 'philosophy' throughout its possible geographical applications.

My own view is that this universality must be preserved – not because philosophy must necessarily develop the same themes or even ask the same questions from one country or continent to another, but because these differences of *content* are meaningful precisely and only as differences of *content*, which, as such, refer back to the essential unity of a single discipline, of a single style of inquiry.

The present chapter will therefore endeavour to develop the conclusions of the first two. In particular, it will attempt to show, first, that the phrase 'African philosophy', in the enormous literature that has been devoted to the problem, has so far been the subject only of mythological exploitation and, second, that it is nevertheless possible to retrieve it and apply it to something else: not to the fiction of a collective system of thought, but to a set of philosophical discourses and texts.

I shall try to evince the existence of such texts and to determine both the limits and essential configurations, or general orientations, of African philosophical literature.

The popular concept of African philosophy

Tempels' work will again serve us as a reference.[1] We will not summarize or comment upon it again but will simply recall the author's idea of philosophy, the meaning of the word 'philosophy' in the phrase 'Bantu philosophy'. More than once Tempels emphasizes that this philosophy is experienced but not thought and that its practitioners are, at best, only dimly conscious of it:

Let us not expect the first Black-in-the-street (especially if he is young) to give us a systematic account of his ontological system. Nevertheless, this ontology exists; it penetrates and informs all the primitive's thinking and dominates all his behaviour. Using the methods of analysis and synthesis of our own intellectual disciplines, we can and therefore must do the 'primitive' the service of looking for, classifying and systematizing the elements of his ontological system. (p. 15)

And further on:

We do not claim that Bantus are capable of presenting us with a philosophical treatise complete with an adequate vocabulary. It is our own intellectual training that enables us to effect its systematic development. It is up to us to provide them with an accurate account of their conception of entities, in such a way that they will recognize themselves in our words and will agree, saying: 'You have understood us, you know us now completely, you "know" in the same way we "know".' (p. 24)

It is quite clear, then: the black man is here regarded, in Eboussi-Boulaga's words, as the 'Monsieur Jourdain of philosophy'.[2] Unwitting philosopher, he is the rival in silliness of Molière's famous character, who spoke in prose without knowing it. Ignorant of his own thoughts, he needs an interpreter to translate them for him, or rather an interpreter who, having formulated these thoughts with the white world in mind, will accidentally drop a few crumbs which will inspire the Bantu, when he picks them up, with boundless gratitude.

We have already mentioned Césaire's criticism. That very necessary political critique, we said, stopped short because it failed to follow up its own theoretical implications. To aim cautious criticisms, 'not at Bantu philosophy, but at the political uses to which it is being put',[3] was to avoid questioning the genealogy of the concept itself and to treat its appearance in scientific literature as an accident, as though its only function were this very political one. It was, in fact, tantamount to shying away from an exposure of the profoundly conservative nature of the ethnophilosophical project itself.

It follows that not only *Bantu Philosophy* but the whole of ethnophilosophical literature must be subjected to an expanded and more profound version of Césaire's political criticism. For if, as a result of what might be called the ethnological division of labour (a sort of scientific equivalent of the military scramble for the Third World by the great powers), Tempels can pass for the great specialist in the

Bantu area, and if, too, his reconstruction of African 'philosophy' is the more sensational because of his one-to-one contrasts between this African pseudo-philosophy and an equally imaginary European philosophy,[4] similar attempts have been made by other European authors for other regions of Africa. To quote only a few, Marcel Griaule has devoted to the Dogons of the present-day Republic of Mali a book currently regarded as a classic of Dogon wisdom, *Dieu d'eau*,[5] followed by another, in collaboration with Germaine Dieterlen, entitled *Le Renard pâle*.[6] Dominique Zahan has made known to the world the religion, the spirituality and what he calls the 'philosophy' of the Bambara.[7] Louis-Vincent Thomas has carried out painstaking research among the Diola of Senegal and has expatiated on their wisdom, their system of thought or, as he calls it, their 'philosophy'.[8]

As might have been expected, the example of these European authors has been widely followed at home. Many Africans have plunged into the same field of research, correcting on occasion – but without ever questioning its basic assumptions – the work of their Western models. Among them is the abbé Alexis Kagamé of Rwanda, with his *Philosophie bantou–rwandaise de l'être*,[9] already cited. Then there is Mgr Makarakiza of Burundi, who published in 1959 a study entitled *La Dialectique des Barundi*.[10] The South African priest Antoine Mabona distinguished himself in 1960 with an article entitled 'African philosophy', then in 1963 with a text on 'The depths of African philosophy' and finally in 1964 with a meditation on 'La spiritualité africaine'.[11] In this concert Father A. Rahajarizafy has sounded the note of the Great Island by trying to define Malagasy 'philosophy' in an article of 1963 on 'Sagesse malgache et théologie chrétienne'.[12] In 1962, François-Marie Lufuluabo, a Franciscan from the former Belgian Congo, appeared in the firmament with a booklet, *Vers une théodicée bantoue*, followed in 1963 by an article entitled 'La Conception bantoue face au christianisme', signing off in 1964 with another booklet on *La Notion luba-bantoue de l'être*.[13] Then, in 1965, his compatriot, the abbé Vincent Mulago, devoted a chapter to African 'philosophy' in his *Visage africain du christianisme*.[14] The former Protestant clergyman Jean-Calvin Bahoken, of Cameroun, was clearing his *Clairières métaphysiques africaines*[15] in 1967, and two years later the Kenyan pastor John Mbiti, probably fascinated by his own childhood, revealed to the world in a now classic work, *African Religions and Philosophy*, the fact that the African ignores the future, hardly knows the present and lives entirely turned towards the past.[16]

Before we go on with the catalogue, let us note that all the authors we have just quoted are churchmen, like Tempels himself. This explains their main preoccupation, which was to find a psychological and cultural basis for rooting the Christian message in the African's mind without betraying either. Of course, this is an eminently legitimate concern, up to a point. But it means that these authors are compelled to conceive of philosophy on the model of religion, as a permanent, stable system of beliefs, unaffected by evolution, impervious to time and history, ever identical to itself.

Let us now turn to the lay authors, with, here again, only a few examples. We cannot but mention Léopold Sédar Senghor, whose chatty disquisitions on 'negritude' are often buttressed by an analysis of what he called, as early as 1939, the black man's 'conception of the world', a phrase which he later replaced, under the influence of Tempels, with the 'black metaphysic'.[17] There are also the Nigerian Adesanya, author of an article published in 1958 on 'Yoruba metaphysical thinking';[18] the Ghanaian William Abraham, author of a book which is remarkable in many ways, *The Mind of Africa*[19] (I believe that a book can be instructive, interesting, useful, even if it is founded on erroneous assumptions); the late-lamented Kwame Nkrumah, whose famous *Consciencism* can hardly be regarded as his best publication;[20] the Senegalese Alassane N'Daw, who devoted several articles to the subject;[21] the Camerounian Basile-Juleat Fouda, author of a doctoral thesis defended at Lille in 1967 on 'La Philosophie négro-africaine de l'existence' (unpublished);[22] the Dahomean Issiaka Prosper Laleye, also the author of a thesis, 'La Conception de la personne dans la pensée traditionnelle yoruba',[23] presented in 1970 at the Catholic University of Fribourg, in Switzerland; the Nigerian J. O. Awolalu, author of an article entitled 'The Yoruba philosophy of life'.[24] And there are many others.[25]

Without being motivated quite so restrictively as the church ethnophilosophers, these authors were none the less intent on locating, beneath the various manifestations of African civilization, beneath the flood of history which has swept this civilization along willy-nilly, a solid bedrock which might provide a foundation of certitudes: in other words, a system of beliefs. In this quest, we find the same preoccupation as in the negritude movement – a passionate search for the identity that was denied by the colonizer – but now there is the underlying idea that one of the elements of the cultural identity is precisely 'philosophy', the idea that every culture rests on a specific, permanent, metaphysical substratum.

Let us now ask the crucial question: is this the usual meaning of the word 'philosophy'? Is it the way it is understood, for instance, in the phrases 'European philosophy', 'nineteenth-century philosophy', etc.? Clearly not. It seems as though the word automatically changes its meaning as soon as it ceases to be applied to Europe or to America and is applied to Africa. This is a well-known phenomenon. As our Kenyan colleague Henry Odera humorously remarks:

What may be a superstition is paraded as 'African religion', and the white world is expected to endorse that it is indeed a religion but an African religion. What in all cases is a mythology is paraded as 'African philosophy', and again the white culture is expected to endorse that it is indeed a philosophy but an African philosophy. What is in all cases a dictatorship is paraded as 'African democracy', and the white culture is again expected to endorse that it is so. And what is clearly a de-development or pseudo-development is described as 'development', and again the white world is expected to endorse that it is development – but of course 'African development'.[26]

Words do indeed change their meanings miraculously as soon as they pass from the Western to the African context, and not only in the vocabulary of European or American writers but also, through faithful imitation, in that of Africans themselves. That is what happens to the word 'philosophy': applied to Africa, it is supposed to designate no longer the specific discipline it evokes in its Western context but merely a collective world-view, an implicit, spontaneous, perhaps even unconscious system of beliefs to which all Africans are supposed to adhere. This is a vulgar usage of the word, justified presumably by the supposed vulgarity of the geographical context to which it is applied.

Behind this usage, then, there is a myth at work, the myth of primitive unanimity, with its suggestion that in 'primitive' societies – that is to say, non-Western societies – everybody always agrees with everybody else. It follows that in such societies there can never be individual beliefs or philosophies but only collective systems of belief. The word 'philosophy' is then used to designate each belief-system of this kind, and it is tacitly agreed among well-bred people that in this context it could not mean anything else.

One can easily detect in this one of the founding acts of the 'science' (or rather the pseudo-science) called ethnology, namely, the generally tacit thesis that non-Western societies are absolutely specific, the silent postulate of a difference in *nature* (and not merely in the *evolutionary stage* attained, with regard to particular types of achievement), of a difference in *quality* (not merely in quantity or *scale*) between so-called 'primitive' societies and developed ones. Cultural anthropology (another name for ethnology) owes its supposed autonomy (notably in relation to sociology) to this arbitrary division of the human community into two types of society which are taken, arbitrarily and without proof, to be fundamentally different.[27]

But let us return to the myth of unanimity. It would seem at first sight that this theoretical consensus postulated by ethnophilosophy among all members of each 'primitive' community should produce a parallel consensus, at the level of results if not of methods, among all ethnophilosophers studying the same community. But, curiously enough, instead of an ideal consensus, a fine unanimity whose transparency would have revealed the spontaneous unanimity of all those 'primitive philosophers', ethnophilosophical literature offers us a rich harvest of not only diverse but also sometimes frankly contradictory works.

We have noted above such divergences between Tempels and Kagamé. It would probably be easy to find similar differences between the many other works relating to the 'traditional' thought of Bantus or Africans in general, if one could overcome one's understandable boredom, read all of them one by one, examine them patiently and juxtapose all the views they contain.

But I can see the objection being raised that such differences are normal, that the diversity of works is a source of wealth and not of weakness, that the internal contradictions of ethnophilosophy can be found in any science worthy of the name – physics, chemistry, mathematics, linguistics, psychoanalysis, sociology, etc. – that they are a sign of vitality, not inconsistency, a condition of progress rather than an obstacle in the path of discovery. It may be added that, as in all sciences, a reality may exist without being immediately understood, and that consequently it is not surprising if an implicit system of thought can be reconstructed only as a result of long, collective and contradictory research.

The only thing this objection overlooks is the 'slight difference' between the sciences cited and ethnophilosophy that they do not postulate anything remotely comparable with the supposed unanimity of a human community; that in these sciences, moreover, a contradiction is never stagnant but always progressive, never final or absolute but indicative of an *error*, of the *falsity* of a hypothesis or thesis, which is bound to emerge from a rational investigation of the object itself, whereas a contradiction between two ethnophilosophical theses is necessarily circular, since it can never be resolved by experimentation or any other method of verification. The point is that an ethnophilosophical contradiction is necessarily *antinomal* in the Kantian sense; thesis and antithesis are equally demonstrable – in other words, equally gratuitous. In such a case contradiction does not generate synthesis but simply demonstrates the need to re-examine the very foundations of the discipline and to provide a critique of ethnophilosophical reason and perhaps of ethnological reason too.

Ethnophilosophy can now be seen in its true light. Because it has to account for an imaginary unanimity, to interpret a text which nowhere exists and has to be constantly reinvented, it is a science without an object, a 'crazed language'[28] accountable to nothing, a discourse that has no referent, so that its falsity can never be demonstrated. Tempels can then maintain that for the Bantu being is power, and Kagamé can beg to differ: we have no means of settling the quarrel. It is clear, therefore, that the 'Bantu philosophy' of the one is not the philosophy of the Bantu but that of Tempels, that the 'Bantu-Rwandais philosophy' of the other is not that of the Rwandais but that of Kagamé. Both of them simply make use of African traditions and oral literature and project on to them their own philosophical beliefs, hoping to enhance their credibility thereby.

That is how the functioning of this thesis of a collective African philosophy works: it is a smokescreen behind which each author is able to manipulate his own philosophical views. It has nothing beyond this ideological function: it is an indeterminate discourse with no object.

Towards a new concept of 'African philosophy'

Behind and beyond the ethnological pretext, philosophical views remain. The dogma of unanimism has not been completely sterile, since it has at least generated a quite distinctive philosophical literature.

Here we must note a surprising fact: while they were looking for philosophy in a place where it could never be found – in the collective unconscious of African peoples, in the silent folds of their explicit discourse – the ethnophilosophers never questioned the nature and theoretical status of their own analyses. Were these relevant to philosophy? There lay the true but undetected problem. For if we want to be scientific, we cannot apply the same word to two things as different as a spontaneous, implicit and collective world-view on the one hand and, on the other, the deliberate, explicit and individual analytic activity which takes that world-view as its object. Such an analysis should be called 'philosophology' rather than 'philosophy' or, to use a less barbarous term, 'metaphilosophy' – but a metaphilosophy of the worst kind, an inegalitarian metaphilosophy, not a dialogue and confrontation with an existing philosophy but a reduction to silence, a denial, masquerading as the revival of an earlier philosophy.

For we know that in its highly elaborated forms philosophy is always, in a sense, a metaphilosophy, that it can develop only by reflecting on its own history, that all new thinkers must feed on the doctrines of their predecessors, even of their contemporaries, extending or refuting them, so as to enrich the philosophical heritage available in their own time. But in this case metaphilosophy does not rely on an exploitation of extra-philosophical data or on the arbitrary over-interpretation of social facts which in themselves bear no relation to philosophy. Metaphilosophy signifies, rather, a philosophical reflection on discourses which are themselves overtly and consciously philosophical. Ethnophilosophy, on the other hand, claims to be the description of an implicit, unexpressed world-view, which never existed anywhere but in the anthropologist's imagination. Ethnophilosophy is a pre-philosophy mistaking itself for a metaphilosophy, a philosophy which, instead of presenting its own rational justification, shelters lazily behind the authority of a tradition and projects its own theses and beliefs on to that tradition.

If we now return to our question, namely, whether philosophy resides in the world-view described or in the description itself, we can now assert that if it resides in either, it must be the second, the description of that vision, even if this is, in fact, a self-deluding invention that hides behind its own products. African philosophy does exist therefore, but in a new sense, as a literature produced by Africans and dealing with philosophical problems.

A contradiction? Oh no! Some may be surprised that, having patiently dismantled the ethnophilosophical machine, we should now be trying to restore it. They have simply failed to understand that we are merely recognizing the existence of that literature as *philosophical literature*, whatever may be its *value* and *credibility*. What we are acknowledging is what it *is*, not what it *says*. Having laid bare the mythological assumptions on which it is founded (these having suppressed all question of its status), we can now pay greater attention to the fact of its existence as a determinate form of philosophical literature which, however mystified and mystifying it may be (mystifying because mystified), nevertheless belongs to the history of African literature in general.

Let us be accurate: the issue here is only *African* ethnophil-osophy. A work like *Bantu Philosophy* does not belong to African philosophy, since its author is not African; but Kagamé's work is an integral part of African philosophical literature. In other words, speaking of African philosophy in a new sense, we must draw a line, within ethnophilosophical literature in general, between African and non-African writers, not because one category is better than the other, or because both might not, in the last analysis, say the same thing, but because, the subject being *African* philosophy, we cannot exclude a geographical variable, taken here as empirical, contin-gent, extrinsic to the content or significance of the discourse and as quite apart from any questions of *theoretical connections*. Thus Tempels' work, although it deals with an African subject and has played a decisive role in the development of African ethnophil-osophy, belongs to *European* scientific literature, in the same way as anthropology in general, although it deals with non-Western societies, is an embodiment of Western science, no more and no less.

A happy consequence of this demarcation is that it emphasizes certain subtle nuances and occasional serious divergences which might otherwise have passed unnoticed and which differentiate African authors whom we initially grouped together as ethno-philosophers. It is thus possible to see the immense distance which separates, for instance, Bahoken's *Clairières métaphysiques africaines*,[29] justifiably assessed as a perfect example of ideological twaddle designed by an apparently nationalistic African to flatter the exotic tastes of the Western public from Kwame Nkrumah's *Consciencism*, written chiefly for the African public and aimed at making it aware of its new cultural identity, even though Nkrumah's book, unfortunately, partakes of the ethnological conception that there can be such a thing as a collective philosophy.[30]

Another even more important consequence is that this African philosophical literature can now be seen to include philosophical works of those African authors who do not believe in the myth of a collective philosophy or who reject it explicitly. Let me cite a few of these. Fabien Eboussi-Boulaga's fine article 'Le Bantou problématique'[31] has already been mentioned. Another Camerounian, Marcien Towa, has given us a brilliant critique of ethnophilosophy in general, the *Essai sur la problématique philosophique dans l'Afrique actuelle*, followed by an incisive criticism of the Senghorian doctrine of negritude, *Léopold Sédar Senghor: négritude ou servitude?*[32] Henry Oruka Odera of Kenya has published a fine article entitled 'Mythologies as African philosophy'.[33] The Béninois (former Dahomeyan) Stanislas Spero Adotevi earned fame in 1972 with his brilliant book *Négritude et négrologues*.[34]

But more than that: African philosophical literature includes works which make no attempt whatever to broach the problem of 'African philosophy', either to assert or to deny its existence. In fact, we must extend the concept to include all the research into Western philosophy carried out by Africans. This broadening of the horizon implies no contradiction: just as the writings of Western anthropologists on African societies belong to Western scientific literature, so the philosophical writings of Africans on the history of Western thought are an integral part of African philosophical literature. So, obviously, African philosophical works concerning problems that are not specially related to African experience should also be included. In this sense, the articles by the Ghanaian J. E. Wiredu on Kant, on material implication and the concept of truth,[35] are an integral part of African philosophy, as are analyses of the concept of freedom or the notion of free will[36] by the Kenyan Henry Odera or the Nigerian D. E. Idoniboye. The same can be said of the research on French seventeenth-century philosophy by the Zaïrois Elungu Pere Elungu, *Etendue et connaissance dans la philosophie de Malebranche*,[37] of the epistemological introduction to *Théologie positive et théologie spéculative*[38] by his fellow countryman Tharcisse Tshibangu. The work of the Camerounian N'joh Mouelle, particularly *Jalons* and *De la médiocrité à l'excellence. Essai sur la signification humaine du développement*,[39] may also be placed in this category, although their subjects are not only universal but also linked with the present historical situation of Africa.

By the same token we may readily claim works like those of the Ashanti scholar Anton-Wilhelm Amo, who studied and taught in German universities during the first half of the eighteenth century, as belonging to African philosophical literature,[40] although this may be regarded as a borderline case, since Amo was trained almost entirely in the West. But is not this the case with almost every African intellectual even today?[41]

The essential point here is that we have produced a radically new definition of African philosophy, the criterion now being the geographical origin of the authors rather than an alleged specificity of content. The effect of this is to broaden the narrow horizon which has hitherto been imposed on African philosophy and to treat it, as now conceived, as a methodical inquiry with the same universal aims as those of any other philosophy in the world. In short, it destroys the dominant mythological conception of Africanness and restores the simple, obvious truth that Africa is above all a continent and the concept of Africa an empirical, geographical concept and not a metaphysical one. The purpose of this 'demythologizing' of the idea of Africa and African philosophy is simply to free our faculty for theorizing from all the intellectual impediments and prejudices which have so far prevented it from getting off the ground.[42]

Final remarks

There can no longer be any doubt about the existence of African philosophy, although its meaning is different from that to which the anthropologists have accustomed us. It exists as a particular form of scientific literature. But, of course, once this point is established, many questions remain. For instance, how shall we distinguish philosophical literature from other forms of scientific literature, such as mathematics, physics, biology, linguistics, sociology, etc., inasmuch as these disciplines also develop as specific forms of literature? In other words, what is the particular object and area of study of philosophy? In more general terms, what relation is there between scientific literature and non-scientific literature (for instance, artistic literature), and why must we include philosophical literature in the first rather than the second?

This is not the place to answer these questions. All that we have tried to do so far has been to clear the ground for questions of this kind, since they presuppose that philosophy is recognized simply as a theoretical discipline and nothing else, a discipline which, like any other, can develop only in the form of literature.

Moreover, such questions can never receive definite and immutable answers, for the definition of a science must be revised constantly in the light of its own progress, and the articulation of theoretical discourse in general – by which we mean the demarcation of the various sciences – is itself subject to historical change. At this point, it is true, a much harder question, or series of questions, arises: how is the object of a science determined? What conditions, economic, historical, ideological or other, contribute to fixing the frontiers of a discipline? How is a new science born? How does an old science die or cease to be considered a science?[43]

This is not the place to answer these questions either. But at least there is one thing we are in a position to affirm: no science, no branch of learning can appear except as an event in language or, more precisely, as the product of discussion. The first thing to do, then, is to organize such discussions in the midst of the society where the birth of these sciences is desired. In other words, whatever the specific object of philosophy may be, the first task of African philosophers today, if they wish to develop an authentic African philosophy, is to promote and sustain constant free discussion about all the problems concerning their discipline instead of being satisfied with a private and somewhat abstract dialogue between themselves and the Western world.[44] By reorienting their discourse in this way, they will easily overcome the permanent temptation of 'folklorism' that limits their research to so-called African subjects – a temptation which has owed most of its strength to the fact that their writings have been intended for a foreign public.

It is indeed a strange paradox that in present conditions the dialogue with the West can only encourage 'folklorism', a sort of collective cultural exhibitionism which compels the 'Third World' intellectual to 'defend and illustrate' the peculiarities of his tradition for the benefit of a Western public. This seemingly universal dialogue simply encourages the worst kind of cultural particularism, both because its supposed peculiarities are in the main purely imaginary and because the intellectual who defends them claims to speak in the name of his whole people although they have never asked him to do so and are usually unaware that such a dialogue is taking place.

On the contrary, it is to be hoped that when Africans start discussing theoretical problems among themselves, they will feel spontaneously the need to gather the broadest possible information on the scientific achievements of other continents and societies. They will take an interest in these achievements not because they will be held to be the best that can be attained but in order to assess more objectively, and if necessary improve, their own achievements in the same areas.

The paradox is therefore easily removed: interlocutors of the same origin rarely feel the need to exalt their own cultural particularities. Such a need arises only when one faces people from other countries and is forced to assert one's uniqueness by conforming to the current stereotypes of one's own society and civilization. Universality becomes accessible only when interlocutors are set free from the need to assert themselves in the face of others; and the best way to achieve this in Africa today is to organize internal discussion and exchange among all the scientists in the continent, within each discipline and – why not? – between one discipline and another, so as to create in our societies a scientific tradition worthy of the name. The difficult questions we have been asking concerning the origins, the definition, the boundaries, the evolution and the destiny of the various sciences, and more particularly the nature of philosophy and its relation to other disciplines, will then find their answers in the concrete history of our theoretical literature.

We must therefore plunge in and not be afraid of thinking new thoughts, of simply *thinking*. For every thought is new if we take the word in its active sense, even thought about past thoughts, provided we are not content simply to repeat hallowed themes, catechetically and parrot-fashion, with a pout or a purr, but on the contrary boldly rearticulate these themes, justify them, give them a new and sounder foundation. Conversely, every blustering declaration of loyalty to a so-called 'modern' doctrine will be at best mere folklore – when it does not turn out to be an objective mystification – unless it is accompanied by some intellectual effort to *know*, *understand* and *think out* the doctrine by going beyond the more sensational formulations to the problematic on which it is founded. We cannot go on acting a part indefinitely. The time has come for theoretical responsibility, for taking ourselves seriously.

In Africa now the individual must liberate himself from the weight of the past as well as from the allure of ideological fashions. Amid the diverse but, deep down, so strangely similar catechisms of conventional nationalism and of equally conventional pseudo-Marxism, amid so many state ideologies functioning in the Fascist mode, deceptive alibis behind which the powers that be can quietly do the opposite of what they say and say the opposite of what they do, amid this immense confusion in which the most vulgar police state pompously declares itself to be a 'dictatorship of the proletariat' and neo-Fascists mouthing pseudo-revolutionary platitudes are called 'Marxist-Leninists', reducing the enormous theoretical and political subversive power of Marxism to the dimensions of a truncheon, in which, in the name of revolution, they kill, massacre, torture the workers, the trade unionists, the executives, the students: in the midst of all this intellectual and political bedlam we must all open our eyes wide and clear our own path. Nothing less will make discussions between free and intellectually responsible individuals possible. Nothing less will make a philosophy possible.

As can be seen, then, the development of African philosophical literature presupposes the removal of a number of political obstacles. In particular, it requires that democratic liberties and especially the right of free criticism, the suppression of which seems to constitute the sole aim and *raison d'être* of the official ideologies, should be acknowledged and jealously guarded. It is impossible to philosophize in Africa today without being aware of this need and of the pricelessness of freedom of expression as a necessary condition for all science, for all theoretical development and, in the last resort, for all real political and economic progress, too.

Briefly, and in conclusion, African philosophy exists, but it is not what it is believed to be. It is developing objectively in the form of a literature rather than as implicit and collective thought, but as a literature of which the output remains captive to the unanimist fallacy. Yet, happily, it is possible to detect signs of a new spirit. The liberation of this new spirit is now the necessary precondition of any progress in this field. To achieve that we must begin at the beginning; we must restore the right to criticism and free expression which are so seriously threatened by our regimes of terror and ideological confusion.

In short, it is not enough to recognize the existence of an African philosophical literature. The most important task is to transform it from the simple collection of writings aimed at non-African readers and consequently upholding the peculiarities of a so-called African 'world-view' that it is today into the vehicle of a free and rigorous discussion among African philosophers themselves. Only then will this literature acquire universal value and enrich the common international heritage of human thought.

4 Philosophy and its revolutions*

I should like to demonstrate three things: First, that philosophy is not a system but a history, essentially an open process, a restless, unfinished quest, not closed knowledge; second, that this history does not move forward by continuous evolution but by leaps and bounds, by successive revolutions, and consequently follows not a linear path but what one might call a dialectical one – in other words, that its profile is not continuous but discontinuous; third, after this rough sketch of a theory of theoretical development, of a theory of theoretical history, of a theory of philosophy seen as a discontinuous theoretical history, that African philosophy may today be going through its first decisive mutation, the outcome of which depends on us alone, on the courage and lucidity we show in bringing it to its conclusion.

Philosophy as history

First, then, philosophy is a history, not a system. I do not consider here the word 'system' in its weak sense of 'methodical knowledge'. If we took it in that sense, it is obvious that philosophy would indeed be a system, simply meaning that one does not philosophize without some method and prior knowledge, that philosophy requires a rather special conceptual ability on the part of the practitioner, that there is a terminology, a vocabulary, a conceptual apparatus bequeathed by philosophical tradition which we can never do without but must, on the contrary, use with profit if we want to be authentic philosophers. It goes without saying that philosophical reflection in this sense inevitably includes a *systematic* aspect, which

* Revised and enlarged version of a lecture given at Lubumbashi on 2 June 1973 on the occasion of the 'Journées philosophiques' of the province of Shaba, organized by the Department of Philosophy at the National University of Zaïre. (See *Cahiers philosophiques africains*, Lubumbashi, nos. 3–4, pp. 27–40.) The lecture was also delivered in Nairobi on 6 November 1973, under the auspices of the Philosophical Association of Kenya.

is both methodical and constantly related to an existing theoretical tradition which may either confirm or confute it, and that no philosophers can evade the rigours of this discipline if they really want to philosophize and not just (in Plato's words) 'tell stories'.[1] In this sense it seems obvious to me that African philosophers, like any others, need have no qualms about philosophizing, methodically and rigorously, in and through the conceptual heritage labelled 'philosophy'. African physicists are not generally ashamed to use the concepts which are proper to their discipline. Likewise, the African philosophers must not shirk the technicalities of philosophical language. We shall never create an authentic African philosophy, a genuine philosophy, genuinely African (that's what I mean by the term 'authentic'), if we skirt round the existing philosophical tradition. It is not by skirting round, and still less by ignoring, the international philosophical heritage that we shall really philosophize, but by absorbing it in order to transcend it.

In this sense, but only in this sense, it seems to me evident that philosophy, whether we like it or not, is a system involving a special method of inquiry.

But in another sense, the strong sense of the word 'system' – that is to say, a set of propositions regarded as definitive, a set of ultimate truths, the be-all and end-all of all thought – philosophy *is not* a system. For philosophy never stops; its very existence lies in the to and fro of free discussion, without which there is no philosophy. It is not a closed system but a history, a debate that goes on from generation to generation, in which every thinker, every author, engages in total responsibility: I know that I am responsible for what I say, for the theories I put forward. I am 'responsible' for them in the literal sense of the word, because I must always be prepared to 'answer' for them; I must be ready to justify them, to attest to their validity. It is as an individual that I take part in this debate, and in doing so I take part in the gradual unveiling of a truth that is not *mine* but everyone's, the outcome of the confrontation of all individual thoughts which constitutes an unending collective search.

The contention that philosophy is a history and not a system means, among other things, that no philosophical doctrine can be regarded as *the Truth*. It follows in a sense that there is no absolute truth in philosophy, or rather, that in this context the absolute is contained in the relative of an infinite, open-ended process. In other words, truth cannot be a set of definitive, untranscendable propositions but rather the process by which we look for propositions more adequate than others. In a way, then, truth is the very act of looking for truth, of enunciating propositions and trying to justify and found them.

In the *Theaetetus*, one of his dialogues devoted to the problem of the nature of knowledge, Plato, having shown that knowledge is not merely true perception or belief, suggests that it may possibly be true belief accompanied by reason or, more accurately, by discourse, by account (*logos*).[2] I say 'possibly', for the remainder of the argument attempts to demonstrate the inadequacy of that definition without, however, substituting another for it.[3]

It is nevertheless interesting to note the importance attributed here to *logos* (i.e. to discourse or *theoretical account*) as the decisive element in *scientific* truth. This clearly suggests that not all truth is necessarily scientific and that science lies less in the result than in the method. In any case, it is in this *logos*, in this discourse, in this infinite quest for proof that science lies, in our view, and also philosophy, which is no more than reflection on the aims of science.[4]

I can foresee the objection: did not many philosophers aspire to build systems? Did not Spinoza or Hegel, to cite only the greatest examples, attempt to think of the Whole as a system of systems, a synthesis of all systems, a totality that was to be the ultimate end of all possible systems?

Maybe. But such reasoning misses the point. In the first place, it omits the fact that the doctrines of a Spinoza or a Hegel owe their systematic character precisely to the philosophers' claim to have summarized, in a single work, the entire history (and not only the actual history but also the possible history, past, present and future) of philosophy: Spinoza's three kinds of knowledge or the stages of Hegel's 'phenomenology of spirit'. The supposed systematicity of these doctrines springs from their having integrated, or their claim to integrate, all possible forms of doctrine in a discourse that both respects and transcends them. They thus recognize, each in its own way,[5] that truth cannot reside in *one* doctrine, that it cannot emerge directly, in a flash, but only at the end of a long journey which takes in all the doctrines in turn until it finally outdoes them all. The philosophies of Spinoza, Hegel, etc., all the philosophies which have taken the form of a system, have always been erudite philosophies, extremely well informed about the history of philosophy. That is precisely why, believing they had discovered the law governing the development of that history and imagining that this law was purely internal and immanent (i.e. that the transition from one stage of thinking to another was purely philosophical and therefore purely conceptual), the philosophers made a deluded attempt to master *a priori* the future course of that history, to reduce their surprises *a priori*, thanks to a system of systems which made it possible to predict the substance of all possible doctrine.

What a mockery it is to compare such ambitious philosophies and their scholarly surveys of the history of philosophy (however mistaken they may have been in thinking that they had put an end to that history) with what anthropologists are today presenting to the world as 'African systems of thought'![6]

That is not all. The concentration on Spinoza and Hegel is liable to make one forget that philosophy did not stop with them and has therefore disproved their claim to have completed it. And this confirms that philosophy is indeed an open-ended story and that any attempt to put an end to it is a dream or a delusion.

It is essential to understand both the necessity for such a dream and its vanity.

Its necessity. It is the expression of an aspiration towards mastery, of a need for security which cannot be divorced from the subjectivity of every thinker because it is a constituent element of all human subjectivity. This dream haunts not only the minds of system builders like Spinoza or Hegel but, in a more or less visible form, those of all philosophers without exception, and not only philosophers but all thinkers and all men when they think. Every one of us likes to think that we pronounce the truth as a court of law pronounces a judgement. We cannot persist in our thought without this belief. The truth of our discourse, like truth in general, is not only an ideological myth but also a necessary and productive ideological myth.

Its vanity. History cannot be stopped. More than that: it cannot be neutralized, and its surprises cannot be reduced. This is true of history in general: while its laws can be established (i.e. the functional correlations between its various levels – for instance, between formations of the economic structure and formations of the ideological superstructure), while therefore a science can be established (and we know that such a science was founded by Marx under the name of 'historical materialism'), knowledge of this science in no way allows us to predict, let alone neutralize, events in their singularity. This is also true of the history of thought in particular. At best one may define the fundamental tendencies of philosophy, as

Engels attempted to do (he reduced them to two); one can, at most, starting from the assumptions of one of these tendencies (the idealist tendency, for instance), offer an *a priori* sketch of some of the possible configurations of philosophical thought, of culture, and of what Hegel called the Objective Spirit. This tells us precious little about the actual succession of philosophical doctrines and even less about their real content as they address each other, refute and confirm one another throughout history.

In this respect what applies to science applies also to philosophy. Husserl attempted for the former what others, more ambitious, have attempted for thought in general (for scientific thought is also a moment in Hegel's 'phenomenology of the spirit'). For the author of the *Logical Investigations* (1900–1)[7] the supreme task of a theory of science was to construct a 'theory of the possible forms of theory', in order to survey *a priori* the entire field of knowledge and so, in a sense, to neutralize the history of science. It is well known that Gödel has demonstrated, in a famous theorem (1931), the mathematical impossibility of such a theory, the impossibility of a universal axiom-system providing an *a priori* determination of all possible axiom-systems. To this should perhaps be added that even if this ideal had been attainable, only the *forms* of possible theories could have so been defined. Nothing would have been learned about the content of future scientific theories or the concrete modalities of their appearance and succession; it would have been of no use in developing techniques based on these theories; it would not have replaced the research, the untiring effort to solve problems, the complex methods of proof and verification. In short, the concrete work of the researcher would have remained unaffected. This is proof enough that science cannot be reduced to a system any more than can philosophy, even if that system were to be a system of all possible forms of systems; science is an endless history, an open and unending process. The actual 'systems' that succeed one another in the history of the sciences or of philosophy, real doctrines with their relative coherence and closure, can never achieve the status of System in the strong sense, System *par excellence*, Absolute Knowledge, the totality of all possible truths, which must remain the ever-receding horizon of an infinite quest.

To say that philosophy is history and not system is to say that there cannot be a collective philosophy and therefore that 'African philosophy', in the sense consecrated by the anthropologists, is a huge misconception. There *is* no philosophy that would be a system of implicit propositions or beliefs to which all individuals of a given society, past, present and future, would adhere. Such a philosophy does not exist, has never existed. The real problem should never have been to define the content of African philosophy in this sense – to identify the essential themes or the fundamental problematic of African philosophy construed as a spontaneous, unreflective, collective world-view. The real problem is a critical one. It is to find out *why* certain Western authors, followed (and this is more serious) by African authors, should from a certain time onwards have felt the need to look for such a collective world-view in the secret recesses of the mysterious African soul. Why, for instance, did Tempels feel compelled to write his *Bantu Philosophy*? How can one explain the extraordinary success of this book in the most serious European philosophical circles and even among African intellectuals? What lies behind the fact that a French philosopher of Bachelard's calibre (to cite only the most disquieting case) should have poured lavish praise on such an equivocal piece of work?[8] There lies the real problem. *Bantu Philosophy* appeared at a specific moment of our history and was the product of the ideological structure of the time. What is worth doing now is to investigate and describe this ideology if we are ever to leave it behind.

The problem is all the more real because Tempels' book itself lagged considerably behind the anthropology of the time. Some twenty years before its appearance Paul Radin had published an altogether more rigorous and scientific work, *Primitive Man as Philosopher*.[9] The American ethnologist was not trying (as Tempels was to do later) to reconstruct a collective 'primitive' world-view through personal and arbitrary interpretation; on the contrary, he was explicitly denouncing the classical prejudice according to which, in 'non-civilized' societies, the individual is entirely submerged in the group, unable and unwilling to think for himself, directly and fully adherent to the thought system of his community. Radin's book was explicitly an 'account of the exceptional man in primitive communities' (p. xiv), an attempt to demonstrate the existence of an 'intellectual class' in 'primitive' societies and to define the role and attitude of this class. His objective was not to reconstruct a collective system of thought, one of gratuitous hypotheses, but simply to transcribe as faithfully as possible the words of those he called the 'thinkers' and the 'philosophers' of 'primitive' communities, to write under their dictation, simply, dutifully, with as little interpretation and even comment as possible.[10]

After Radin Marcel Griaule also attempted, as is well known, to write under the dictation of a 'primitive' thinker, the Dogon Ogotemmeli. It is true that the French ethnologist's book, *Dieu d'eau. Entretiens avec Ogotemmeli*, was not written until 1946–7 and was published in 1948 – that is to say three years after the first and limited edition of *Bantu Philosophy* in Elisabethville in the then Belgian Congo (1945) and one year before the Présence Africaine edition (1949).[11] There is therefore no point in upbraiding Tempels for having failed to take his cue from Griaule's method. Nevertheless, in comparing these two almost simultaneous texts one cannot help noticing how different they are from the point of view of rigour and cogency. It is remarkable that the less consistent of the two should have received the more enthusiastic welcome, at least on the part of the African public.

There is only one explanation: the public of the time was ready for a work of that kind, which might momentarily please everybody, passionate detractors as well as zealous defenders of African culture, even if it were to be at the cost of a gross misunderstanding. By asserting the existence of a 'Bantu philosophy' Tempels, at little cost, satisfied the Africans' aspiration to see their culture rehabilitated. By simultaneously asserting the collective and unreflective character of this 'philosophy', the inability of its exponents to formulate it adequately for themselves, he was indirectly confirming the contentions of Lévy-Bruhl. Everybody was happy: not only the conventional nationalists (and their accomplices, the 'progressive' European anthropologists or intellectuals), for whom cultural authenticity coincided with an exclusive revaluation of the past, but also the traditional ethnologists, who were quite prepared to trade the word 'mentality' for the word 'philosophy' as long as the adjective 'primitive' remained and the structure was regarded as immutable, ahistorical and inert. Thus the miracle came to pass, thanks to the mirage of a *word*, a simple word deliberately misused. It was a tragedy of haste and thoughtlessness, the nationalists being in a hurry, like their accomplices the ethnologists. Neither could be satisfied with the transcription of the thoughts of an individual like Ogotemmeli or of several comparable individuals. For them African philosophy could not possibly lie in this disorderly plurality of individual thought; they could not engage, in order to study it, in an examination demanding endless patience, in a ceaseless search doomed to meditate on an infinite series of irreducible doctrines, and never to arrive at anything better than provisional, revocable syntheses. Each in his own way needed something more massive, more definite, that could be taken in at a glance, something that could be objectivized and manipulated at will so that he could claim it passionately (the nationalist), or recognize it frankly as the story of his own intellectual childhood (Bachelard *et ceteri*), or find in it confirmation of the inferiority of 'exotic' cultures (the conventional ethnologist). Tempels' book met these multifarious expectations. It was praised to the skies.

It is also worth noting that Griaule, who had tried so hard to transcribe the words of *one* man, felt it necessary to deny in his preface that the thought they conveyed was the property of Ogotemmeli and that, rather than granting him originality and responsibility, he preferred to look on him as the simple guardian of ancestral tradition, the slavish mouthpiece of group wisdom. In order to justify his book to the public, he had at all costs to avoid letting it believe that 'here was an individual speculation of second-rate value' (p. 4); on the contrary, he had to emphasize its collective character, to show that this doctrine was the birthright of the whole Dogon society and even, beyond the Dogon, of all the populations of the Sudan:

Bambara thought rests on a metaphysic as ordered and rich as that of the Dogon, and its principles are comparable. . . . It is the same with the Bozo, fishermen of the Niger, with the Kurumba, farmers in the middle of the Loop, with the enigmatic ironsmiths of the same region. . . . We are therefore not in the presence of an isolated thought-system but of the first link in a long chain. [12]

So Griaule, in spite of his concrete method of investigation, shared Tempels' refusal to accept that a non-Western society could contain a plurality of opinions that might conceivably diverge. In the presence of *one* thinker, he believed that this man's thought acquired value only as the expression of a diffuse collective thought; that the thinker in question was therefore not a real thinker but a *griot* of some sort because it was assumed from the outset that the individual was completely immersed in the group or, rather, that the individual and individuality as such could not exist in a supposedly primitive society.

From this point of view, Radin's work is still, to the best of my knowledge, the most lucid ethnological critique of the theoretical assumptions of ethnophilosophy. By pointing out the variations in the different versions of the same myth, by showing how they express each narrator's individual fancy, by vigorously denouncing the classical prejudice according to which there is only one good version of a myth or a rite and all deviation or variation is due to lapse of memory, ignorance or general degradation,[13] by asserting the profound individualism of 'primitive' man, his thirst for prestige and recognition, his consequent complete 'freedom of thought' (this phrase is the title of Chapter 5), by interpreting myths and proverbs as the personal creations of poets and thinkers, rather than as a collective, immemorial and anonymous heritage[14] – by these means the American anthropologist completely reverses the habitual practice of his colleagues and allows us to see the possibility of a plurality of opinions and beliefs, of theoretical individuality in 'primitive' societies and their profound resemblance, in this respect, to Western societies.

Unfortunately, this reversal has its limits, and our author persists in referring to 'primitive' man and 'primitive' society, to 'aboriginal' peoples, etc. – an unmistakable sign that he still believes in an essential difference between Western and other cultures, even if the difference is displaced, determined in a new way.

For instance: Radin duly begins by rejecting the conventional statements 'about the tyranny of the group and about the complete lack of individualism found in primitive communities',[15] but a couple of pages later he asserts that primitive man has a conception of social reality that is radically different from that of Western man, that for the 'primitive' 'social reality is. . .something unique and definitely distinct from the individual and no more emanates from him than does the external world'.[16] And again:

The individual and the group are in primitive society strictly incommensurable units, each with a separate and independent existence. We have nothing even remotely comparable with primitive man's sense of an objective social world, a world which is just as real as the external world and which is conceived of as being just as independent of the individual as the external world is.[17]

It is this conception of social order which, according to our author, explains the apparent conformism of the 'primitive', 'the

absence of consistent sceptics or unbelievers and. . .the non-exist-
ence of revolts against the real structure of society',[18] the many facts
which would otherwise remain inexplicable in view of the intellectual inventiveness and independence of which the same 'primitive'
is also capable.

In other words, in a 'primitive' society thought never has any real
subversive effect. It is purely individual, impractical and aesthetic:

The freedom of thought encountered here is not due to any secondary
emancipation from the shackles of traditional dogmatism, as among us [us
Westerners, of course]. It is due to the recognition of personality and the
right of personality to expression and to the clear perception of a lack of
contact between thoughts, ideas and opinions on the one hand and the
social realities on the other. The life of thought does not dominate and
tyrannize even the most intellectual of primitive people as it does some of
the least intellectual among us.[19]

As is apparent, the difference remains as monolithic and radical
as ever. The 'primitive' is still, in Radin as in Lévy-Bruhl, the
'absolute other' of the 'civilized' man. His otherness is simply
redefined. The American anthropologist has been incapable of, or
has shrunk from, demolishing the thick wall of ethnological
prejudice, despite the considerable breach he has made in it. Not
daring to pursue his critique to its conclusion, he has preferred to
enclose himself within another circle by substituting for the old
myths of primitive unanimity, of immersion of the individual in the
group and other inventions of the same water, new myths no less
gratuitous and pernicious. Evidently, it would have been too simple
to recognize the capacity of the 'primitive' for responsible thought
and have done with it – too simple and too dangerous, for the
'primitive' would then have ceased to appear as a primitive and to
feed the Western taste for spice, sensation and exoticism. So he had
to daub, to depict non-Western man in the likeness of an absorbed
individualist devoted to 'prestige-hunting', to naïve self-glorifica-
tion', whose rapport with his society was totally different from the
Westerner's with his own: a strange relationship of exteriority and
mutual exclusion – and this, by the same token, severely restricted
the primitive's individualism and relegated his celebrated 'freedom
of thought' to the limbo of dreams, imagination and art. And thus
the essential fine irresponsibility of the primitive was preserved,
along with his good-natured insouciance, his passivity, his

impotence; and at the end of this prodigious journey the classical (ethnological) attributes of the primitive were restored.

Thus the only real effect of Radin's critique was on the aesthetic plane. It does indeed validate the idea of individualized art in non-Western societies (in the form of the verbal arts, of poetry, singing, storytelling, etc.) as against the contemporary anthropologists' vision of a collective, anonymous art. On all other planes this critique stops short.

We are now at the heart of the matter. An individual art of discourse is not yet a philosophy. Individual discourse (as opposed to silent group discourse), the discursive intervention (as opposed to passive acquiescence) are no doubt necessary conditions; but they cannot in themselves create the act of philosophizing.

On the social level the last proposition means this: granted that philosophy can exist historically only through a literature, that it is properly speaking a special kind of literature, it does not follow that all literature is philosophical.

Therefore even if Griaule had the merit, which Tempels lacked, of giving the 'primitive' a *right to speak* (although he obstinately reduced Ogotemmeli to the role of mere spokesman), and even if Radin went so far as to recognize that, in the last analysis, all wisdom is irreducibly personal and to demonstrate the existence of a *littérature de pensée*,[20] produced by those whom he calls its 'intellectuals' in every non-Western society and transmitted orally from generation to generation, it does not automatically follow that this literature of thought is a *philosophical* literature, any more than discourse in general is automatically *philosophical* discourse. Radin and Griaule, in affirming this, were in much too much of a hurry.

With this in mind, if we read Ogotemmeli's narratives in *Dieu d'eau*, we shall easily be persuaded that they constitute a mythological rather than a philosophical discourse. They reflect a vast and ambitious cosmogony, but cosmogony is not philosophy. Let us read this Ewe funerary hymn, for instance, translated by Radin:

Sing me a song, a song of death,
That I may guide it by the hand.
Sing me a song of the underworld.
Sing me a song, a song of death,
That I may walk to the underworld!

Thus speaks the underworld to me,
The underworld speaks thus:
'O beautiful it feels in the grave,
O lovely is the underworld!
But yet no palm wine you can drink.'
Therefore I take you by the hand
And journey to the underworld.[21]

Or this doleful lament of an Amerindian warrior:

Mighty, mighty, great in war,
So was I honoured,
Now behold me old and wretched![22]

If we read about the feats of the great 'Earthmaker' in the cosmogony and mythology of the Winnebago Indians,[23] we can readily see that this literature is infinitely closer to poetry than to philosophy. That this poetry conveys a thought makes no difference, for poetry is not necessarily pure wordplay but can be profound as well as beautiful. Every thinker is not a philosopher. This point must be made clearly so that we can rid ourselves of the common illusion once and for all.

But, of course, I know what's waiting for me around the corner – the trick-question, the question of questions that divides all philosophers: what is philosophy? If it is not poetry or narrative, not myth or proverb or any other kind of aphorism, neither history nor biography, if it belongs to none of the genres into which the oral literature of so-called primitive peoples is customarily divided, then what is it?

I am in no hurry to answer this question, and this is my right, for I am not an anthropologist. I am content for the moment to show what philosophy is *not*. As for the rest, we shall come to that later. But let me clarify just one point: in speaking of poetry, I do not mean to reduce the oral literature of non-Western peoples to pure wordplay. Poetry is not just wordplay, as I have already remarked. Furthermore, not all of the texts are 'poetry'. I am only pointing out a similarity, a kinship, so as to show that if these texts cannot all be equated with poetry, they cannot *a fortiori* be characterized as philosophical. Objectively, they are closer to poetry than to philosophy. Tables, fables, legends, myths, proverbs, biographies and autobiographies, etc., are 'literary' genres in the ordinary sense of the word, genres of what we shall call *artistic* literature as distinct from *scientific* literature. Philosophy, on the other hand, belongs to scientific literature. Its lifeblood and rhythm are the same as those of mathematics, physics, chemistry, biology, linguistics. That is why the texts cited by Radin are nearer to poetry than philosophy. That is how a way of thinking may belong to art rather than to science.

If we wish to articulate the difference more accurately, we shall have to call, once again, upon the notion of history. Roughly speaking, one can say that a poem or a novel is valuable in itself; it is independent of the general history of poetry or the novel. A philosophical or mathematical work, on the other hand, is intelligible only as a moment in a debate that sustains and transcends it. It always refers to antecedent positions, either to refute them or to confirm and enrich them. It takes on meaning only in relation to that history, in relation to the terms of an ever-changing debate in which the sole stable element is the constant reference to one self-same object, to one sphere of experience, the characterization of which, incidentally, is itself part of the evolution. Scientific literature, in short, is thoroughly historical.

Artistic literature, on the other hand, knows only of an extrinsic history which is not essentially related to its content. It is an endless accumulation of works, each of which is a perfectly autonomous unit, significant in and of itself, a finished totality which might have appeared at any time in empirical history and the date of whose actual appearance is due to no internal necessity. One poem or novel does not refute another unless it be a poem or a novel *à thèse*, but then it is more than an ordinary poem or novel. From a purely artistic point of view, Valéry's *Cimetière marin* (1920) could have appeared before Baudelaire's *Fleurs du mal* (1857). Césaire's *Armes miraculeuses* (1946) could have appeared in the nineteenth century. Neither content nor form assigns these works to particular appointed places in a historical sequence, or if they do, the relation of these works to others is accidental, not essential, and it does not define them as literary works.[24] In the strictest sense of the term, art has no history, although it unfolds in history. Philosophy, on the other hand, like any other science, is historical in its very substance. It has the intrinsic historicity of a pluralistic discourse, in which different interlocutors question and answer one another within a generation or from one generation to another.

Compared with this kind of debate, it is clear that the discourse of a man like Ogotemmeli, inasmuch as it aspires to convey a wisdom that is eternal, intangible, a closed knowledge sprung from the depths of time and admitting of no discussion, opts out of history in general and, more particularly, from that groping, endless history, that unquiet, forever incomplete quest we call philosophy.

Philosophical revolutions

We have perhaps said enough to illuminate our first contention: that philosophy is a history, not a system. It goes without saying that in making this contention 'history' is placed above 'system'. To be more precise, we wish to make the point that philosophy cannot reduce itself to dumb acceptance, a contented purring, to the catechistic repetition of intangible dogmas without denying itself, and moreover, that philósophy not only exists *within* history, like a substance in a container, but is itself a second-order history borne by empirical history, a *productive* process (producing something as yet undefined), a *progress*. In this sense philosophy does not have a history; structurally, it is history itself.

Some readers may think that this is an overestimation of philosophy and its power. While conceding at most that philosophy, like science, exists only as a theoretical history, such readers will object that the history of philosophy, unlike the history of the sciences, is repetitive, circular, that it creates nothing, that in the last resort it is a pointless history, a pointless discourse. The objections may find support in the history of philosophy – in Kant, for instance, and in a certain sense, in Marx and then Lenin.

First, Kant. As is well known, the immense project of the *Critique of Pure Reason* rests on the painful observation that human reason has failed every time it has sought to grapple with transcendental problems. For Kant the history of philosophy is nothing but the story of those failures. Philosophy is the battlefield (*Kampfplatz*) on which, from time immemorial, irreconcilable doctrines have been fighting. Essentially, they can be reduced to two main types: dogmatism and scepticism. To put an end to this sterile and exhausting confrontation, it was necessary to undertake a complete examination of the power of the human mind as an instrument of knowledge and to define its true scope and the limits of its legitimate exercise. The Kantian project thus puts the history of philosophy on one side: what use is it if after so much toil it has failed to bring to light a single universally recognized truth and has never been more than a theatre of pointless quarrels, the closed field of a generalized war of all against all (*bellum omnium contra omnes*, as Husserl was to say).

Let us then make a *tabula rasa* of the history of philosophy. Already evident in the Preface (the *two* Prefaces), this move becomes increasingly precise and explicit in the Introduction to the *Critique of Pure Reason*. We know that this Introduction concentrates on raising and articulating the problem to which the whole work is devoted: how are synthetic, *a priori* judgements possible? We also know that this all-embracing question is immediately divided into three: how is pure mathematics possible? How is pure physics possible? How is metaphysics possible?

What is most remarkable here is that the third question (which in a way is the first, since it prompts the general question and consequently the first two particular questions) appears from the outset to be crippled by a hopeless equivocation. While Kant regards pure mathematics and physics as real sciences and attempts, by regressive analysis, to determine the conditions of their possibility, he believes that metaphysics exists not as a science but merely as a 'natural disposition', so in this case it is necessary to demonstrate the conditions of possibility not of a science and an actuality but of a painful absence. The analysis indicated by this little word 'possible' may be 'regressive' only because of this discontinuity in the real, because of the different status of the objects to be analysed: 'sciences' on the one hand, 'natural disposition' or 'need' on the other. Conversely, if the third question is formulated in the same terms as the first two (how is metaphysics possible *as a science*?), the similarity of form is only superficial. The problem is no longer to move back from an *existing* science to the conditions of its possibility but to specify the conditions for the emergence of a *future* science. The little word 'possible' has changed its meaning: it no longer calls for a regressive analysis but for a prospective exploration.

This equivocation, we have said, is remarkable. Why? Because the thesis of the non-scientificity of metaphysics (of pre-critical metaphysics, of course) has a specific effect in Kant's text: it annuls, invalidates the whole history of Western philosophy, considered as the untiring repetition of the same dogmatism generating contradictory theses interspersed with occasional sceptical doctrines:

[Reason's] dogmatic employment. . .lands us in dogmatic assertions to which other assertions, equally specious, can always be opposed – that is, in scepticism. . . .

We may then, and indeed we must, regard as *abortive* [our emphasis] all attempts, hitherto made, to establish a metaphysic dogmatically.[25]

This dismissal of a history whose diverse productions 'we must' regard as 'abortive' is complemented by the thesis of the universality of metaphysics seen as a 'natural disposition': 'There has always existed in the world, and there will always continue to exist, some kind of metaphysic, and with it the kind of dialectic that is natural to pure reason.'[26]

Kant's effort aims precisely at explaining the possibility of this 'natural metaphysics', of these questions which, it seems, spontaneously and universally command the attention of human reason. If all men are natural metaphysicians, it is by virtue of the very nature of reason, which irresistibly impels it to break out of the field of experience by following up the series of its conditions as far as the ultimate Unconditional. This motion is irrepressible in all men, in all cultures. In this respect, Western civilization enjoys no special privilege: reason is doomed to the same fate everywhere, the perpetual sifting of the same problems. So long as a 'tribunal' has not been instituted to 'uphold the legitimate claims of reason' and 'to condemn any unjustified usurpations', so long as a *critique of pure reason* has not been established, the history of metaphysics will be a pointless history. The subtle debates, the enormous literature devoted for centuries by the West to problems of this order will be nothing but vain theoretical agitation, sterile diatribe in no way preferable to the mindless mumbo-jumbo of the so-called primitive mythologies. In Europe as elsewhere, metaphysics exists merely as a 'natural disposition'. Nowhere does it exist as a science. We are all in the same boat, at the same level of theoretical indigence.

How reassuring to see our mythologies, cosmogonies, theogonies, anthropogonies, eschatologies, etc., our conceptions of the world, our wisdom thus up to a point rehabilitated. It suggests that all those forms of thought that a little while ago we were contrasting with philosophy conceived as history, because of their systematic closure, can be regarded as modes of this universal 'natural metaphysics' and, to that extent, as rehabilitated.

But if we take a closer look, the Kantian critique itself is a moment in the history which it rejects; it appears at a particular stage in its evolution and is carried by its momentum. Of this Kant himself is fully conscious. It is no accident that he so frequently takes his bearings with reference to Hume. The Humean analysis of the concept of cause, the psychologistic reduction of all predicative relations to the level of simple effects of association, the *a priori* subjectivist determination to explain objective relations between phenomena in terms of the laws of the human mind and the resulting impossibility of science as of metaphysics, all of these had exerted a profound impression on Kant which, in the celebrated remark of the *Prolegomena*, were to rouse him from his dogmatic slumber.[27]

This is true to such an extent that the *Critique of Pure Reason* may be read as a methodical solution of Hume's unique problem, reformulated and placed on a level of generality which Hume had not been able to attain: *how is causal judgement possible?* In this respect it is worth reading and rereading the enthusiastic pages devoted to Hume in the Introduction and the text of the *Prolegomena*, and then the numerous, the dozens of passages in which his problematic is evoked inside the *Critique*, to realize how personally Kant felt *challenged* by Hume and to what extent his work, far from simply taking its place alongside that of the great Scottish sceptic in an external history, is actually based intimately on it, both in continuity and in opposition – in a *dialectical* relation in the strict sense. This is proof enough that despite his thorough obliteration of the history of thought, or rather because of it, because of his patient destruction of the finest monuments of speculative reason, Kant takes his place in a current of that history – or, rather, it is through Kant that we are able to grasp the precise theoretical function of that current as distinct from all the others. Scepticism, the father of all critical philosophy, is not a philosophy among others. It cannot be placed on the same level as the various constructions of dogmatic metaphysics; it functions in the history of metaphysics as a force of negation and uncertainty, somewhat like a bad conscience. Above all, scepticism is what enables metaphysics to escape from the simple juxtaposition or confrontation of irreducible closed systems and to take its place in a history of thought, in a history of philosophy, which includes metaphysics as well as its opposite.

One can find in the last pages of the *Critique of Pure Reason*, in that 'Transcendental Doctrine of Method' which is supposed to constitute the second part of the book but is very much shorter than the first, the Transcendental Doctrine of Elements, an outline of what Kant calls a 'History of Pure Reason'.[28]

This history may present us with nothing but 'structure in ruins', rotting systems stripped of all credibility and powers of persuasion, but these ruins are nevertheless instructive, and they have a history that is not purely negative, since it was to nurture the idea, the project of a critique of pure reason; moreover, the creator of these ruins, the corrosive element that demolished all structures and neutralized all dogmatic systems, reinvigorating reason and inspiring it with the will to criticize, is none other than scepticism. This makes it tempting to account for the nuances of the Kantian position on this point by carefully separating metaphysics from philosophy, by generalizing Kant's explicit opposition between dogmatic metaphysics and transcendental philosophy. If there is no history of metaphysics as such because the subject is pure repetition, the sterile confrontation of opposing dogmatisms, there exists on the contrary a history of philosophy – the history of the question of the possibility of metaphysics that can, with hindsight, incorporate and integrate the various productions of dogmatic metaphysics. The history of philosophy so understood follows an internal necessity, a logic. As Kant writes, in a chapter entitled 'The discipline of pure reason':

The first step in matters of pure reason, marking its infancy, is *dogmatic*. The second step is *sceptical* and indicates that experience has rendered our judgement wiser and more circumspect. But a third step, such as can be taken only by fully matured judgement, based on assured principles of proved universality, is now necessary, namely, to subject to examination not the facts of reason but reason itself, in the whole extent of its powers, and as regards its aptitude for pure *a priori* modes of knowledge.[29]

There is therefore something like an internal rationality, a teleology, in the history of pure reason that leads to the gradual emergence of the need for self-knowledge, for criticism. In this respect Kant is fully of his time. The progress of philosophy is just an aspect of the progress of Enlightenment. The very intention of the *Critique* is deeply rooted in the spirit of the century: of this we are warned in the Preface.[30] Kant defined Enlightenment as 'man's release from his self-incurred tutelage, for which he is himself responsible'.[31]

There are examples other than the relation of Kant to Hume, less direct perhaps, less favourable sometimes, but just as decisive. Thus Locke is often cited as the real founder of modern empiricism, later raised by Hume to its highest level of coherence. The notion of a Category, in the Transcendental Analytic, is taken from Aristotle but redefined and reassessed from a critical perspective. Plato,

Berkeley and occasionally Descartes function in Kant's discourse as negative models, pitfalls to be avoided, and so of course does the rationalism of Leibniz and Wolff, which Kant himself long professed (the famous 'dogmatic slumber') before subjecting it to a particularly radical critique based on corrosive Humean empiricism.

We could now call it a day, the example of Kant being proof enough of our point that no philosophy, however new, ever appears *ex nihilo*, that every philosophical doctrine is a reply to foregoing doctrines in the double mode of confirmation and refutation or, better still, as a call for further developments, an appeal for future confirmation or refutation, so that every philosophy looks forward and backward, to the inexhaustible history of the discipline.

But then we should still have to account for the Kantian move mentioned above, for his reduction of the history of philosophy on which the critical philosophy was based, a reduction which seems to be belied by the multiple real relations which continue to bind it to this same history.

It is not only in Kant that we observe this equivocation. We find it in diverse degrees in all the great classical philosophers, in all those who were conscious of the fact that they were deliberately trying to change the course of the history of philosophy. In the seventeenth century Descartes ruthlessly blue-pencilled the whole of scholastic doctrine, which had failed to give him the certainty he required, and on this basis he turned fiercely to the *cogito* as the ultimate source of all truth. Closer to us, Husserl, tired of empiricist prattle about the psychological origins of the laws of logic, demands, in a celebrated formula, a 'return to things themselves', beyond the learned discourses which have tried to dissolve them in the flow of subjective consciousness. At this initial stage of phenomenology the history of philosophy could be understood only as the story of an omission, of the loss of what was essential, of alienation. Husserl's entire project was to seek to restore original contact with the reality of things, to seek an opening to the meaning by which consciousness invariably defines itself. Hence this rule, formulated in 'Philosophy as rigorous science': 'The impulse to research must proceed not from philosophies but from things and the problems connected with them.'[32]

But the sequel to the story is well known. Beyond its break with the scholastic heritage and its radical return to the *ego cogito*, Cartesian philosophy deployed a number of concepts and themes inherited from the scholastic tradition. Many of Descartes' most crucial (and sometimes least convincing) moves, like his celebrated reification of the *cogito*, his hasty provision of substantial support for the pure activity of thought (defined as the *res cogitans*) with which Kant and then Hegel, Husserl and many others, each in his own way, were to reproach him, are intelligible only in terms of the implicit logic of Aristotelian and medieval metaphysics. In his turn Husserl, in breaking with the dominant psychologism of his time, in returning to the transcendental ego for a methodical definition of its intentional structures, is conscious of repeating, essentially, the initial move of Descartes' philosophy. Moreover, in contemplating the crisis in European science and humanity in his last works, he was to place his own philosophy in perspective, interpreting it as the manifestation of a *telos* inherent in history itself.

Kant's position is therefore far from unique. Every great philosophy begins by inserting within parentheses, by practically rejecting the history of philosophy. Every great philosophy is a rebirth, a radical questioning. But the break itself appears only after the event, through a kind of recursion which is also essential to all philosophy, as a necessary moment in the history of philosophy, a turning, renascence, revolution, mutation taking place *within* that history and not a suppression or annihilation that comes from the outside.

So the fact is that the history of philosophy is not cumulative as a consequence of the addition of new thoughts to old ones. It moves between successive levels separated by pits and ruptures; it cuts its way through crises, radical requestionings, and when its end seems on the point of being engulfed it rises up, transformed. Thus the structure of the history of philosophy is similar to that attributed by Bachelard to science: 'What happens is not a *development* from old doctrines to the new; but rather an *envelopment* of old thoughts by the new.'[33] This is probably a typical structure in the history of thought, the *after-the-event* structure of hindsight, the recursion that enables each figure of science, as those of philosophy, to reinterpret the previous figures, after first rejecting them, and to replace them in a reorganized theoretical space. In philosophy, as in the sciences, one does not simply move from an old theory to a new one by a process of elaboration. One must have already accepted the new theory in order to discover the limits of the old theory and, at the same time, its relative validity.

So far we have been content with describing this *fact*, calling on a few classic examples. There remains the task of accounting for it, of explaining why the history of philosophy does not move in a straight line but steers a zigzag course, as it were; why every great philosophy, in order to establish itself, must ravage the existing theoretical space; what laws, regularities or series of conditions govern these upheavals. To ask such questions, let us note, is to abandon philosophy, in a way, and to treat it as an object, to provide an account of it, anticipating perhaps the 'non-philosophical theory of philosophy'[34] which Althusser looks forward to. Such questions are impossible *inside* philosophy. The philosopher can only *observe* this kind of articulation of doctrines; he cannot *explain* it for the simple reason that anything he might say would necessarily refer, in the last analysis, to the universal essence of discourse as the basis for the articulation of philosophy in history. The reasons he would give could help to explain why philosophy has a history – or, rather, that it is itself a history – but they could not explain why this history is structurally disjointed rather than continuous.

We must therefore approach the question from a point of view outside discourse, and this is precisely what Marx and Engels invite us to do in *The German Ideology*. Their position on this point is concise and well known: philosophy has *no* history! Of course, one is tempted, after what has been said of Kant, Descartes and Husserl, to dismiss this theoretical rejection of the history of philosophy as a figurative expression of its rejection in practice which is always part of the negative move that institutes every new philosophy. And it remains true that this thesis cannot without absurdity be taken literally: Marx and Engels were aware of the *actual* succession of philosophies and of the complex tangles of their reasons and arguments. They knew that in this succession everything is interwoven, that in the end every philosophy is a link in the chain that carries it, referring to the whole set of past, present and future philosophies.

Nevertheless, it does not follow that this thesis can be reduced to a rhetorical figure. What Marx and Engels are asserting is that neither the succession nor the theoretical interdependence of doctrine is enough to make a history. In the pure domain of thought every mutation or revolution, every *event* in the strong sense, refers to some event in the material world and owes its own occurrence as an event to this relation. This is what the young Hegelians did not understand. Taking the history of thought for the whole of history,

they overestimated the importance of their own intellectual effervescence, saw in the Germany of their time 'the scene of an un-
precedented upheaval' and believed that they were promoting 'a
revolution beside which the French Revolution was child's play, a
world struggle beside which the struggles of Diadochi would appear
insignificant'.[35] Marx and Engels retorted to these pretentious
ideologues that their theoretical revolutions were dreams, fantasies
without any grip on reality, that real history was taking place
elsewhere, in the material world where people were forever *producing* the means of their existence. They oppose their own method
in *The German Ideology* to the Hegelian conception of history.

In direct contrast to German philosophy which descends from heaven to
earth, here we ascend from earth to heaven. That is to say, we do not set out
from what men say, imagine, conceive, nor from men as narrated, thought
of, imagined, conceived, in order to arrive at men in the flesh. We set out
from real, active men, and on the basis of their real life process we demonstrate the development of the ideological reflexes and echoes of this life
process. The phantoms formed in the human brain are also, necessarily,
sublimates of their material life process, which is empirically verifiable and
bound to material premises. *Morality, religion, metaphysics, all the rest of
ideology* and their corresponding forms of consciousness, *thus no longer
retain the semblance of independence.* They have no history, no development; but men, developing their material production and their material
intercourse, alter, along with their real existence, their thinking and the
products of their thinking. *Life is not determined by consciousness, but
consciousness by life. . . .*
    Where speculation ends – in real life – there real, positive science begins:
the representation of the practical activity, of the practical process of
development of men. Empty talk about consciousness ceases, and real
knowledge has to take its place. *When reality is depicted, philosophy as an
independent branch of knowledge loses its medium of existence.*[36]

This long quotation is necessary in order to give the context of
certain formulations, now classic, that have been so often repeated
mechanically out of context that they have lost any real meaning
and have ceased to function except as incantations. Incidentally,
this passage is fatal for some of our official 'Marxists', for if one
cannot start 'from what men say, imagine, conceive. . .to arrive at
men in the flesh', if on the contrary one must judge their word in the
light of their practice, it is equally clear that it is not enough to
proclaim oneself a Marxist to be one; that official declarations of

authority – even and especially if that authority calls itself revolutionary – must be assessed in the light of its real practice; that the major problem in the sphere of political analysis is to know not so much how a regime defines itself as what objective function this self-proclaimed definition has in the political game which the regime is playing; that beyond the declaration, real or feigned, of loyalty to Marxism the real problem concerns the historical mode of appropriation of Marxism, the concrete role which it is made to play and, in a word, the way in which it *functions*: is it an agency of liberation or of enslavement, a catalyst of energy or an ideological opiate, theoretical matrix of political and scientific debate or monologue of power, language of the masses or mystifying discourse carried on behind their backs? But enough of this problem.

It is more important for our purpose to measure the exact scope and meaning of that paradoxical but by now classic statement 'Philosophy has no history.' Addressed to pretentious intellectuals shut up in their theoretical universe and, like their master Hegel, regarding the development of the Idea as the motor of world history, the purpose of this thesis was simply to relativize the history of ideas itself, to replace it in the context from which the ideologists had extracted it to hypostatize it, and to show that of itself it has all the characteristics of a game but that it really can be organized by reference to the real history of the material world. There is no *Idea* in itself, no Spirit that is not the human spirit, no Consciousness that does not refer to a specific subject. Therefore there is no autonomous development of the Idea imagined as a living being endowed with spontaneity and drawing from itself the law of its own growth. Ideas are always products of human thought, of the mental activity that is inseparable from the material activity of men.

We are therefore now presented with a reversal of perspectives. Marx and Engels do not really deny that philosophy can have a history. On the contrary, they explicitly accept that 'men, developing their material production and their material intercourse, alter, along with their real existence, their thinking and the products of their thinking', and this is a way of recognizing the existence of such a history. They add, however, that this history is not autonomous and does not draw from itself the law of its own development, which is determined in the last analysis by the history of the production of material goods and that of the social relations of production.

The precise modalities of this determination, which we know to be a determination only *in the last instance*, are not defined in *The*

German Ideology. In order to give a theoretical account of them we must refer to other texts and place *The German Ideology* in the context of the whole of Marx's work. One then realizes how enigmatic are the trenchant formulations of this book and how mistaken one would be to give it a literal interpretation in view of the theory developed in later works. On this matter Louis Althusser has said things that one can no longer afford to ignore: the Marxist conception of history is not a simple reversal of the Hegelian conception, an almost mechanical substitution of a materialistic (economistic) monism for an idealistic monism. Marx did not 'borrow' the Hegelian concept of history and alter its content or determinations: he constructs another concept of history on the basis of a totally different conception of the social whole. Whereas for Hegel society was a homogeneous whole, of which each part was *pars totalis*, equally qualified to express the internal essence of the whole and manifesting, each in its own way, the self-presence of the concept at any given historical moment, the Marxist whole is complex, hierarchical, decentralized and has distinct and comparatively autonomous levels. Each level of this whole evolves according to its own rhythm, and every instance possesses a different kind of historical existence so that it is not possible to conceive these different levels or instances in the same historical time. Strictly speaking, therefore, there is no such thing as a single, unitary 'history' of society, let alone a 'general history' of mankind, a sort of neutral milieu in which different events might successively reside, like clients in the bed of a prostitute. But for each mode of production there exist the differential histories of the different levels or instances: an economic history with its own rhythm, a political history, a history of religions, a history of ideologies, a history of philosophy, a history of the sciences, a history of art, etc., each also with its own rhythm. The idea of continuous and homogeneous time disappears. Abstract history splinters into a plurality of differential histories stripped of all reference to a common time (the abstract time of the clock) but articulated one into the other according to the specific nature of the relevant whole (of the relevant mode of production) and determined by the economic 'base' only *in the last instance* through a series of completely unavoidable mediations.[37]

This is surely not the place to develop this theme. We have broached it simply to locate properly (that is, to relativize) the abrupt statements of *The German Ideology* and also of *Theses on Feuerbach*, which date from the same period, by reference to the works of Marx's maturity (in particular *The Poverty of Philosophy, The Contribution to the Critique of Political Economy* and *Capital*). In these texts of 1845 the whole of philosophy is cast aside as part of ideology and thus condemned to a joyous death in the cause of the only science, which itself owes its escape from ideology to the fact that it is conceived, in accordance with the classical model of empiricist theories of knowledge, as a carbon copy of reality and not as a conceptual exercise creating its own objects. To understand these enigmatic texts, one must remember that they belong to the period of the 'break' (Althusser), when Marx undertook, in his own words, to 'settle accounts with [his] erstwhile philosophical conscience', and that they are inevitably marred by exaggeration and polemical violence. Reacting against the idealism of Hegel, Marx and Engels could not, in 1845, bother with niceties. They could only invert its propositions, term for term, and counter Hegel's idealist monism with a brutal materialism that was still mechanistic, pending the development of new concepts that were to enunciate the new science and philosophy founded on this break.

Whatever these later revisions, however, the inversion effected in that extract from *The German Ideology*, even attenuated and refined by the works of Marx's maturity, refers to a different concept of history from the one from which we started. At the outset we could not imagine any other history than that of discourse. History was for us nothing but the developed form of articulated speech, its distribution over time and, consequently, the developed form of the linkage of letters in writing, of the linear display of words on papyrus. For us history was the history of *logos*, and in fact it was no more than another name for *logos*: discourse, reasoning, reason. We could therefore confidently treat the historicity of philosophy and of the sciences as modes of *logos*, but we could conceive of the history of art only by reducing it to the history of discourse about art. Still less could we conceive of economic history, the history of material production, what Marx and Engels in the extract above call the 'real life process', the 'material life process', 'material production' and the 'practical process of development of men'.

Let us not shun the word: our concept of history was an *idealistic* concept. Underlying our analysis was the Hegelian conception of philosophy as the pure development of the Idea, a conception which makes the history of thought the rational core and finally the whole of history. Marx's critique sends that naïve concept of history flying and compels us to refer the linear development of ideas, the concatenation of discourse, the theoretical interdependence of doctrines, to a more fundamental history, decisive in the last instance – the history of production.

Of course, it would be foolish to ignore the theoretical difficulties of this new concept of history. It lacks the massive persuasiveness of the metaphor of the *line* or, more exactly, the *chain*. It is infinitely less transparent and limpid than the earlier concept. Marxist history is not the simple articulation of a linear discourse slightly complicated by the plurality of divergent theoretical traditions, which are nevertheless ultimately reducible to one another through mathematical laws of transformation and conversion. It is the complex articulation of 'levels' or 'instances', each of which has its own legitimacy and mode of existence, all consequently heterogeneous and irreducible to one another. The unity of the concept of history, which seemed so secure in Hegel's conception is lost in this deployment of 'levels'. At the same time a new difficulty arises, unknown to Hegel: that of the transition from one historical moment to another. These transitions were self-explanatory within the idealist philosophies, being nothing more than the flow of speech itself, the evocation, affirmative or contradictory, of one idea by another, what the empiricists interpreted mechanistically in terms of 'association'. But the transition from one economic structure to another? From one mode of production to another?

We shall not attempt here to solve this problem, nor even to state it fully.[38] Let us simply point out that in fact this problem of transitions does not concern material history alone. It exists also at the level of intellectual formations, although it is partially concealed by the assumption of continuity of the idealistic and logocentric conception of history. The difficulty posed by this problem is therefore no argument against materialism; on the contrary, it is materialism which *reveals* the problem and thereby makes its solution possible, whereas previously it was unseen, suppressed.

We shall also add this: the difference of status between the two concepts of history means not that one must be renounced in favour of the other but that each must be integrated with the other, as the part with the whole or the particular with the general, or, as Bachelard puts it, as an old theory is 'enveloped' by a new one. The Hegelian concept of history enables one to understand the specific mode of existence of philosophy and the sciences as opposed to the repetitive discourse of daily life or art. For us its sole meaning lies in this polemical, discriminatory capacity, and it is only in this sense that we have used it above. But having specified the theoretical level (scientific as well as philosophical), having defined what we shall venture to call the theoretical instance, it has been necessary – in order to render intelligible the specific mode of development of this instance – to locate it in the complex, hierarchical whole which is society. Hence our recourse to another, infinitely richer and more complex, concept of history.

Let us put forward, in conclusion, a few abrupt hypotheses, which we shall not be able to justify fully here. We offer them for what they are, i.e. possible elements of an answer to the problem, stated above, of the conditions of possibility of revolutions in philosophy. In the light of our earlier analyses, this problem may be formulated thus: what, outside philosophy, determines the transitions which are the stuff of its history? How, by what mediations, is philosophical practice finally determined by material practices?

Our answer is based once more on an extremely valuable remark of Althusser. Returning in *Lenin and Philosophy* to one of the arguments of his unpublished 'Course in Philosophy for Scientists', he warns us that the great philosophical revolutions are always the sequel of great scientific revolutions, so that philosophy is organically linked, in its growth and evolution, with the birth and development of the sciences:

Philosophy has not always existed; it has been observed only in places where there is also what is called a science or sciences – science in the strict sense of theoretical discipline, i.e. ideating and demonstrative, not an aggregate of empirical results. . . .
. . . For philosophy to be born or reborn, it is necessary that sciences be. That is why, perhaps, philosophy in the strict sense began only with Plato, goaded into being by the existence of Greek mathematics; was blown up by Descartes, roused into its modern revolution by Galilean physics; was recast by Kant, under the influence of the Newtonian discovery; was remodelled by Husserl, stung by the first axiomatics, etc.[39]

In other words, philosophy does not get up until dusk: we know that from Hegel, in the Preface to *The Principles of the Philosophy of Right*. But this tardiness is here defined as a lagging behind science, as the belated aftermath within philosophical discourse of the great events in the history of the sciences.[40]

Now, if this hypothesis is correct, it gives us the answer to our question. Philosophical revolutions are functions of scientific revolutions, of the great 'breaks' through which the problematics of existing sciences are reorganized and new sciences sometimes thrown up. These breaks are not, of course, in themselves purely discursive events but rather theoretical effects in the field of discourse, of experimental practices which inform science throughout, practices organically linked to human material practices as a whole, employing various technical processes and hence dependent on the development of technology and therefore of the productive forces. If we want to understand the possibility of revolutions in philosophy, we must go so far as to accept that philosophical discourse, while not a mechanical reflection of the economic structure (as vulgar materialism would have it), is strictly modelled on the model of scientific discourse (though it is not, of course, a simple replication of it) and in this way hinges upon the history of material practices. To be sure, this is as yet only a hypothesis. To give it substance, new and difficult analyses in the history and philosophy of science will be needed, which would in particular emphasize the experimental nature of all sciences, mathematics included.[41] We also need new analyses of the history of philosophy in order to discover the specific relation between each great philosophical problematic and an actual, or at least emergent, science. Such an approach promises to be fruitful and in any case offers the only hope at present of a solution to the difficult problems stated above.

We can now state what we have been driving at: if our hypothesis is correct, if the development of philosophy is in some way a function of the development of the sciences, then African philosophy cannot be separated from African science and we shall never have, in Africa, a philosophy in the strict sense, a philosophy articulated as an endless search, until we have produced, in Africa, a history of science, a history of the sciences. Philosophical practice, that peculiar form of theoretical practice that is called philosophy, is inseparable from that other form of theoretical practice called science.

Rather than noisily claim the existence of an African 'philosophy' which would save us the trouble of philosophizing, we would therefore be better advised to work patiently and methodically for what we could call African *science* or African *scientific research*. It is not philosophy but science that Africa needs first. If philosophy can also be of use, it is only by helping to liberate a genuine theoretical tradition on this continent, an open scientific tradition, master of its problems and of its themes, and also to the extent that it proves capable, once this tradition is established, of contributing in one way or another to its enrichment. *That* philosophy – that theoretical quest strictly hinged upon science – will carry us a thousand miles away from the preoccupations which have inspired and shaped the myth of a so-called traditional African 'philosophy'. It will get us far away from the metaphysical problems of the origins of the world, the meaning of life, the wherefore of death, human destiny, the reality of the beyond, the existence of God and all those insoluble problems which really belong to mythology, yet are the usual fodder of philosophical rumination. But it will open up new theoretical problems concerning the essence of scientific discourse, its history and the conditions that render it possible.

The first precondition for a history of philosophy, the first precondition for philosophy as history, is therefore the existence of a scientific practice, the existence of science as an organized material practice reflected in discourse. But one must go back even further: the chief requirement of science itself is writing. It is difficult to imagine a scientific civilization that is not a civilization based on writing, difficult to imagine a scientific tradition in a society in which knowledge can be transmitted only orally. Therefore African civilizations could not give birth to any *science*, in the strictest sense of the word, until they had undergone the profound transformation through which we see them going today, that transformation which is gradually changing them, from within, into literate civilizations.

Let us be quite clear about this: pre-colonial Africa had undoubtedly amassed a wealth of true knowledge, of effective techniques which have been transmitted orally from generation to generation and continue to this day to ensure the livelihood of a large part of the population of our countryside and cities. It is probably one of the most urgent tasks facing our generation to record this precious heritage, to test and systematize it. But precisely because we speak of recording and systematizing it in order to integrate it into our modern knowledge, it must be that this heritage has not yet been *recorded, systematized, integrated*. It must be admitted that of itself it could not have produced that specific form of knowledge that we refer to, very vaguely, as 'modern knowledge'. We have first to accede to this 'modern' knowledge before we can recognize retrospectively the possibility and necessity of such a recovering our heritage. It is a matter not of the spontaneous development of traditional wisdom into the modern *episteme* but of the envelopment of the first by the second, as Bachelard would say. Incidentally, the correct execution of this project of envelopment (integration, reclamation, etc.) presupposes the elaboration of a methodology that may not be the exclusive business of scientists but that of philosophers also.

I shall add one more remark. Pre-colonial Africa was certainly not, or not quite, a society without writing. Theophile Obenga has recently described, in his excellent work *Africa in the Ancient World*,[42] some of the systems of writing practised on our continent before the European invasion – for instance, among the Vai of Sierra Leone, the Bamun of the Cameroun, not to mention the more ancient and better-known systems such as that of ancient Egypt. But this does not solve our problem. It is not enough to know that systems of writing existed in certain societies in certain parts of Africa. The question is how these systems were used, what the concrete purposes were that they served, and what place they had in the spiritual and material culture of these societies. Were they reserved for a privileged class (the priests, for instance), and did they on that account convey an esoteric or aristocratic kind of knowledge, or were they on the contrary within the reach of the masses? That is the real problem.

One can also, with Cheikh Anta Diop, advocate the thesis of historical regression, according to which Africa, in the remotest antiquity, knew a most brilliant scientific civilization, as witnessed in particular by the spectacular achievements of the Egypt of the Pyramids. In th.is view the present penury of Africa on the scientific and technological planes is not original but the result of a regression, a decadence.[43] I shall not dwell on the difficulties confronting this thesis, which seems to me extremely fruitful but is likely to remain speculative, until definitive arguments, as opposed to impressionistic or conjectural ones, can be given for the biological and historical continuity between the populations of ancient Egypt and those of present-day Africa. The most important point is that even if this hypothesis is. true, it does not explain why such a cultural regression should have taken place. One possible explanation is the hieratic, esoteric character of science and literacy in a society in which these were monopolized by a tiny class of priests who made them instruments of their domination. This is, of course, speculation, into which I do not care to venture further. But what remains certain is that the first and most basic requirement of *philosophy*, as of *science* (in the strict sense of these words), is the broad, democratic practice of writing – a necessary, if not sufficient, condition.

African philosophy today

It should not now be necessary to linger over my third point: African philosophy may now be undergoing its first decisive transformation under our very eyes. To understand the meaning of this proposition, it is necessary to bear in mind, first, that African philosophy *exists*; second, that it is different from what it is thought to be (that is, from what ethnological literature has said it is for so long).

The present theoretical transformation, which is rich in the most unsuspected promise, must therefore consist in a recognition of what philosophy *is not* and a vigorous denunciation of earlier illusions concerning the historical mode of existence of African philosophy.

Indeed, it is now beginning to be understood that African philosophy is not the supposedly collective, spontaneous, unreflective and implicit world-view with which it has hitherto been confused. It is coming to be accepted that it is not a system of tacit beliefs which are accepted, consciously or unconsciously, by all Africans in general or, more especially, by all the members of a particular ethnic group or a particular African society. It is now recognized that in this sense 'Bantu philosophy', 'Dogon philosophy', 'Diola philosophy', 'Yoruba philosophy', 'Fon philosophy', 'Wolof philosophy', 'Serer philosophy', etc. are so many myths invented by the West, that there are no more spontaneous African 'philosophies' than there are spontaneous Western, French, German, Belgian or American 'philosophies' creating silent unanimities among all Westerners, all the French, all the Germans, etc. African philosophy can exist only in the same mode as European philosophy, i.e. through what is called *literature*.

It is now agreed: African philosophy *is* African philosophical literature.[44] The only problem, then, is whether this literature must be understood in a narrow sense or whether non-written statements and that long tradition called oral literature should be added to the writings.

This broadening of the concept of literature does not seem, at first sight, to raise any difficulties. Indeed, it might seem that the concept of oral literature should theoretically precede that of written literature, as speech precedes writing. A written text appears to be simply the transcription of a previously oral statement, one that is not supposed to modify the content and scope of that statement at all.

One could even be tempted to enlist, in support of this thesis, the authority of Jacques Derrida – especially the analyses in his celebrated *Of Grammatology*.[45] One could invoke the way in which this book enlarges the concept of writing, beyond its narrow sense of phonetic, alphabetical writing. Indeed, we know with what vigour Derrida denounces Western ethnocentrism and its celebration of alphabetical writing, i.e. essentially European writing, as *the* universal model of writing. One could be tempted, by way of legitimately reacting against that ethnocentrism, to say that after all speech is also a form of writing and that its finest inventions, passed on orally from father to son and prodigiously preserved in the memory of so-called illiterate peoples, have nothing to envy the archivally transmitted achievements which take the form of material, visible, manipulable documents. After all, oral tradition is already the beginning of writing, since speech, as Derrida has shown, presupposes articulation, phonological contrast and therefore an interplay of differences which are substantially the same as those of writing; moreover, speech, conveyed from father to son without archival support, is possible only through mnemonic techniques which, as aids to memory, play the same objective role as documents or archives.

The argument is attractive, but it merely pushes the problem into the background. After all, if one ignores the classic distinction between speech and writing, if one asserts, as Derrida rightly does, that writing in the ordinary empirical and voluntaristic sense is no more than a mode derived from a form of supra-writing that is also present in speech, there is still the problem of deciding whether these two modes or forms of writing are strictly equivalent, play the same part and fulfil the same function in the history of culture. Derrida never asserts such an equivalence. Even less would he agree to reduce empirical writing to the status of a mere aid to speech, of a mere transcription of an already complete and self-sufficient thought, in short to an insignificant technique deprived of the slightest effect on the content to which it is applied. Far from warranting such an assertion, the author of *Of Grammatology* expressly warns us against it by identifying it as the central thesis of a specific ideology which he calls *logocentrism*, an ideology according to which *logos*, or speech, is the most perfect form of language and writing a mere technique of conservation or memorization and in which speech is taken to precede writing and, being 'live' and 'full', to constitute the most spontaneous and reassuring manifestation of life, self-presence, self-consciousness and conscience. For Derrida this logocentrism (or 'phonocentrism') is the most ancient and most constant of the illusions of Western civilization. Personally, I should be inclined to say that it is not so much a specific taint of Western civilization as a universal prejudice, probably due to the demands of social life as such.

But let us return to our problem after this apparent digression. We were speaking about African philosophy or, more exactly, of what it is *not*. Having rejected the classical illusion by which it is reduced to a collective, unreflective and implicit system of beliefs, we were saying that it could exist only in the form of explicit discourses, that is to say, above all in the form of a literature. The problem then arose of the meaning to be given to this word 'literature', whether it should be reduced to 'written' literature (in the usual empirical sense of the word 'writing') or whether 'oral' literature should be included also. Eventually it became clear that this question envelops another, the question of the respective roles and status of 'written' and 'oral' literature or, in other words, of writing in the empirical and derivative sense of 'book writing' and of writing as pure memorization (mental writing, as it were).

Having stated the problem in these terms, I should like to risk a hypothesis: oral tradition favours the consolidation of knowledge into dogmatic, intangible systems, whereas archival transmission promotes better the possibility of a critique of knowledge between individuals and from one generation to another. Oral tradition is dominated by the *fear of forgetting*, of *lapses of memory*, since memory is here left to its own resources, bereft of external or material support. This forces people to hoard their memories jealously, to recall them constantly, to repeat them continually, accumulating and heaping them up in a global wisdom, simultaneously present, always ready to be applied, perpetually available. In these conditions the mind is too preoccupied with *preserving* knowledge to find freedom to *criticize* it. Written tradition, on the contrary, providing a material support, liberates the memory, and permits it to forget its acquisitions, provisionally to reject or question them, because it knows that it can at any moment recapture them if need be. By guaranteeing a permanent record, archives make actual memory superfluous and give full rein to the boldness of the mind.

From this point of view, it is impossible to be satisfied with Lévi-Strauss's distinction between European societies and the so-called illiterate societies and his claims that the former produce a 'cumulative', 'acquisitive' history, constantly endeavouring to increase their wealth and discoveries, whereas the latter have a passive, 'cold', 'non-cumulative', 'non-acquisitive' history.[46] Strictly speaking, one should reverse the terms of this opposition. The so-called illiterate societies (which, as we have seen, often do possess a form of writing, even in the most empirical sense of the word, but are characterized by the fact that they do not use it as the chief means of transmission and diffusion of knowledge) are compelled to store their inventions and discoveries jealously in their memories, to accumulate and hoard them. Their history is therefore, paradigmatically, *cumulative*, if this word has any meaning. On the contrary, the history of the West is not directly cumulative but *critical*: it moves forward not through a mere plurality of knowledge, through the accumulation of discoveries and inventions, but through the periodical questioning of established knowledge, each questioning being a *crisis*.

But such crises, as we have seen, are founded on the confidence, the assurance, that it will always be possible to retrieve the past if need be, thanks to the visible traces and material landmarks which have been carefully preserved. Nothing is lost: the title-deeds of the positions attacked with critical and iconoclastic verve are safe in the bank.

Such is the real function of (empirical) writing. It leaves the task of conservation to matter (books, documents, archives, etc.) and liberates the mind to make innovations that may shake established ideas and even overthrow them completely.

Now if it is accepted, as we have advocated, that philosophy is history rather than system, a perpetual movement of critique and counter-critique rather than quiet certainty, it is clear that philosophy can flourish and fulfil itself only in a civilization with writing (in the empirical sense). Purely 'oral' writing, on the other hand, without of course entirely prohibiting criticism, tends to contain it within narrow limits and to perpetuate a conservative, traditionalist culture, jealous of its heritage and exclusively concerned to increase it quantitatively, without ever questioning it: a *cumulative* culture if ever there was one. Philosophy, a critical reflection *par excellence*, cannot develop fully unless it 'writes its memoirs' or 'keeps a diary'. Again, it would not be impossible as an intellectual activity in an 'oral' civilization, but it would be confined to a specific time and place and would survive in the collective memory only in the impoverished form of a *result*, a *conclusion*, cut off from the train of thought that has led to it.

Little by little, we have narrowed down the circle of our definitions. African philosophy, which Tempels and his disciples, as heirs to a long ethnophilosophical tradition originally conceived as a collective, implicit and possibly unconscious world-view, is now beginning to reject the definition which has been foisted on it and to take cognizance of itself as discourse, explicit thinking, as the unfinished history of a many-sided debate. It is beginning to see itself as a specific kind of literature. A number of texts very explicitly bear witness to this revolution. Some of these texts are signed by the Camerounians Eboussi-Boulaga, Towa and N'joh-Mouelle, by the Ghanaian Wiredu, by the Kenyan Odera or occasionally by myself, and some are collective manifestoes, but that is unimportant. What matters is that all these texts, despite their real divergences, announce and delineate a new theoretical structure in the history of our philosophy.

What we have however attempted to establish in the present discussion is that this definition of African philosophy as a set of explicit discourses produced by African philosophers is only a *minimal definition* and that, strictly speaking, it is still too broad and needs to be made more accurate by reference to documents, archives, visible traces that exist in the form of empirical writing. In other words, we must be extremely careful about trying in some way to cut off slices of philosophy from our oral literature. We must know that these slices, having been not merely preserved but repeated from father to son and piously transmitted to us across the centuries, without having had to undergo the test of criticism and what one might call tactical forgetting, represent at best the results of a remote process of thinking that has not itself been recorded. These moral tales, didactic legends, aphorisms and proverbs are the expression not of an intellectual quest but at best of its results, not of a philosophy but at most of a wisdom; and it is only in our time that it may prove possible, by transcribing them, to confer upon them the value and status of philosophical documents, that is to say, of texts capable of sustaining free and critical reflection.

By way of conclusion, I would like to put the present analysis in the context of my own previous work. In an article published in 1970 (substantially reprinted in this volume as Chapter 1) I wrote abruptly, without prior justification: 'By "African philosophy" I mean a set of texts, specifically the set of texts written by Africans and described as philosophical by their authors themselves.' I was thereby rejecting the ethnological conception of African philosophy, reduced to a collective, unreflective vision of the world. But since then I have often been asked whether the philosophical discourses of our forebears, which did not have the good fortune to be transcribed, are not an integral part of African philosophy – in other words, whether a thought must be written down in black and white in order to deserve the description 'philosophical'. We are now in a position to answer. The absence of transcription certainly does not intrinsically devalue a philosophical discourse, but it prevents it from integrating itself into a collective theoretical tradition and from taking its place in a history as a reference point capable of orienting future discussion. There may therefore have been *African philosophers* without an *African philosophy*, although the converse, as I hope to have shown, is strictly impossible. Thousands of Socrateses could never have given birth to Greek philosophy, however talented they might have been in dialectics. So thousands of philosophers without written works could never have given birth to an African philosophy. Socrates was able to enter the theoretical history of Greece because his disciples or fellow citizens took the time and trouble to write down his thoughts, to discuss, sometimes to criticize and often to distort them. Similarly, we Africans can probably today recover philosophical fragments from our oral literature, but we must bear in mind that so far as authentic philosophy goes, everything begins at the precise moment of transcription, when the memory can rid itself of cumbersome knowledge now entrusted to papyrus and so free itself for the critical activity which is the beginning of *philosophy*, in the only acceptable sense of the word.

That is not all. We have also tried to establish that African philosophy is inseparable from African science, African scientific research; that it cannot exist as a specific form of literature except in its ordered difference from, and articulation with, scientific literature; that the only fruitful prospect for our philosophy today is to attach itself closely to the destiny of science by integrating itself with the immense movement towards the acquisition of scientific knowledge that is now developing on the continent.

We have shown how this process of acquiring the international scientific heritage conditions the actualization and, as it were, the reappropriation of our pre-colonial knowledge. In the same way, it is clear that a systematic appropriation of the international philosophical heritage, which is inseparable from that scientific heritage, is absolutely necessary to any reappropriation of our philosophical past and to any reconstitution of our theoretical history. In this sphere our task is complex, our responsibility overwhelming. We must be ambitious for Africa and for ourselves; we must be careful not to nip in the bud the unparalleled promise of our history or to prune it prematurely. We must on the contrary open it up, liberate it. The inspired short circuit of nationalism and pseudo-revolutionary lies has, at best, only limited effectiveness. Beyond all facile solutions, beyond all the myths, we must have the courage to make a fresh start.

Part Two
Analyses

5   An African philosopher in Germany in the eighteenth century: Anton-Wilhelm Amo *

Axim is an old African town situated on the 'Gulf of Guinea', in present-day south-west Ghana, not far from the Ivorian frontier. It was there, in the first years of the eighteenth century, that the black philosopher was born who signed himself in Latin *Amo-Guinea-Afer* or *Amo Guinea-Africanus* (Amo the Guinean), as though he was afraid that his long European adventure might make him or his circle forget his African origins and ties.

Amo's philosophical career took place principally in Germany, where he received a training that he in turn was destined to dispense as a teacher in the universities of Halle, Wittenberg and Jena between the years 1730 and 1740, before returning to his home country where he died.

His work is almost entirely written in Latin. These are the main titles: *Dissertatio inauguralis de jure Maurorum in Europa* (The Rights of Africans in Europe), 1729 (this text is lost); *Dissertatio de humanae mentis apatheia* (On the Impassivity of the Human Mind), 1734; *Tractatus de arte sobrie et accurate philosophandi* (On the Art of Philosophizing with Sobriety and Accuracy), 1738 (this is Amo's most important text and runs to 208 pages). An English translation of these works was published in 1968 by the English Department of the Martin Luther University of Halle, under the title *Antonius Gulielmus Amo Afer of Axim in Ghana, Translation of his Works*. For the sake of completeness one should add *Disputatio philosophica continens ideam distinctam eorum quae competunt vel menti vel corpori nostro vivo et organico* (A Philosophical Discussion Distinguishing between what Belongs to the Mind and to the Living and Organic Body). This brief dissertation of sixteen pages is a memoir presented under Amo's supervision and defended before Amo on 29 May 1734 by a student named John Theodosius Meiner.

* This article appeared in *Les Etudes philosophiques*, no. 1 (Paris: PUF, 1970). It is based on a paper given at the Institut d'Histoire des Sciences et des Techniques, Paris, on 16 January 1969, during a seminar directed by M. Georges Canguilhem.

It is in fact a development of the main ideas of *De humanae mentis apatheia*.

The work of the 'Ghanaian'[1] philosopher has not yet been systematically studied. To my knowledge, the only attention it has so far attracted is biographical and contains no analysis of his philosophical works. Nkrumah, it is true, refers quite pertinently to *De humanae mentis apatheia* in the long polemic against idealism which opens his philosophical essay *Consciencism*.[2] But this is only an allusion and cannot be regarded as a historical and theoretical analysis of the work.

The time has probably not yet come for such an analysis. It would be necessary not only to read (in the immediate sense of the word) Amo's works, which would not be very difficult, but also to locate them accurately in the theoretical context of their time in order to define their co-ordinates or, in other words, what they are really about. Such historical research, which is an indispensable pre-condition of a critical reading, would require more time and effort than I, and possibly more than anyone, could devote to it. But I think it should be attempted one day.

It is the dissertation *De humanae mentis apatheia* that I have decided to present here, laying emphasis on Amo's method and doctrine as well as on the present significance of his career. In doing so, I am not in any way prejudging the theoretical importance of the work. Perhaps we should even accept from the outset that within the framework of European philosophy, and given that he was conscious of belonging to another civilization, Amo could not but be an author of the second rank – that is to say not an original thinker but an honest teacher and professor of philosophy whose sole merit may have been at most that, like a mirror, he reflected the thought of his time in terms of his theoretical choices within it.

One day it will probably be necessary to state clearly and to elaborate systematically the question underlying all 'history' of philosophy. Answers to this question determine the choices and exclusions which constitute this history, though the historians may not be aware of them: how does one measure the importance of a philosopher, and what are the criteria that determine the choice of particular names and works for the attention of posterity?

This is not the place to tackle this question, and I will therefore set it on one side. Without prejudice to any future judgement of the *philosophical interest* of Amo's work, I shall simply point out its existence and try to understand its problematic, if only because of the author's singular career and its general historical interest.

Elements of a history

Today the biographers of Amo have an appreciable number of historical documents at their disposal. The earliest date from Amo's time. They are, in particular: the register of baptisms of the chapel of Brunswick-Woltenbüttel, where the young Amo was baptized in July 1708, according to the rites of the Lutheran Church, and the financial register of the court of the Duke of Brunswick-Wolfenbüttel, which mentions grants made to Amo between 1716 and 1720 (these two registers are now in the Wolfenbüttel State Archives); a journal of the time, the *Hallische Frage-und-Anzeigen Nachrichten*, and the archives of the University of Halle, which contain many items of information concerning Amo for the period 1727–37 and even a single final reference dated 1747; a few issues of another journal, published in Hamburg, the *Hamburgische Berichte von neuen gelehrten Sachen*, especially the issues dated 2 June 1733 and 24 November 1739; finally, a congratulatory speech delivered by John Godefroi Kraus, Rector of the University of Wittenberg, on the occasion of the defence of *De humanae mentis apatheia*, and a congratulatory epistle written on the same occasion by Löscher, Amo's thesis supervisor (both the speech and the letter were published as appendices to an edition of *De humanae mentis apatheia*, copies of which are held today in the Library of the Free University of Berlin and another in that of the University of Ghana, in Accra).

To this contemporary evidence must be added more recent references to Amo's life and work dating from the end of the eighteenth century and the beginning of the nineteenth. The first is in a text written by Winckelmann in 1782 in memory of the Dutch physicist David Henri Gallandet and based on notes written by the latter but now lost. Gallandet was the doctor on a ship which called at Axim, on the Gold Coast, in 1753. There he met Amo, who had returned to his country after forty years spent in Europe and was leading the life of a hermit. The mention of Amo in Winckelmann's obituary of Gallandet is therefore incidental.

There is a further reference to Amo in a text by Blumenbach which appeared in 1787 in Gotha under the title 'Von den Negern' in the *Magazin für das Neueste aus der Physik und Naturgeschichte*. Without stating its own sources, this text informs us, among other things, that towards the end of his stay in Germany Amo lived in Berlin as a counsellor at the royal court.

Finally, the abbé Henri Grégoire, constitutional Bishop of Blois during the French Revolution, devoted to Amo four pages in his book *De la littérature des Nègres* (Paris, 1808).[3]

The last three documents were the sources for an entry on Amo in the *Nouvelle biographie générale*, published by Firmin-Didot et Cie (Paris, new edition, 1859), volume II.[4] Incidentally, the entry contains an error, to which we shall refer again later.

In addition, there is a third group of documents consisting of essays written on Amo since the beginning of this century and based on the sources cited above.[5]

It appears from Winckelmann's obituary that Amo was born *circa* 1703, since he is described as being 'about fifty' when Gallandet visited him in 1753.

The Ashanti philosopher's place of birth gave rise, even in his lifetime, to a confusion that testifies eloquently to the inadequacy of contemporary knowledge. Some gave his birthplace as Abyssinia (now Ethiopia) instead of the Gold Coast. Thus, Rector Kraus in the aforementioned congratulatory speech said that Amo was born *in ultimo Africae, qua spectat in Orientem, recessu* ('at the farthermost point of Africa, whence she looks to the Orient'), a phrasing that unmistakably refers to the easternmost part of our continent, which was supposed, in the geographical mythology of the times, to be the most distant from Europe (*recessus* = distance, remoteness).

The *Nouvelle biographie générale* follows Kraus but makes the error more precise: it places the meeting between Amo and Gallandet at Axum in Abyssinia and asserts that that was Amo's birthplace.

Both texts contain a contradiction, however. In his speech Kraus calls Amo *Antonius-Gulielmus Amo Guinea-Afer*, whereas East Africa has never been called Guinea. In the *Nouvelle biographie générale* article, shortly after the passage referred to, we read that in 1753 Amo's father and sister were living in the interior of the country, 'at several days' journey from the Gold Coast'. This statement would be unintelligible, in the context, if the Gold Coast were not where Gallandet met Amo.

The truth is that there was confusion between Axim, a town on the Gold Coast in West Africa, probably little-known by the geographers of the period, and the Ethiopian town of Axum, which was then better-known. So we should rely not on Rector Kraus's congratulatory speech but on Löscher's letter, which places Amo's birth very precisely 'in Guinea, that distant region which Europeans once called the Gold Coast, because of its abundant production of gold, but which *we* call your Fatherland, where you first saw the light of day'. Indeed, Amo himself, when he registered at the University of Halle in 1727, is said to have added to his name the following words: *Ab Aximo in Guinea-Africana* ('from Axim, in Guinea, Africa').[6]

The reasons why Amo left for Europe are a matter for conjecture. Abraham lists three possibilities: (1) he was kidnapped by sea pirates who took him to Europe; (2) he was bought as a slave and taken to Europe; (3) he was sent to Europe in order to train as a preacher in the Dutch Reformed Church. Without entering into the details of Abraham's discussion, we can accept with him that the third hypothesis is the most probable.

Anyway, Amo arrived in Amsterdam in 1707. The same year he was introduced to Duke Anton Ulric of Brunswick-Wolfenbüttel[7] who, according to Winckelmann, presented him to his son Augustus Wilhelm. It will be noticed that Amo took his very name, Anton-Wilhelm, from these two protectors. It was in this name that he was baptized in the castle chapel on 29 July 1708, with the two dukes as sponsors.

Thirteen years later, in 1721, he was 'confirmed' in the same chapel. The register of worship, in which the ceremony is recorded, then calls him 'Anton Wilhelm Rudolph Mohre', the third name being taken from Ludwig Rudolph, another Duke of Brunswick who was to succeed Augustus Wilhelm as the head of the Duchy, and the fourth probably originating (as Abraham argues) from the German word *Mohr*, which means 'black man' (and not just 'Moor'). Abraham rightly remarks that the African name 'Amo' does not figure on that register. It may be supposed that the clergy had deliberately rejected it because of its 'pagan' origin, as often happens even to this day in Africa.

However that may be, the court's financial records show that even before the confirmation Amo had received grants amounting to sixty-four thalers for the period from Easter 1716 to Easter 1717 and thirty thalers for the period Easter 1720 to Christmas 1720.

Why these allocations? Abraham refutes the idea that they represented a salary (for instance, for his services as a page at the court of

Wolfenbüttel) and argues that they were pocket-money for use while he was at court. Consequently, it is reasonable to conclude that Amo was not at court from Easter 1717 to Easter 1720 but probably at school, where he would have received his grant directly.

We are reduced to the same kind of conjecture for the period 1720–7, the date of Amo's registration at the University of Halle. It may be assumed that during this interval he pursued his studies and for a while attended a university other than Halle, which Abraham, following Löchner, identifies as Helmstedt.

What is known for certain is that Amo registered at the University of Halle on 9 June 1727. We know that this new university, only founded in 1694, had already acquired a brilliant reputation and was regarded as one of the capitals of the Aufklärung (Enlightenment). The celebrated Leibnizian Christian Wolff had occupied the chair of mathematics there from 1706 to 1723 and there composed his *Thoughts*, the first major philosophical work published in German. It is true that in November 1723[8] Wolff had eventually been dismissed from the university and expelled from Prussian territory by Frederick William I, as a victim of the clerical and obscurantist reaction led by Joachim Lange. But his influence had continued to spread, as witness the declarations of Lange himself, who continually deplored the dangerous appeal which his opponent's teaching had for German youth. On the other hand, Christian Thomasius, also known for his liberalism and anti-clericalism, was still teaching at Halle and was to remain there until his death in 1728.

It was thus a flourishing university (despite important points scored by the obscurantist party) that Amo joined in 1727 in order to read law. In 1729 he defended his 'inaugural dissertation' on 'The rights of Africans in Europe' under the direction of the dean of the Faculty of Law, P. von Ludewig. This text is lost, but there is a brief summary of it in the *Annals* of the University of Halle for 2 November 1729.

The significance of this article is that it shows Amo's profound awareness of his position as an African and his preoccupation with the problem of slavery and of the social condition of blacks in Europe. In this dissertation, basing himself on law and history, he showed how the kings of Africa had once been vassals of the Roman Emperor, enjoying an imperial franchise, which Justinian in particular had renewed. He also made a detailed examination of the question how far the freedom or servitude of Africans living in

Europe after being bought by Christians was in conformity with the laws commonly accepted at this time.

We have another clue to Amo's political preoccupations: the abbé Grégoire mentions him in the long list of dedicatees of *La Littérature des Nègres* as one of 'all those courageous men who have pleaded the cause of the unhappy Blacks and half-breeds, either through their writings or through their speeches in political assemblies, and to societies established for the abolition of the slave trade, and the relief and liberation of slaves'.

For reasons that remain obscure, Amo soon left Halle and, on 2 September 1730, registered at the University of Wittenberg. There he studied medicine and psychology (then called pneumatology) under the direction of Martin Gotthelf Löscher, who presided when Amo defended his second dissertation, *De humanae mentis apatheia*, in April 1734. Meanwhile, on 10 October 1730, Amo received the degree of 'Master of Philosophy and Liberal Arts', which presumably entitled him to give in the University the private lectures mentioned in Rector Kraus's congratulatory epistle. This is probably what also entitled him to supervise and present Meiner's *Disputatio philosophica* on 29 May 1734.

Two years later Amo was back at Halle. A document dated 1736 authorizes him to give public lectures in the University of Halle, 'in certain domains of philosophy, as he did previously in the locality of Wittenberg'. Furthermore, the *Annals* of Halle, dated November 1736, inform us that 'the Master Amo, who hails from Africa and more particularly from Guinea, and is a genuine Negro but a humble and honourable philosopher', had, alone of all the examiners, publicly used his veto against the acceptance of a thesis in anatomy. Finally, there exists a poem by Amo in German, published as an appendix to a thesis in medicine which was successfully defended by one Moses Abraham Wolff in 1737.

According to Abraham, Amo devoted one series of his lectures to a critical exposition of Leibniz's principle of sufficient reason, and another to Christian Wolff's political thought. It was in Halle in any case, that he wrote and published, in 1738, his *Tractatus de arte sobrie et accurate philosophandi*, a work on logic and the psychology of knowledge. Copies of this book are available in the university libraries of Erlangen and Bamberg in Bavaria and, according to Abraham, in the Library of the Soviet Academy of Sciences in Leningrad.[9]

Once more, however, Amo was about to leave Halle. On 27 June

1729 he sends an application to the Faculty of Philosophy at the University of Jena for permission to give public lectures there. His candidature is quickly accepted, and a note dated 17 July gives a list of his lectures, including a series of 'the valid fields of philosophy' (*sic*) and another on the refutation of superstitious beliefs.

There is also a brief note written in Amo's hand in the album of a certain Gottfried Achenwall, which can be consulted today in the Library of the University of Göttingen. In this album Achenwall was in the habit of collecting autographs from notable scholars and men of culture. Amo's autograph is dated 5 May 1740, Jena, and begins with the following quotation from Epictetus: 'He who consents to necessity is wise and has a divine perception of things.'

If we are to believe Blumenbach, followed on this point by the abbé Grégoire, Amo became a counsellor at the court of Berlin after leaving Jena. But there is no extant contemporary document to confirm this information.[10]

The last existing contemporary reference to Amo is to be found in an issue of 1747 of the *Hallische Frage-und-Anzeigen Nachrichten*. It mentions the presentation of a satirical play entitled 'A comic student, the false academic virgin and the intentions of Master Amo'. This suggests that Amo had returned to Halle after 1740 and that he was still in Germany around 1747.

But it is certain that by 1753 he had returned to his native land, 'to Axim on the Gold Coast, in Africa' where, according to Winckelmann, Gallandet found him living like a hermit and with the reputation of a soothsayer. His father and sister were still living at a place four days' journey inland, and he also had a brother who, according to Winckelmann, was a slave in Surinam.

At an unknown date after meeting Gallandet Amo left Axim for Chama, another coastal town and settled there in a fort of the Dutch West Indies Company. The date of his death is also unknown.

Amo's problem in *De humanae mentis apatheia*

De humanae mentis apatheia must be seen in the broad context of the great debate of the time: the quarrel of the mechanists and vitalists. Amo, through his dissertation, takes part in the debate, siding against the vitalists. In a polemic clearly aimed at the doctrine of Stahl, he tries to show that the human mind is 'impassive', or in other words, as he himself explains in the subtitle, that it is not the seat of sensation and cannot in itself possess the 'faculty of sensation', both attributes which can belong only to our living and organic body.

Amo's argument is in two stages, one negative and the other positive. On the one hand, the human mind is insensible or, more exactly, 'apathetic', i.e. it has nothing to do with passion in the strict sense (negative moment); on the other hand, sensibility belongs to the body (positive moment). The second moment complements the first but is also less developed. Amo does not study seriously *how* sensation is effected in the body; he does not use physiology but merely defines the domain of physiology as that of the body, of living matter, rather than of the mind. His target is the confusion of categories, that *metabasis eis allo genos* which leads some scholars to use the language of pneumatology in the sphere of physiology because they have failed from the start to make the basic ontological distinction between mind and matter.

At least, though the Stahlians were not unaware of the distinction, they did not make it with sufficient rigour. But for them it was a question of living matter, which must after all be distinguished from inert matter. The problem that faced contemporary 'medicine' of the time was to decide in which of the two substances, spiritual and material, divided by a mysterious ontological barrier, lay the basis of the phenomenon of life. To this question Stahl had answered that the principle of life was the soul, meaning by that not only Aristotle's sensitive or animal soul but the rational soul itself, mind in the true sense of understanding or *logos*. It followed that the phenomena of life, including sensation itself, must be explained, in the last resort, by the action of understanding. Physiology consequently became a pneumatology or, rather, a hybrid discourse incapable of sustaining its own intelligibility and without identifiable status in the world of theory.

It is not certain that Amo had read Stahl, for he never quotes him in *De humanae mentis apatheia*. But there is no doubt that he knew him at least through his disciples, such as George Daniel Coschwitz, author of an *Organismus et mechanismus*, whom we know to have been Stahl's pupil. He is cited by name by Amo in his *Status controversiae* ('The state of the question'). Amo takes Coschwitz and others to task for their lack of rigour and coherence, and it is clear that this reproach, in a sense, was a reflection on Stahl, whose basic idea was that matter was inert, passive, and could not therefore move itself – hence his resort to an active, non-material principle that is supposed to communicate life, or motion, to the body.

For Stahl the terms 'instinct' or 'sensitive soul', which were ordinarily used to signify the vital principle, merely named the problem without solving it. The true vital principle was to be found in the only active substance, which is the rational soul.

In this brief text Amo turned the vitalists' own argument against them: it is precisely because the soul is an active substance that it cannot be responsible for all the vital functions, particularly those which imply passivity or receptivity. Sensation, for example, is a passive process, consisting above all in receptivity or affect. It cannot proceed from the mind but from the only passive substance in us, the body.

It cannot be denied that this is a cogent argument, all the more remarkable since sensation is clearly a very special example, being not one vital function among others but the most characteristic manifestation of life. This is what Amo himself suggests: 'To live and feel are two inseparable attributes. Proof of this lies in the convertibility of these two propositions: all that lives necessarily feels, and all that feels necessarily lives, so that the presence of the one implies the presence of the other.'[11] Life itself may consist not in motion, that motion which the vitalists claim to explain by attributing it to the soul, but in receptivity, permeability, openness to the world.

If this is so, however, there remains the problem of deciding whether this receptivity of living matter is the same as the passivity of inert matter. Amo did not formulate the question in these terms, but he was aware of it, and his answer was in the negative. In a remark immediately following our last quotation he explicitly distinguishes between 'life' and 'existence'. While life and sensation are two 'inseparable attributes', living and existing, on the contrary, 'are not synonyms. All that lives exists, but all that exists does not live. Spirit and stone both exist, but it would be wrong to say that they live, for the spirit exists and acts intelligently, matter exists and suffers the action of an agent. But humans and animals exist, act, live and feel.'[12]

The juxtaposition, in this remark, of spirit and stone is really very surprising. But it conveys tellingly Amo's secret intention: the insensibility of spirit is not a quality but a defect, a lack, exactly like that of stone. Each lacks the 'faculty of feeling'. This faculty resides in a specific type of organization or arrangement (*dispositio*, or the adjective *organicum*), i.e. a particular structure which specifically belongs to living matter and is lacking in inert matter as well as in spirit.

One could pursue Amo's reasoning in these terms: it is this particular structure that 'medicine' (which was the word for what we now call 'biology') must study. The field of that science is thus clearly defined, and the scientist will no longer have to resort to the mysterious action of spirit to explain physiological processes. Henceforward, medicine must be an independent science.

Amo did not go beyond defining its possibility and its theoretical status. It was not his purpose to enter that field, which probably explains why the positive moment of his thesis, his attribution of the faculty of sensation to the 'living and organic' body (one can now readily understand how these two adjectives are pleonastic), is so little developed. Indeed, the concept of organism, which was a recent addition to the arsenal of scientific concepts and which stood in need of theoretical justification, is not discussed at all, although Amo invokes it several times. It functions almost as a theoretical stopgap in his discourse, a *flatus vocis* destined to cover up an omission. Generalizing a little, one could say the same of the whole of this part of his treatise (its positive moment), which is little more than a formal repetition of theoretical elements contained in the preceding moment. But this could not be otherwise in view of the basic aim of the work, which was not to create a physiology but to dispel certain confusions concerning its object, i.e. to clear the way for a physiological theory worthy of the name. The aim was to demonstrate the impossibility of a psychology of sensation,[13] as well as of a psychology of vital functions in general, and to prove the ideological (to use this recent term somewhat anachronistically) nature of any discourse that attributed to the spirit properties belonging to the body.

This polemical intention commands the whole work. It alone is expressed in the title, which refers to the insensibility (or, literally, to the non-passivity) of the human mind, relegating to the subtitle the positive attribution of a receptive structure to the body. This explains the development of the negative moment of the thesis. The negation is dual, consisting of two complementary propositions carefully and insistently distinguished by Amo for reasons which should now be clear: the apathy of mind signifies, on the one hand, that mind does not have sensations, and, on the other hand, that it lacks the faculty of sensation. The second proposition is not a mere repetition of the first in another form; it completes it and makes it more precise. The faculty of sensation is not just the mere possibility of actual sensations, a kind of vague intellectual hypothesis that is meant to 'explain' the possibility of sensations in the sense that the 'dormitive virtue' was supposed to explain the action of opium. No, it is not a rational entity or intellectual fiction but a positive structure, a specific organization genuinely belonging to the living body and distinguishing it from inert matter. The faculty of sensation is, in Amo's own terms, 'a specific arrangement (*dispositio*) of the living and organic body, thanks to which animated beings are affected by material and sensible things, given in immediate presence'.[14]

We have already noted the absence in Amo's work of a theoretical justification for the notion of organism. But he does in fact make a brief incursion into the field of physiology, on two occasions.

In the first place, in order to show that mind does not experience sensations, he appeals to the authority of all doctors and other scientists 'who accept that sensation takes place in the nervous system and fluid'. Among these are mentioned by name Johann-Gottfried von Berger, whose *Physiology* is cited, Martin Gotthelf Löscher, cited for his *Summary of Experimental Physics*, and Senners, for his *Summary of Natural Science*.

Secondly, one page further on, in order to prove that mind does not possess the faculty of sensation, he is led to state that this faculty, like the principle of life in general, depends upon the circulation of the blood. Here again he refers to Berger and Löscher, but also to one Christian Vater, author of another *Physiology*. In both cases he quotes abundantly from Holy Scripture, as if to demonstrate the harmony between authentic Christianity and his own philosophical position and the scientific doctrines on which it is based.

The reference to the nervous system and the circulation of the blood suggests that both were regarded at the time, by the school of physiological thought with which Amo was connected, as the essential elements of that 'organization' of living matter. One may wonder, of course, how the two were related. Amo does not say. However, to take him at his word, 'the nervous system and fluid' are the seat of sensation, the place in the body where it takes place, while the circulation of the blood, which is responsible for the faculty of sensation and for life in general, is what makes the nervous system possible.

Thus the concept of organism, although it does not find theoretical justification (which would have required an investigation into its metaphorical origin), is nevertheless given a positive content and is thus more than a mere intellectual fiction.

From now on, to argue that the human mind is deprived of the faculty of sensation is tantamount to saying that it lacks something, which is the specific organization that makes life possible, in other words, the circulation of the blood, together with the nervous system. It is in this respect that the second 'negative thesis' contains something more than the first and also reveals more than the first, the real intention of the work, which is not to valorize the mind by attributing to it higher perfections than those of the body but, on the contrary, to devalue it, or at least to reduce its importance in human existence as much as possible, by insisting on the importance of bodily functions.

A methodical irony

Once this is stated, we can more clearly perceive the irony pervading the earlier part of Amo's work.[15] He begins by reproducing all the commonplaces of scholastic theology on the attributes of mind: 'We mean by spirit any substance that is purely active, immaterial, always understanding through itself and acting spontaneously, intentionally, in pursuance of a conscious and specific end.' The entire argument rests on this definition: the various attributes are listed, to be developed in the first part of the first chapter. It is soon clear that Amo has succeeded in his object and has demonstrated his thesis: 'Spirit is a purely active substance; this means that in itself it suffers no passion.'

But if we look closer, we see that this development concerns spirit in general (*spiritus in genere*) and not the human mind in particular (*mens humana in specie*). The spirit in general is above all the spirit of God or of the angels, disembodied or, in Amo's words, 'free from all commerce with matter' (*extra materiam positus*). In such a spirit, if it exists, non-passivity is the reverse of pure activity and, therefore, a perfection. Here Amo deliberately uses the language of theology. God, precisely because of his omnipotence, cannot be passive and content merely to experience things as they are. But simply in the act of thinking them God creates, or recreates, things. It is in this sense that he is impassive or insensible, these terms implying perfections. But when Amo comes to apply these same terms to the human mind, they will designate a lack rather than a perfection. Why? Because, the human mind is embodied; its non-passivity is no longer the reverse of pure activity but expresses its dependence on the body, which alone enables it to know sensible things. Thus the notion of passivity, which is really the central point in Amo's text, on which the whole argument turns (since sensation and the faculty of sensation are denied to the human mind solely on account of the passivity they would imply), is ambiguous and has different meanings when applied to the divine spirit and the human mind.

Amo's irony consists precisely in playing on this ambiguity by extending to the human mind the attribute of non-passivity that was initially a property of the divine spirit but inflicting a *transvaluation* on it in the passage from God to man. Non-passivity, when applied to man, is no longer a quality but a defect because it implies the total absence of receptivity in a mind which, deprived of the power of creating things, is reduced to a mediative and purely representative relationship with them.

It is true that this transvaluation is not actually discussed by Amo, but this is precisely where the irony lies. In this way he unmasks without saying so the internal contradictions of vitalist spiritualism. He uses the assumptions of his opponents to argue against them, thereby showing up the theoretical inconsistency of their system. Let us remember that in their breathless disquisitions on the attributes of the divine spirit the spiritualists were wont to endow it with every possible quality, including pure activity (or absolute non-passivity). And whenever they attempted to define the human mind directly, they endowed it with these same qualities, simply stripped of infinity. But when they moved to discuss the human mind as an explanation of the phenomenon of life, they automatically attributed to it functions that were incompatible with the *essence* that they had previously assigned to it. Amo clearly brings this inconsistency into the open while provisionally adhering, or pretending to adhere, to his opponents' premises for purely methodological or strategic, not dogmatic, reasons.

In the end it is the conclusion that matters, not the premises. Amo's premises are invoked with polemics in mind and with the sole aim of showing his vitalist opponents the conclusions to which their own spiritualistic assumptions lead – conclusions which anyone else would acknowledge as the basic axiom of physiological science without necessarily starting from these same premises.

In some ways too Amo's text gives these premises a hard knock. It discreetly questions the idea that the divine spirit and the human mind belong to the same genus. We are surprised to see the author, who wants to define 'spirit in general', go so far as to attribute to it a quality that he expressly denies the human mind, that of 'being always intelligible to itself': 'Every spirit always understands through itself (*per se semper intellegit*), i.e. it is aware of itself and of its operations, as well as of other things.'[16] This is the affirmation of the independence and self-sufficiency of the soul in general in the act of cognition. But Amo immediately adds, in a footnote, that the human mind is deprived of this fine faculty and that it can acquire knowledge only through the mediation of the body and the senses. This is tantamount to saying that the human mind cannot be regarded as a particular species of the genus spirit and, moreover, that this genus itself does not really exist because what is called 'spirit in general' is always in fact the perfect spirit, 'God's or the angels' (the same thing) or, in Amo's words, spirit 'without commerce with matter'. The relation between divine spirit and human mind is not in reality that of two species of the same genus but of two radically different genera, their heterogeneity being suggested by the Latin, which selects one of two different terms according to context: '*spiritus*' *divinus* and '*mens*' *humana*.

Here again Amo's irony is perceptible in the subtle use he makes of the two terms and in the apparent paradox of the assertion with which he introduces his long preamble on the spirit in general: *mens humana in genere est spirituum*. In fact, this dogmatic proposition is constantly questioned throughout the text. Here its role is merely strategic, aiming as it does at allowing the extension to *mens humana* of the attribute of non-passivity. But later Amo will reveal some essential differences between the spirit in general and *mens humana* in particular.

These essential differences are differences of kind, not of degree, and are due to the embodiment of the human mind, which is what puts it in a genus of its own, completely new and irreducible to the supposed essence of pure spirit. By the same token, embodiment also causes the change of sign, or the transvaluation as we have called it, suffered by the attributes of spirit in general when, removed from their primary theological function, they are applied to human beings.

Theological discourse itself is incidentally questioned when Amo writes: 'Although I do not know in what manner God and disembodied spirits understand themselves and their operations and external things, I do not think it probable that they do it through ideas.'[17] This amounts to a clear profession of agnosticism, and for all its piety it is nevertheless ruinous for theology. One might call it a retreat into a negative theology in the name of the unfathomable mystery of God and of the weakness of our cognitive power: but negative theology is always bound to be exactly that: a retreat. Its pious renunciation of any discourse about God, its refusal to define God's essence and nature, make it the practical accomplice of atheism, which denies His very existence. This secret complicity was to become, a few decades later, the main theme in that masterpiece of irony, Hume's *Dialogues concerning Natural Religion*.

Amo does not actually discuss this complicity but is content with practising it. Of course God exists, but I know nothing of Him and can say nothing of Him. In any case, I cannot guess His mode of thinking; I cannot understand how a spirit can relate to things directly and commune with them through an immediate presence. So my exclusive concern must be humanity and the methods and limits of human thought.

It is impossible not to see irony too in the *Status controversiae*, in which Amo successively demonstrates the self-contradiction in an author like Descartes and in doctors and scientists as renowned in their time as Senners, Jean Leclerc, Coschwitz, etc. If one of the most constant effects of irony is to trap one's interlocutors into manifest avowed contradictions which compel them to renounce one of their premises, then *The State of the Question* makes explicit the latent irony of the first part of the book – it exhibits the author's real method.

Finite knowledge

We must, however, return to that concept of *ideas* through which Amo attempts to express the limitations of human knowledge: 'The idea is an instantaneous operation of our mind, through which it represents to itself, i.e. regards as present (*praesentes sistit*), things previously perceived by the senses and sense organs.'[18] It is precisely in this sense that conceptual thought supposes the body and could not belong to God or to pure spirits. In this sense also, it reveals the finitude of the human mind, with its inevitable, functional dependence on the organism.

This is why human thought is representative, in a literal sense. The human mind has only *mediative* knowledge of things. It cannot feel them but can only reflect them. Their presence constantly recedes from it, leaving behind an abstract evocation, the paltry substitute for a vanished plenitude. 'Representation', says Amo in effect, 'supposes the absence of its object.' It occurs after the event, when the object is no longer there, unless the mind itself performs the paradoxical feat of distancing the object by the simple 'act of thinking of it. This is why also we must accept that 'in God there is no representation', for God is impervious to past or future, the temporal forms of absence, 'but in his knowledge, all things are present'.

Thus, representation is exclusively a human faculty. Human thought does not directly communicate with things; it does not create them by thinking them; it reproduces but does not produce, except in the sense that it produces intellectual fictions in the form of ideas.[19] However, an intellectual fiction is not a real entity but its pale reflection in a finite mind whose sole power is to repeat the sensations of the body or, if one prefers, to reactivate them. An idea, as Amo suggests, is merely a *sensatio repetita*, a reactivated sensation. It supposes both passivity in the body and spontaneity in the mind; it is a secondary operation based on a primary receptivity. The idea is ambiguous and, as such, peculiarly human:

God and other spirits understand themselves, their operations and other things directly, without ideality, i.e. without the help of reactivated sensations that are called ideas (*sine ideis et sensationibus repetitis*); it is the peculiarity of the human mind that it understands and acts through ideas, because it is very closely tied to the body.[20]

This brief *remark* provides us with one of the most powerful moments of this short text. It unites in one discourse the idea of finitude and the idea of the body. Amo was to treat this theme at length in his *Tractatus* but insisting there on the finitude of ideas, whereas here emphasis is laid on both the fundamental inadequacy of ideas and the importance of the body in giving us an immediate relation to the world, an affective, almost umbilical link.

Such is, in our view, the essential significance of the work as philosophy. Its importance must not, of course, be exaggerated: *De humanae mentis apatheia* was meant to be, and is, essentially a kind of academic exercise, a display of stylistic skill, as much as a piece of philosophical reflection. This partly explains the abundance of formal remarks and methodological justifications which the reader may not always regard as indispensable (one example is the 'remark on the title of this part' which opens the first part of the first chapter). From this point of view, the *Tractatus* is much more fluent. The author, surer of himself, speaks no longer like a student but like a master.

It must be added that this abundance of formal remarks is also a sign of didactic fastidiousness and an insistence on clarity, both qualities which Amo, in common with all Wolffians at the time, regarded as essential to philosophy. In all his works Wolff interlocks definitions with methodological considerations in chains of mathematical reasoning of exemplary rigour. His originality consisted precisely in the fact that he revived scholasticism by subjecting philosophical reflection to the severe discipline of a coherent discourse governed by the laws of formal logic. Kant himself was to pay him tribute for this, however opposed he was to what he called Wolff's metaphysical dogmatism.[21]

Amo was part of this movement. The first condition of philosophy is clarity and coherence. However scanty our knowledge, we must first of all put it into order, proceed methodically from the simple to the richer and more developed, with sobriety and precision. The first term means that we must accept, at least provisionally, the limitations of our present knowledge; the second points to the most important of the rules we must observe to increase it. The *Tractatus* is therefore, above all, a work of philosophical methodology intended to reflect, and through discussion to clarify, the rigour attempted (not without some clumsiness) in the *De humanae mentis apatheia*.

We are now left with one question,* the last and most difficult: what does this work contain that can be called African?

Disappointing though it may be, the answer must be: nothing. But we must understand correctly the meaning of this 'nothing' and properly assess the meaning of our inevitable disappointment: what could the Africanness that is so sadly lacking in Amo's work have consisted in? And, in general, what can be meant by the Africanness of a philosophical work?

Let us say this clearly: our regret does not lie in our failure to detect in Amo *theses* that we could claim to be of African origin, concepts and themes that could be said to be characteristic of 'African metaphysics' or simply of 'negritude'. On the contrary, one

---

* Here the original conclusion of the article is recast.

should readily see how unacceptable, how highly contradictory such an expectation would be. To require thinkers to be content with reaffirming the beliefs of their people or social group is exactly the same as prohibiting them from thinking freely and condemning them in the long term to intellectual asphyxia. Deep down in such a demand lies radical scepticism and stubborn relativism; and, perhaps worse still, behind the apparently anti-racial and anti-Eurocentric stance lurks a secret contempt for non-Western thinkers, who are thus subtly excluded from any claim to universality – that is to say to *truth* – and denied the right to any authentic research, simply being expected to display the peculiarities of their culture in philosophical form. No, we do not regret, in Amo, the absence of such a particularism. We would very much prefer to cite as an example his direct and frank dialogue with the great philosophical works of his time and his unaffected and questioning relationship to them. Africans today should be capable of doing the same, of freely seizing the whole existing philosophical and scientific heritage, assimilating and mastering it in order to be able to transcend it.

But there you are: throughout his long intellectual odyssey Amo the African could find no other partners but Europeans. Cut off from his people at the age of four, thrown into a world which inevitably saw him as different, he was unable to appeal to any but the European scientific tradition, unable to measure himself against other classics or debate with interlocutors other than those put forward by Western society. Amo the African wrote in Latin for a European public, could be read and possibly appreciated, discussed, criticized only by that European public. He forged his own problematic from themes and concepts integral to the history of European philosophy and contributed by his work to the enrichment of that history at a time when there was no comparable theoretical tradition in his own country. This is surely a prefiguration of the present state of African literature in English or French which, with very few exceptions, is much better known outside than inside Africa.

Therefore our disappointment concerns not the content of Amo's work but its social insertion. What we regret about the work of this *African* philosopher (for African he was and remained, in origin and in personal destiny, he who voluntarily returned to his people after his long European adventure and ended his days among them), is that it belongs entirely to a *non-African theoretical tradition*. What we regret is the exclusive ascription of this work, by virtue of its references and of the public to which it was addressed, to the history of Western science. Obviously Amo was not responsible for this painful isolation. He was the victim of an historical situation, and it is clear that he did everything that it was humanly possible for him to do. The times were not ripe. Failure was inevitable. But this failure, meditated today, could prove infinitely instructive, for it shows us, in relief, all that remains to be done. It prescribes for us the most precise tasks: to put an end once and for all to the monstrous extraversion of our theoretical discourse, to cease to be satisfied with individual participation in the great scientific debates of the industrialized world and instead to create progressively, in our various countries, those structures of dialogue and debate without which science is impossible.

6 The end of 'Nkrumaism' and the (re)birth of Nkrumah*

A year ago, on 27 April 1972, in Bucharest, the capital of Romania, one of the greatest Africans of this century died. I should like to analyse, on the occasion of this anniversary, one of the most neglected aspects of the rich heritage he left us – a heritage whose importance we have hardly begun to appreciate.

The major works

Nkrumah was not only a politician of the first rank but also, as is too often forgotten, a writer, a creator of a considerable body of work.[1] True, some have claimed that the work attributed to him was not really his. But the fact is that it *exists*, with a specific unity and indisputable *coherence*, so it cannot simply be by-passed. Nkrumah may have dictated some of his books to his private secretary or supplied one or another of his collaborators with some basic ideas to work into shape, but he was responsible, directly or indirectly, for all the books attributed to him (even where his authorship has been disputed, for ill-concealed political reasons).[2]

Such disputes are possible only as long as one refuses actually to *read* the works in question. As soon as one has done so and has been exposed to their *logic* and their *content*, this meaningless issue vanishes, giving way to the only theoretical problem: *how* should one read Nkrumah's works? What kind of reading will reveal their coherence, and indeed, what kind of coherence is it?

Before tackling this question, let us briefly recall the main titles of his considerable output.[3]

Towards Colonial Freedom. A book drafted at the end of his ten years in the United States (1935–45) and printed in London a few months later; republished by Heinemann (1962) and later by Panaf.

* An article published in the daily *Daho-Express*, no. 1127 (5 May 1973), on the occasion of the first anniversary of the death of Kwame Nkrumah, under the title 'L'Oeuvre théorique de Kwame Nkrumah'.

What I Mean by Positive Action (Accra 1949; reissued Panaf). An ephemeral booklet.

Ghana. Autobiography of Kwame Nkrumah (Nelson 1957; re-edited Panaf).

I Speak of Freedom: a Statement of African Ideology (Heinemann/New York; Praeger 1961; reissued Panaf). A collection, with commentary, of extended extracts from speeches made by Nkrumah between his return to the Gold Coast in 1947 and his Declaration at the General Assembly of the United Nations in September 1960.

Africa Must Unite (Heinemann 1963; reprinted Panaf).

Consciencism. Philosophy and Ideology for Decolonization and Development, with Particular Reference to the African Revolution (Heinemann 1964; 4th reprint 1966; Panaf, new, revised edition 1970).

Neo-colonialism, the Last Stage of Imperialism (Nelson 1965; reissued Panaf).

Challenge of the Congo (Nelson/New York: International Publishers 1967).

Dark Days in Ghana (New York: International Publishers 1968; reissued Panaf). This is a reconstruction of the events of the *coup* of 24 February 1966 and an interpretation of these events in the light of the world strategy of imperialism. The fifth chapter has been published separately by Panaf under the title *The Big Lie*.

Handbook of Revolutionary Warfare (Panaf 1968; New York: International Publishers 1969).

Class Struggle in Africa (Panaf 1970).

Voice from Conakry (Panaf 1967). This is a collection of talks broadcast by 'The Voice of Revolution', Conakry.

Axioms of Kwame Nkrumah (Nelson 1967; reissued Panaf). A collection of quotations taken from various works, articles or speeches by Nkrumah and classified under various headings.

I have omitted the articles, pamphlets and tracts. But I shall also be drawing on two other texts of considerable theoretical value, 'African socialism revisited' and 'The myth of the "Third World" ', which appeared as articles in 1966 and 1968 respectively and were reprinted by Panaf in 1968 and in 1970 as a pamphlet entitled *Two Myths*.[4]

Nkrumah's development

How to read Nkrumah's works

Let us return to our problem: how should Nkrumah's works be read, and what kind of unity do they possess? The question is important, for it has been common to give a static or, if one prefers, a systematic reading of Nkrumah. His works are read as though they were all written at the same time, and an abstract and strangely simplistic and dogmatic system called 'Nkrumaism' is extracted from them. But a different reading is possible, emphasizing the discontinuities and the points which indicate developments or even drastic reorientations in the author's career. Only this reading, which may be called *historical*, seems to me true or acceptable today. It enables us to go behind the appearances of a systematic 'Nkrumaism' and to identify the actual problems that this doctrine attempted to solve. At the same time, it enables us to detect the occurrence within Nkrumah's problematic of displacements whereby certain theses are explored in different contexts and implicitly, and even explicitly, rejected.

At the risk of shocking some readers, I must add that a first reading, the one that flattens Nkrumah's works into a system, is objectively a rightist reading. Indeed, it is interesting to note, as Samuel Ikoku does in his *Mission to Ghana*, that the term 'Nkrumaism' was in fact invented by the right-wing elements of what was then the only party, the Convention People's Party (CPP).[5] The anti-socialists coined the word to describe the supposed absolute originality of Nkrumah's doctrine and to mask its socialist content. It gave them a pretext for denouncing militants who dared speak of 'socialism' instead of 'Nkrumaism' as traitors, disloyal to the Master. This compelled the left-wingers who, among other organs, controlled the party's ideological weekly, the *Spark*, to accept the word 'Nkrumaism', although they tried to give it a strictly socialist content. From then on the quarrel was over not the word but its meaning.

One can now readily see that this was a very serious concession by the left-wingers. By accepting the term 'Nkrumaism' into their political and theoretical vocabulary and by constantly trying to redefine this supposedly new system instead of firmly repudiating the word, together with the idea that it represented (namely, the absolute originality of the *Osagyefo*'s doctrine), the progressives in the CPP unwittingly contributed to the consolidation of the personality cult in Ghana. At the same time they helped to obliterate what was living but unfinished in the writings of their comrade. They schematized, simplified, mummified and buried it alive in an enclosed system. For after all, whatever content may be given to the word 'Nkrumaism', whether one defines it as a socialist or a non-socialist doctrine, an anti-Marxist socialism or a variety of 'scientific socialism', it is still seen as a closed system, a finished doctrine, with every point clearly defined and cohering with all the rest. It is true that at one time Nkrumah persuaded himself that he had effectively invented a new doctrine which he called 'consciencism', this strange neologism being intended to indicate the novelty of the system. But this illusion was short-lived, and it is important to note that Nkrumah reconsidered his position to the extent that all his works after *Consciencism* bear witness to a patient and systematic re-examination of the ideological assumptions of his earlier works. And this self-criticism was initiated even before his fall from power, as we shall see.

To read Nkrumah today, then, is to rediscover the unfinished text of a thought in search of itself beneath the system in which it has been trapped, willingly, for a while. It is to restore to the work its hesitations, its internal contradictions, its life, avoid smoothing the rough edges or blurring the contradictions and to recognize, where necessary, both that the text may not always work on the same level but may pass from one to another and that it is essential for us to identify and define these levels with accuracy.

Now, a careful reading reveals a considerable change of perspective between the early works and the later ones. The early works are attacks on colonialism; their sweeping assertions bear witness to the relative simplicity of that struggle; their tone, often enthusiastic, even euphoric, expresses certainty about a victory to come or joy over a recent success. The later works, by contrast, are a critique of neo-colonialism. Their problems are more complex, their analyses more rigorous and refined. The initial passion gives way to painstaking discussions of the new strategies of imperialism, the nature of neo-colonialism as a world conspiracy and the new imperatives of the liberation struggle.

So the problems changed, and there was a remarkable *dislocation of the system*, I should say almost a *destruction of the system*, (a dismantling, a de-construction). Nkrumah, faced with new questions, found himself compelled in his answers to contradict theses which had seemed solidly secure in the original system. I shall cite three examples of this displacement.

The problem of violence

In the early works Nkrumah advocated what he called *positive action*, meaning all methods of resistance that are legal and non-violent (this at least is the definition given in *What I Mean by Positive Action* and in the *Autobiography*, although the meaning was later broadened to include revolutionary action in general, even violence). In these early works Nkrumah readily declares himself a disciple of Gandhi.

The latest works, however, assert that the only effective method of resistance is armed struggle. The reason for this change is that Nkrumah regarded imperialism no longer as just the control by one nation of another but as a world conspiracy to subjugate one part of the world to another.

This remarkable change took place, as we have said, before his fall. Thus *Neo-colonialism, the Last Stage of Imperialism*, written in 1965, focused on the subtle but real links between the great capitalist corporations that are exploiting the soil and subsoil of Africa. He showed that beneath the various labels and denominations these corporations are in reality one huge enterprise. Their control is concentrated in the hands of a few big international financiers; their operations are therefore aspects of a unified international design to impoverish the 'Third World'. Neo-colonialist exploitation was thus unmasked. At the same time the struggle against imperialism also appeared in a new light: as a 'class struggle on an international scale'.

The extent, the gravity and the strength of this kind of neo-colonialism, so understood, necessitated armed struggle. Thus Nkrumah, who had been a timid pacifist, now developed to construct a whole theory of continental guerrilla warfare in the *Handbook of Revolutionary Warfare*. The distance between the *Autobiography* of 1957 and the *Handbook* of 1968 is considerable, but one cannot appreciate it if one insists on reading Nkrumah's works as a system.

The class struggle

There is a comparable development on the question of the class struggle. The early works asserted that there was no class struggle in Africa. The later ones emphasized the importance of this phenomenon, the concealed struggle, without reference to which the political events and upheavals of modern Africa are unintelligible.

In this respect *Consciencism* appears as the last work of the first period and also as that in which the assumptions of this first period are most clearly formulated. *Consciencism*, indeed, insists that traditional African society was egalitarian, a communal society in which land and the means of production belonged not to individuals but to the community. Nkrumah calls the ideology of such a society 'communalism'. This thesis enables him to argue that in Africa the transition to socialism can be effected without a revolution and in perfect continuity with traditional African ideology:

> Revolution is thus an indispensable avenue to socialism, where the antecedent social-political structure is animated by principles which are a negation of those of socialism, as in a capitalist structure. . . . But from the ancestral line of communalism, the passage to socialism lies in reform, because the underlying principles are the same. . . . Because of the continuity of communalism with socialism, in communalistic societies, socialism is not a revolutionary creed, but a restatement in contemporary idiom of the principles underlying communalism.[6]

So *Consciencism* asserts that in pre-colonial society the exploitation of man by man and class struggle were unknown. In a more general way the 1964 work is pervaded by what might be called an *ideology of continuity* – continuity between 'traditional' African culture and present and future African culture, continuity between the communal organization of the pre-colonial economy and the socialist organization of the new African economy envisaged by African revolutionaries. In fact, according to the logic of *Consciencism*, these revolutionaries are the truest traditionalists.

Nkrumah's later works, however, assert the existence of class struggle in Africa and treat the struggle against neo-colonialism as class struggle on an international scale. This is what we read in the 1965 work:

> Marx had argued that the development of capitalism would produce a crisis within each individual capitalist State because within each State the gap between the 'haves' and the 'have nots' would widen to a point where a conflict was inevitable and that it would be the capitalists who would be defeated. The basis of his argument is not invalidated by the fact that the conflict, which he had predicted as a national one, did not everywhere take place on a national scale but has been transferred instead to the world stage.

World capitalism has postponed its crisis but only at the cost of transforming it into an international crisis. The danger is now not civil war within individual States provoked by intolerable conditions within those States, but international war provoked ultimately by the misery of the majority of mankind who daily grow poorer and poorer.[7]

If we read this text carefully, we find two points in it: first, that neo-colonial Africa is no freer from class struggle than any other society; second, that this class struggle has been introduced into Africa from the outside, that it is simply an extension of the class struggle occurring in Western industrial societies. So Nkrumah has not really renounced his earlier thesis that 'traditional' African society did not know class struggle. The same thesis survives even in his last work, *Class Struggle in Africa*.

Emphasis, however, is laid no longer on the absence of class struggle in so-called traditional Africa but rather on the importance, gravity and irreducibility of class struggle in modern Africa. This is an important shift of emphasis. Nkrumah is no longer claiming, as he has claimed in *Consciencism*, that the transition to socialism can be made without a revolution; on the contrary, he emphasizes how the violence of the reigning bourgeoisies (military *coups*, bloody repression, etc.) will force the exploited classes to resort to armed struggle, the *sine qua non* of successful revolution.

Furthermore, at several points in these writings of the second period Nkrumah actually questions the first thesis too. The pamphlet entitled *Two Myths* is particularly instructive in this respect; it takes up a far more advanced, radical and categorical position than *Class Struggle in Africa*, although it was written earlier. Nkrumah rejects the common expression 'Third World' for implying that colonized and neo-colonized countries constitute a world apart. For the same reason he rejects Senghor's and Nyerere's prattle about 'African socialism' (which, incidentally, is of a similar nature and is based on the same assumptions as the discourse one finds in *Consciencism*):

Today, the phrase 'African socialism' seems to espouse the view that the traditional African society was a classless society imbued with the spirit of humanism and to express a nostalgia for that spirit. Such a conception of socialism makes a fetish of the communal African society. But an idyllic, African classless society (in which there were no rich and no poor) enjoying a drugged serenity is certainly a facile simplification; there is no historical or even anthropological evidence for any such a society. I am afraid the realities of African society were somewhat more sordid.[8]

This is a radical criticism if ever there was one, but it is also, as we have said, a self-criticism. Nkrumah would never again present Africa as a world apart, but he accepted that our societies are subject to the same laws as every other society in the world and that African revolution, properly understood, is inseparable from world revolution. This explains why he preferred to use the more neutral phrase 'socialism in Africa' rather than the equivocal expression 'African socialism'.

African unity

Let us now take a third example, African unity. In the earlier works, and particularly in *Africa Must Unite* (1963), Nkrumah had advocated the immediate formation of a continental African government. He believed that the creation of the United States of Africa was the most urgent necessity in the struggle against neo-colonialism because the main instrument of neo-colonialism was, in his view, Balkanization. Unfortunately, this project, bold though it was, took no account of the differences in political and ideological orientation between the various African states.

In the later works, however, these conflicts are clearly recognized and identified as the main obstacle to African unity. Between African governments firmly dedicated to the anti-imperialist struggle and the puppet regimes totally committed to the defence of neo-colonialist interest there could be no compromise. It is from this point of view that in his *Handbook* Nkrumah is severely critical of the Organization of African Unity (OAU), which might have seemed at least a partial and timid realization of the scheme that he himself was expounding, at about the same time, in *Africa Must Unite*. Thus the criticism must be attributed to a change of perspective. One could say that the later Nkrumah regarded the OAU as premature because the African states of which it was composed lacked a real community of political views and choices. It was a heterogeneous and incoherent body.

Genuine African unity presupposed the elimination of puppet regimes, and this increasingly required the use of force. Consequently the first priority had become the co-ordination of the activities of the various liberation movements fighting in different territories rather than unrealistic attempts to form a continental government.

Nkrumah devoted a whole book, the *Handbook*, to this problem. He proposed the creation of the following instruments of co-ordination: The All-African People's Revolutionary Party (AAPRP), The All-African Committee for Political Co-ordination (AACPC), The All-African People's Revolutionary Army (AAPRA).[9] Thus while African unity was still an important objective, the means to achieve it were no longer the same. Unification must take place, not at the top but at the base; not at the level of governments or official diplomatic relations but at the level of populations and of the political organizations which really represent them. The reason for this change of strategy was that Nkrumah had become convinced that the people's will is not always expressed by their governments and that autonomous popular organizations are by far their most faithful representatives.

What these three examples show is that Nkrumah's work is not a closed system but open, attentive, pertinent and subject to constant revision. His thought was far more alive, restless and demanding than the abstract, dogmatic faith called 'Nkrumaism'.

For the reader who succeeds in identifying this life in the texts, the secret breath of his writing, the real Nkrumah is not dead. Beneath the stereotypes which had already begun to close in on him during his lifetime, behind the screen of conventional phrases, the empty, would-be revolutionary declarations of faith, the protestations of loyalty of those who are ready to sell themselves to the first comer, behind the thick walls of servile adulation, the painful isolation of the man called *Osagyefo*, the Redeemer, we can now see the face of the true militant, the open face of the comrade, whose hesitations and anxieties bring him infinitely closer to us. We discover a text.

What died in Bucharest was not Nkrumah but 'Nkrumaism'. That closed system and deceptive assurance, that body had to die in order to release the element of universality they contained. Nkrumah himself probably thought this, for he requested in his will that his body should not be embalmed and preserved but that his ashes should be scattered over the whole African continent, 'in the rivers, the torrents, the deserts, the savannahs, etc.'.

As it happens, his body is now in his native town, Nkroful, moved there from Conakry on 9 July 1972. But Nkrumah has nevertheless achieved the omnipresence he wished for, since at last his real text, freed from its shackles, can now be read and understood in its open incompleteness and so stimulate other thoughts that will in turn become part of the eternally incomplete text into which is woven the increasingly complex theoretical tradition of our continent.

7 The idea of philosophy in Nkrumah's *Consciencism**

In Chapter 6 I tried to present Nkrumah's literary works as a whole.[1] I argued that they should not be read as a closed system but that serious account should be taken of the author's development. I proposed discarding the usual reading, which one might call static or systematic, in favour of what might be called a historical reading. And, finally, I suggested that the first type of reading could perhaps be regarded objectively as a rightist reading, in the strongest sense of the term: if Nkrumah is locked into a closed system and we fail to consider the remarkable development that led him in his later works to question certain concepts he had used frequently in his early works, then his works are objectively reduced to a dogmatic, harmless system, and their critical and subversive implications, which become apparent only in terms of their development, are completely concealed.

The Nigerian Samuel Ikoku, who was one of the Ghanaian leader's closest collaborators, informs us in his remarkable book *Mission to Ghana*[2] that the word 'Nkrumaism' was invented by right-wing members of the Convention People's Party, which controlled the one-party state. They were trying, by this means, to disguise the socialist content of the Master's doctrine and to neutralize its subversive power in the name of its allegedly irreducible originality.

Nkrumah himself, it is true, once thought that he was inventing an original system to which he gave – precisely to emphasize its originality – the strange name of 'Consciencism'.[3] But it must not be forgotten that later he more and more openly declared his allegiance to scientific socialism, that is to say Marxism–Leninism,

* A revised and enlarged version of a lecture given on the campus of the University of Lubumbashi (Zaïre) on 8 June 1973 and at Cotonou, under the sponsorship of the National Commission for Philosophy of Dahomey, on 23 August 1973. The text of this lecture appeared in *Daho-Express*, no. 1235 (15 September 1973), under the title 'L'Oeuvre philosophique de Kwame Nkrumah'.

though, of course, without in any way repudiating the authentic African cultural tradition.

The two versions of *Consciencism*

Consciencism must be read with an essentially critical eye, as evidence of a particular stage in the development of Nkrumah's thought. Above all, one must avoid treating it as the author's last word in philosophy. In the fifth and last edition, dated 1970 (Panaf, London), the original (1964) text underwent profound modifications.

Nkrumah himself explains the meaning of the revisions in an Author's Note:

Since the publication of the first edition of *Consciencism* in 1964, the African Revolution has decisively entered a new phase, the phase of armed struggle. In every part of our continent, African revolutionaries are either preparing for armed struggle, or are actively engaged in military operations against the forces of reaction and counter-revolution.

The issues now are clearer than they have ever been. The succession of military *coups* which have in recent years taken place in Africa have exposed the close links between the interests of neo-colonialism and the indigenous bourgeoisie. These *coups* have brought into sharp relief the nature and the extent of the class struggle in Africa. Foreign monopoly capitalists are in close association with local reactionaries, and have made use of officers among the armed forces and police in order to frustrate the purposes of the African Revolution.

It is in consideration of the new situation in Africa that some changes have become necessary in this edition. They occur principally in Chapter III.[4]

It was therefore in the light of what he regarded as the new phase in the African revolution that Nkrumah felt the need to revise the original text of *Consciencism*. A comparison of the two editions shows that the author had completely changed his mind about the structure of African societies. I pointed this out in chapter 6, where the change was cited as an example of the conceptual revolution which, I suggested, had taken place in Nkrumah's thought in 1965. From that year on, and more precisely after the appearance of the work entitled *Neo-colonialism, the Last Stage of Imperialism* (note the Leninist sound to this title, which consciously echoes Lenin's famous *Imperialism, the Highest Stage of Capitalism*),[5] Nkrumah explicitly rejected his earlier view that there was no real class struggle in Africa.[6]

The first edition of *Consciencism* took it for granted that traditional African society had been free of class struggle, being organized on a communal, egalitarian basis which Nkrumah, following ethnological tradition, called 'communalism'. The view is totally reversed in *Neo-colonialism*, when Nkrumah explicitly writes that class struggle is one of the fundamental characteristics of contemporary African society and that in the last analysis the struggle against imperialism, whether colonial or neo-colonial, is nothing but a 'class struggle on an international scale'.[7] And so while the early works looked upon the anti-imperialist struggle as isolated and unique, interpreting it in a romantic way, as it were, and appealing only to moral principles (personal rights, etc.), the later works emphasize the close links between the efforts of colonial and neo-colonial peoples to liberate themselves and the continuous class struggle in the industrial societies. Consequently, the later works also reinterpret the main political developments in colonial and neo-colonial societies. For instance, the succession of military *coups* in Africa becomes a manifestation of the class struggle. No doubt Nkrumah's concrete explanations can be criticized on points of detail, but the basic principle can hardly be contested.[8]

Thus in the new edition of *Consciencism* Nkrumah totally recast all the passages in the original text which had exaggerated the uniqueness of African societies and had presented their functioning as independent of the universal laws governing the history of human society in general. On the other hand, brief additions reflect some of his new preoccupations (the conditions of socialist revolution, criticisms of the welfare society, etc.).

To illustrate this point, a comparison of the two versions of the same passage may be useful. In the first edition (1964) Nkrumah wrote:

Revolution is thus an indispensable avenue to socialism, where the antecedent social-political structure is animated by principles which are a negation of those of socialism, as in a capitalist structure (and therefore also in a colonialist structure, for a colonialist structure is essentially ancillary to capitalism). Indeed, I distinguish between two colonialisms, between a domestic one, and an external one. Capitalism at home is domestic colonialism.

But from the ancestral line of communalism, the passage to socialism lies in reform, because the underlying principles are the same. But when this passage carries one through colonialism the reform is revolutionary since the passage from colonialism to genuine independence is an act of revolution. But because of the continuity of communalism with socialism, in communalistic societies, socialism is not a revolutionary creed, but a restatement in contemporary idiom of the principles underlying communalism. The passage from a non-communalistic society to socialism is a revolutionary one which is guided by the principles underlying communism.

In my autobiography, I said that capitalism might prove too complicated a system for a newly independent country. I wish to add to this the fact that the presuppositions and purposes of capitalism are contrary to those of African society. Capitalism would be a betrayal of the personality and conscience of Africa.[9]

In the last edition (1970) this became:

Revolution is thus an indispensable avenue to socialism, where the antecedent socio-political structure is animated by principles which are a negation of those of socialism, as in a capitalist structure (and therefore also in a colonialist structure, for a colonialist structure is essentially ancillary to capitalism). Indeed, I distinguish between two colonialisms, between a domestic one and an external one. Capitalism at home is domestic colonialism.

But because the spirit of communalism still exists to some extent in societies with a communalist past, socialism and communism are not, in a strict sense of the word, 'revolutionary' creeds. They may be described as restatements in contemporary idiom of the principles underlying communalism. On the other hand, in societies with no history of communalism the creeds of socialism and communism are fully revolutionary, and the passage to socialism must be guided by the principles of scientific socialism.

The nature and cause of the conflict between the ruling class and the exploited class is influenced by the development of productive forces, that is, changes in technology; the economic relations which these forces condition; and the ideologies that reflect the properties and psychology of the people living in that society. The basis of a socialist revolution is created when the class struggle within a given society has resulted in mass consent and mass desire for positive action to change or transform that society. It is then that the foundation is laid for the highest form of political action – when a revolution attains its excellence, and workers and peasants succeed in overthrowing all other classes. I have explained how society's desire to transform nature reflects itself in different socio-political theories.[10]

Of the three paragraphs of the original text, the first has been retained *verbatim*, the second modified and the third deleted and replaced by another, which reflects preoccupations that were entirely absent from the first edition.

It will be noticed, however, that these changes destroy the original coherence of the text. The overall implication of the passage in the 1964 edition was that there could be a peaceful transition to socialism by way of reforms. The second paragraph was strongly antithetical to the first and suggested a reassuring alternative to the prospect of violent revolution. The new text, however, reduces the antithesis. Nkrumah is no longer able to claim, in the second paragraph, that the transition to socialism can be effected through reforms. Indeed, he no longer mentions a 'transition to socialism', that is to say, to a specific form of the relations of production, but is content with an abstract comparison between two 'creeds'. There is no longer any assertion of continuity between a *communalist* organization and a *socialist* organization of production but only between the two corresponding 'creeds' or *ideologies*, and tentatively at that: in a society with a communalist past, socialism and communism are not revolutionary doctrines 'in the strict sense of the word', which means that they may be revolutionary in the broad sense, both as doctrines and *a fortiori* as modes of social organization. The new edition also avoids the use of the very word 'reform' and of the hybrid notion of 'revolutionary reform'. However, the effect of these revisions is to upset the original balance of the text by the cutting off of one of the limbs of the 'reform–revolution' antithesis.

But that is not all. In the new text Nkrumah is careful to avoid the suggestion that African societies are still communalist today. In fact, he expressly says that this communalism belongs to their past and now survives only as a memory ('the spirit of communalism').

The third paragraph in the first edition is simply deleted. This is a significant cut, for careful reading shows that this paragraph may have seemed like an aside but in fact expressed the whole design of the book. Long before writing *Consciencism* Nkrumah had proclaimed his commitment to socialism. Article 8 of the CPP's earliest political programme, drafted in 1949 and adopted in 1951, stated clearly that the party aimed at founding 'a Socialist State in which all men and women [would] have equal opportunity and where there [would] be no capitalist exploitation'.[11] Nkrumah made the same declaration in his *Autobiography*, published in 1957. The 1964 essay is therefore an attempt to justify a long-standing commitment. More exactly, it is an answer to a classic objection: that in adopting socialism, Africa would be delivering herself to an imported ideology and betraying her original civilization. It was precisely this issue, inspired by the most traditionalist cultural nationalism, that Nkrumah tried to address in *Consciencism*. The object of the book was to link socialism with the purest African tradition by showing that socialism, far from being a betrayal of this tradition would actually be its best possible translation into modern idiom.

This little paragraph therefore played a crucial strategic role in the original text. The fact that he later suppressed it suggests that Nkrumah had lost some of his confidence in the rationale of his project, perhaps because he now realized that 'the assumptions and designs . . . of African society' were really a highly fanciful hypothesis.

On the other hand, the 1970 text contains an entirely new paragraph, discussing the practical conditions for socialist revolution, a strange revision in a text whose coherence depended entirely on the idea that a revolution was not a necessary condition for the transition to socialism in Africa.

This comparison shows, then, that the new version of *Consciencism* destroys in places the original coherence of the work. The only possible explanation for this discordance is to be found through reading the other works of the same period, i.e. post-1964. In these Nkrumah explicitly develops themes which are only touched upon in *Consciencism*. These provide a political discourse whose coherence is of a very different order from that of the earlier texts. What is stressed now is the need for revolutionary violence (though in his *Autobiography*, for instance, Nkrumah made it clear that he believed in non-violence and regarded himself as a disciple of Gandhi), the universality of class struggle (previously denied), the importance of political and ideological conflicts within Africa (previously ignored), etc. For the later Nkrumah the laws governing African society are the same as those governing every other society in the world. He even goes so far as to reject the notion of the 'Third World', because it particularizes the ex-colonies, lumping them together as a monolith globally opposed to capitalist societies on the one hand and to socialist countries on the other. In reality, he says, there is no third way.[12] In more general terms, any phrase or concept that explicitly or implicitly gives African societies absolute specificity in relation to other societies in the world is theoretically unacceptable.

It is in the light of this development in Nkrumah's thought that

Consciencism must be reread today. And when we find present-day commentators confidently asserting that the Ghanaian leader's considered view was that there was no such thing as class struggle in Africa, we can only lament the fact that they have not read what Nkrumah wrote after 1964.

The limits of the project

Despite the important changes made in the 1970 edition of *Consciencism*, it remains largely dependent upon many pre-1965 ideological assumptions. Nkrumah might have avoided many inconsistencies if, instead of patching up the original text, he had simply scrapped it and written an entirely new book on the same subject – or rather, since it could not really be about the same subject, a new book designed to show exactly why such a subject was no longer viable.

Indeed, what *is* the subject of *Consciencism*? In order to explain this somewhat bizarre title, the author added the subtitle *Philosophy and Ideology for Decolonisation and Development, with Particular Reference to the African Revolution.*[13] But on close scrutiny, the subtitle is even more obscure than the title. What is *the* African Revolution in the singular? Is it simply a national revolution, aimed at political liberation from the colonial powers, or is it a social revolution, aiming to overthrow the dominant relations of production for the benefit of the proletariat? And what does 'development' mean? Development surely implies moving from a stage that is no longer adequate towards another that is more desirable. In this instance, what are the first and the final stages?

The third and most serious problem, and the only one we can really tackle here, is the strange coupling of 'Philosophy *and* Ideology'. Are the two terms synonymous? Do we have here a mere repetition, a pleonasm, or is some distinction intended? Is philosophy the same thing as ideology, or are they different? And if they are different, what is the relation between the two terms, and what ought it to be? It must be said that *Consciencism* is unclear on this important point, not because Nkrumah did not answer the question but because his answer is extremely obscure.

The question is expressly put at the beginning of the third chapter, which is entitled 'Society and Ideology'. Nkrumah quotes a text from Mazzini:

Every true revolution is a programme; and derived from a new, general, positive and organic principle. The first thing necessary is to accept that principle. Its development must then be confined to men who are believers in it, and emancipated from every tie or connection with any principle of an opposite nature.[14]

His own comments are as follows:

Here Mazzini asserts the connection between a revolution and an ideology. When the revolution has been successful, the ideology continues to characterize the society. It is the ideology which gives a countenance to the ensuing social milieu. Mazzini further states the principle to be general, positive and organic. The statement, elucidation and theoretical defence of such a principle will collectively form a philosophy. Hence philosophy admits of being an instrument of ideology.[15]

Nkrumah thus explicitly embraces an instrumental conception of philosophy. Philosophy, for him, exists merely to translate spontaneous ideological theses into a more refined language, to elucidate, enunciate and justify, after the event, the decisions of the ideological instance. This conception of philosophy explains the whole project of *Consciencism*.

Once he has defined the relation between philosophy and ideology, Nkrumah proceeds to show that traditional African societies were not without ideology; and, forestalling the objection that could easily (but incorrectly)[16] be raised – namely, that African societies lacked writing – he proclaims: 'What is crucial is not the paper, but the thought.'[17] On closer scrutiny, it becomes obvious that Nkrumah is here banging at an open door. For anyone who has heard of Marx – I shall not say *read* – and is minimally informed about the fundamental theses of historical materialism, it goes without saying not only that pre-colonial Africa had its ideology but also, and more accurately, that it had a plurality of competing ideologies, like any other society in the world. In his obdurate attempts to demonstrate that African society had a single ideology, however, Nkrumah in fact links up with the vast majority of Africanist anthropologists and accepts the classic ethnological ideology. In this way he neglects the pluralism of pre-colonial African culture, forcing an artificial unity upon what is really irreducibly diverse, and hence impoverished – the classic African tradition.

This over-simplification is serious, but there are at least two others: Nkrumah also simplifies Western and Arab-muslim culture; he ignores the pluralism and the great internal conflicts which have always constituted the splendour of these civilizations.[18] It is on the basis of this triple simplification that Nkrumah then makes the following (ideological) observation: present-day African society has lost its identity; it is buffeted by three rival ideologies or cultural currents, the traditional, the Euro-Christian and the Muslim, the coexistence of which generates what he calls 'the African crisis of conscience'. Note the wording: there is a crisis *because of* the pluralism of creeds, ideologies and cultural currents. And to convey the gravity of the crisis, Nkrumah compares it with 'schizophrenia'.[19] In short, the arch-enemy is pluralism, and the crisis will be overcome only if we can evolve a new ideology charged with the function of effecting a synthesis of the three old rival ideologies. This synthesis will be 'consciencism'.

In spite of the strangeness of this name, Nkrumah could not have made a better choice, for 'consciencism' is a direct response to the classic project of a philosophy of consciousness, in the sense that in the Western philosophical tradition 'consciousness' has always been the ultimate unifying principle, the agent for the unification and synthesis of quite diverse beliefs. 'Consciencism' is a classic philosophy of consciousness, in that it aims at restoring the lost unity of African consciousness and at articulating three separate ideologies into a single, unified system of thought. 'Consciencism' thus presents itself as a philosophy of consciousness, that is to say, of ideological unity.

This is not the place to dwell at length upon this theme. It will suffice to remind the reader that various recent or contemporary authors, like Marx, Freud, Lacan and Althusser or, from another point of view, Heidegger, Levinas, Derrida, Foucault, etc., have developed criticisms of this current of classical thought, the philosophy of the consciousness, the metaphysic of self-presence and the ideology of voluntarism. This is the measure of the frailty of Nkrumah's doctrine, which to his mind will, by tomorrow, if it is not already, be the collective philosophy of Africans, the African philosophy. The crucial weakness of the project resides in the basic assumption that Africa *needs* a collective philosophy. It is deeply regrettable that Nkrumah, usually such a lucid thinker, should have failed to realize that this assumption was untenable. It is a matter of deeper regret that in the revised edition of 1970 he did not perceive

the close link, the indissoluble complicity, between this philosophical project and the thesis he had meanwhile abandoned,
namely, that there were no classes in pre-colonial African society.

A philosophy in the image of the CPP

On this last point, though, some distinctions must be made. *Consciencism* does not categorically deny the existence of classes in
contemporary Africa but only in pre-colonial Africa. Nkrumah
readily accepts that colonialism introduced important changes in
the egalitarian structure of the old society. He recognizes that
colonization, by throwing up African cadres in the service of a
foreign administration, 'groups of merchants and traders, lawyers,
doctors, politicians and trade unionists', produced in fact 'a class
which was now associated with social power and authority'.[20] But he
says no more. What interests him is less the economic and political
function of this class as such than its secondary cultural function as a
conveyor belt of European civilization.

Thus Nkrumah conjured away the practical problem of class
struggle and ducked the theoretical problem of the internal composition of colonial and post-colonial African societies. The
indigenous bourgeoisie comes into the analysis only to illustrate the
previous assertion that the three cultural currents in Africa are
borne by three 'different segments'[21] of society. Its exploitative role
is thus sublimated in a more neutral, purely cultural, role.

More generally, the cultural conflict described by Nkrumah may
be understood as the sublimated form of a class struggle which he is
reluctant to recognize. No wonder he identifies only one of the three
rival 'segments', the one bearing the European current. His assimilation of this 'segment' to a specific 'class' leads us to expect a similar
identification for the other two 'segments'. He does not make it: no
wonder, since sublimation is not, in this context, a simple trans-
position of each of the suppressed elements into a corresponding
representation in the order of the imaginary; it is rather the transition of a different order, which has its own structure and logic and
is not reducible to a systematic inversion of the original order. Thus
it would be difficult simply to assimilate to a class the fraction of
African society which has remained faithful to 'our traditional way
of life',[22] and still more the Islamic segment. For it would soon
emerge that each of these ways of life is common to 'traditional'
rulers and their subjects, to feudal lords and their domestic slaves.

Nkrumah confines himself to the easiest, the most obvious identification, but in spite of this, the real order (economic and political)
can still be detected behind his cultural discourse.

The consequences of this sublimation can now be measured. The
most important of them is that the three 'competing ideologies',
which are in fact cultural substitutes for economic class conflicts, are
seen by Nkrumah as easily reconcilable. The aim of *Consciencism* is
precisely to effect such a reconciliation, to fuse the three hitherto
juxtaposed systems into a single system. In other words: just as in
the book cultural pluralism is the index of a social cleavage, so its
abolition would in fact be the index of a suppression of classes. The
synthesis of the systems should express a harmonization of class
interests. And the great advantage is that such a harmonization
would have taken place without violence, without a political
struggle, solely through the power of dialectical reasoning.

Better still, it so happens that the ideological synthesis can be
presented as socialist. And to the extent that it is collective and that
all Africans, without exception, are expected to commit themselves
to this new system in order to recover their authentic cultural
personality, they will all automatically be socialists and will all
reject, out of conviction, the exploitation of man by man. Africa
will have permanently recaptured its fine village unanimity and will
thus offer the world the unique spectacle of a society without
conflict, division or dissonance.

It is a remarkable fact that if one scrutinizes Nkrumah's political
practice during the entire period of his leadership, one finds in it this
same will to synthesize, the same desire for reconciliation, the same
stubborn refusal to sacrifice any element of the whole. The structure
of the CPP is a clear reflection of this tendency: Nkrumah always
wanted it to become a mass organization, uniting the widest
possible spectrum of Ghanaian society around a common programme for what he called 'positive action'. He explicitly rejected
the idea of a vanguard party,[23] which would have necessitated a
more homogeneous social base and a more precise ideological
perspective. The CPP belonged to everybody: agricultural workers,
labourers, small traders, office workers and 'verandah boys', as well
as rich planters, feudal chiefs, industrialists, compradores, etc.
With hindsight it is easy to see that if such a party can take the credit
for the swift success of the struggle for independence, it must also,
because of its incoherence and its internal contradictions, the power
struggles that subsequently undermined it and the inevitable

eventual disarray, take the blame for the ultimate bankruptcy of 'Nkrumaist' politics.[24] As Ghana's leader, Nkrumah genuinely believed that he could use a socialist programme and ideology to rally social strata whose economic interests would, in the long term, be threatened by the realization of that programme. This was idealism. This was voluntarism. This was contempt for class struggle. Nkrumah did not realize this until it was too late.

Consciencism reflects this same voluntarism. No wonder, since the book was written for the rank and file of the CPP and was intended to provide the philosophical doctrine which the party still lacked. But the doctrine was founded, in the last analysis, on the same assumptions and illusions as the party itself. The enforced synthesis of rival ideologies, the simplification of the cultural history of Europe, Africa and Islam, the attempt to embrace each of these histories in a single unified view, the expectation that all three would live together in a single consciousness, the enclosure of thought into a standard and supposedly collective system, the interpretation of philosophy as the 'subtle instrument of ideology'[25] – all these positions pervade *Consciencism* and are the metaphysical equivalents of Nkrumah's attempts in practice to unite in a single mass organization different social strata with frequently irreconcilable interests.

The doctrine

We are now in a position to attempt a brief summary of the doctrine of consciencism – brief, because our primary aim was to throw light on the ideological assumptions of Nkrumah's project, not to dwell upon the content of the proposed system.[26] However, to give some idea of what it is like, let us say that it is essentially a materialist metaphysic that responds to the age-old question of the origin of being by asserting the priority of matter over mind.[27] This does not mean, says Nkrumah, that matter is the only reality but merely that it is the fundamental reality from which all others derived. This derivation is, he claims, the result of a process which he calls 'categorial conversion' – a term reminiscent of logic. This is the process through which a given reality generates a reality of a higher category. Thus mind is supposed to be generated by matter; and God himself, if He exists, should be conceived as a higher form of matter. So Nkrumah presents his doctrine as a form of materialism whose novelty is that it does not exclude the existence of God:

'Even though deeply rooted in materialism, Consciencism is not necessarily atheistic.'[28]

We cannot now go into the question of the consistency of such a materialism.[29] It will be far more pertinent to note the way in which Nkrumah tries to base a complete ethic and a political doctrine on this metaphysic. In this respect *Consciencism* professes an egalitarian and humanistic ethic strongly marked by the influence of Kant.[30] Politically, it adopts the central demand of nationalist ideology by reaffirming the right of self-determination for all peoples[31] on the one hand and calls for the construction of socialism in a liberated Africa on the other.[32] The most interesting point, however, is the author's assertion that the three panels of the triptych (metaphysical, ethical and political) are closely linked and inseparable. *Consciencism* thus appears as a vast ideological structure in the fullest sense, a complete system of thought, with multiple but interdependent aspects. The relation of metaphysics to politics is presented as one not of simple juxtaposition or even of complementarity but of logical implication. On this point, Nkrumah is categorical: 'There are two real philosophical alternatives. These alternatives coincide with idealism and materialism. . . . Idealism favours an oligarchy, materialism favours an egalitarianism.'[33]

In other words, every political stance is ultimately founded on a metaphysical stance and, conversely, every metaphysical assertion calls for a specific political choice. This is an infinitely hazardous view. Moreover, through his many examples drawn from the history of Western philosophy, he himself gives us the rope with which to hang him. For instance, he overlooks Descartes' idealism and attributes to him an implicit political doctrine of 'co-operative socialism' which is said to be the opposite of oligarchy.[34] Such an ascription is highly surprising, but it illustrates how, in his case studies, Nkrumah could propose interpretations that are in fact implicit refutations of his own initial hypothesis.

But what is most controversial is Nkrumah's wish to put the various figures of metaphysical discourse into one-to-one correspondence with the figures of political discourse. Any such correspondence is implausible, *generally and in itself*, whatever its concrete specification. It is just as arbitrary to found socialism on materialism as on idealism, as arbitrary to found oligarchy on idealism as on materialism (or on any other metaphysical system for that matter). Our political choices stand on their own feet.[35] If they need justification, it must be political justification, belonging to the same level of discourse and not to what is the completely different (*ex hypothesi*) level of metaphysical speculation.

If this were not so, it would be difficult to understand how, in the heroic days of the anti-colonial struggle, Africans of such diverse religions, of totally opposed metaphysical views, could have fought together so spontaneously and effectively against the common oppressor. And it would be equally difficult to understand how, in our own time, inside and outside Africa, people can struggle side by side for the construction of socialism in spite of enormous scientific and philosophical disagreements. A plurality of beliefs and theoretical choices does not preclude commitment to the same political ideal. The only necessary basis for commitment is that common interests are at stake: national interests in the case of the anti-colonial struggle, class interests in the case of the struggle for socialism.

Now, if this is so, then the project of *Consciencism* rests on the misconception that every political ideal depends on a specific metaphysical system. It was this illusion that led Nkrumah to attempt, by hook or by crook, to reduce the plurality of metaphysical beliefs and choices within African society.

Conclusion

As a whole, Nkrumah's book is founded on two closely linked ideological assumptions; one the author noticed and corrected in the second edition, while to the other he remained blind. The first was the denial of the existence of class struggle in Africa. History was to make short work of that one. The second was the idea that there were no ideological conflicts in pre-colonial Africa on the one hand, and, on the other, that this illusion should be valorized by making theoretical unanimity into a value to be struggled for. Let us call this the unanimist illusion.

Our final point has been that this illusion constantly feeds on *l'esprit de système*, or on what could be called more accurately the metaphysical illusion: the idea that every political project requires a specific metaphysical basis. Our own contention, on the other hand, asserts the autonomy of the political as a level of discourse, and we think it unnecessary to try to base this on any other discursive authority.

The problem with *Consciencism* in its second version is that it preserves the unanimist illusion although it has discarded the first assumption on which in part it rested. But we can now see that this has happened because unanimism has another source in the metaphysical illusion, the ideological thesis that politics has a metaphysical level.

If we can overthrow this thesis, we will be able to achieve a double liberation:

1   The liberation of political debate, at last rescued from metaphysics' thrall and henceforth able to be stated in terms of interests and conflicts of interests. To be fair, we must recall that Nkrumah himself contributed enormously to this clarification, in particular in the later works where he showed the importance of class struggle as the motor of contemporary history on our continent.

2   The liberation of philosophical debate, as it recovers both its indispensable pluralism and its specific object as freely developing discussion around a specific problem.

This is not the place to dwell on the nature of this problem, which in our view constitutes the proper object of philosophy. Without offering any arguments for it, I will simply propose the working hypothesis, that in the last analysis philosophy has always been a reflection on science, so that it is closely dependent on the real development of scientific knowledge.[36] It follows that it will not really take off in Africa until the other disciplines have done so. In any case, it seems to me a serious mistake to consider the problem of philosophy separately from the more general problem of science. It is wrong to examine the conditions in which an African philosophy might thrive without examining at the same time the possibility of an African science and, even more relevant, the legitimacy and meaning of the phrase 'African science'.

Nkrumah's blindness to the essential conjunction of science and philosophy, and his substitution of politics for science as the key determinant of philosophical discourse, drove him, little by little, to rehabilitate the ethnographic notion of 'collective philosophy' at a different level. A reading of *Consciencism* has forced us to denounce this notion once again and to reaffirm the value of pluralism – that is to say, of the free exploration and confrontation of ideas as a precondition of a real African philosophy.

8 True and false pluralism*

'Cultural pluralism' generally means three things: (1) the *fact* of cultural plurality, understood as the coexistence of cultures belonging, at least in principle, to different geographical areas; (2) the *recognition* of this fact; (3) the *advocacy* of this plurality and the *will* to make use of it in one way or another, either by preserving these cultures from mutual contamination or by organizing a peaceful dialogue among them for their mutual enrichment.

In this now classic form cultural pluralism is a reaction against the cultural exclusivism of the West, and it is important to note that this reaction itself came from the West. The Europe that produced Lévy-Bruhl also produced Lévi-Strauss. The Europe that produced Gobineau also produced Jean-Paul Sartre. The Europe that produced Hitler had previously produced Marx – a sign that European culture is itself pluralistic, a criss-cross of the most diverse tendencies, so that, when we speak of Western civilization we may not be clear what we are talking about, and there is a danger that we will confuse currents that are opposed and irreconcilable.

But whether imaginary or real, this 'Western civilization' has been created as a unitary civilization and has become the yardstick by which the civilizations of other continents are deprecated and devalued. The cultural achievements of other societies have been destroyed for its sake. This attitude bears a name: ethnocentrism. It has had its day of glory – the second half of the nineteenth century and the beginning of our own; and today nobody would seriously dispute that it was linked historically to colonization. It has also had its professional ideologues, one of the most illustrious of them being Lévy-Bruhl (who, by the way, has the distinction of being 'entirely francophone').

---

* A paper read at the AUPELF (Association of Partially or Entirely Francophone Universities) colloquium, held at Louvain-la-Neuve (Belgium) from 21 to 25 May 1973, on 'The Universities and the Plurality of Cultures'. Published in the *Acta*, pp. 53–65, and in *Diogène*, no. 84 (October–December 1973).

From 'progressive' ethnologists to the Third World 'nationalists'

It was as a reaction against this cultural imperialism that it began to be asserted at least fifty years ago,[1] and continues to be today, that European civilization is only one of a number of ways of organizing people's relations to each other and to nature. Thus was recognized the plurality of cultures. Thus was rejected, at least in principle, the myth of Western superiority as a result of a new awareness that the technical and economic advancement of a society did not automatically produce social or moral superiority. Some even went so far as simply to invert the scale of imperialistic values and to valorize the non-technicity of 'exotic' societies by interpreting their lesser technological development as a condition of greater 'authenticity', i.e. of a greater transparency in human relations. As early as 1930 Malinowski wrote:

Many of us . . . see a menace to all real spiritual and artistic values in the aimless advance of modern mechanization.
   One of the refuges from this mechanical prison of culture is the study of primitive forms of human life as they still exist in remote parts of our globe. Anthropology, to me at least, was a romantic escape from our over-standardized culture.[2]

Closer to our own time, Lévi-Strauss has adopted the same Rousseauist tone, arguing that 'primitive' societies are more 'authentic' than 'civilized' societies because they are free from exploitation, because their human relations are less anonymous and more personal, because they are small enough for everyone to know everyone else and to enjoy perfect unanimity on all the most important problems.[3]

So we are now witnessing the valorization of a cultural plurality, the very existence of which was inconceivable to imperial ethnology. The evolutionism of Tylor or Morgan and the brash and reactionary ethnocentrism of Lévy-Bruhl could not accept the idea that non-European cultures might actually exist. They could not conceive of the cultural life of 'primitive' societies except as representing the early stages in a single cultural process of which Europe represented for them the most advanced stage. Today, however, Western anthropology accepts the existence of other cultures; and, more than that, it sees them as representing the possible salvation of a Western civilization suffering from an excess of technology and standardization and yearning for what Bergson called a 'heighten-ing of the soul'.

It is remarkable how quickly the nationalists of the 'Third World' began to follow in the footsteps of the ethnologists of the new school. Césaire was one of them. Many African intellectuals of my generation read with fervour and delighted in those admirable stanzas from his *Cahier d'un retour au pays natal*, and my nostalgia for past enthusiasms forces me to quote them at length:

Those who did not invent gunpowder or the compass
Those who never knew how to tame steam or electricity
Those who have explored neither the seas nor the sky
But those without whom the earth would not be the earth
A hump of greater bounty on earth-forsaking earth
A silo to preserve and ripen the earthmost in earth,
My negritude is not a stone to rush unhearing at screaming daylight
My negritude is not a film of dead water on the dead eye of the earth
My negritude is neither a tower nor a cathedral
It dips in the red flesh of the earth
It dips in the burning flesh of the sky
It pricks the blank torpor of its direct patience

Eia for the royal mahogany!
Eia for those who have never invented anything
For those who have never explored anything
For those who have never tamed anything
But they yield, possessed, to the essence of all things
Blind to surfaces but possessed of the motion of all things
Careless to tame but gamesters of the world
Truly the elder sons of the world
Porous to all the world's breathing
Drainless bed for the world's waters
Spark from the world's sacred fire
Flesh of the flesh of the world pulsating with the world's self-motion![4]

These lines are remarkable for their poetic sweep, capable of moving the most frigid temperament; but they are also of great historical interest, since they include what I think is the first occur-rence of the now famous neologism: 'negritude'[5] in a context capable of bringing out its significance.

But even more remarkable is the fact that they display a black poet spontaneously employing a mode of argument originally devised in white society to express his revolt against white racism.

The *Cahier d'un retour au pays natal* was published in 1939.[6] At that time functionalism was no novelty, since Malinowski's classic work *The Argonauts of the Western Pacific* had appeared in 1922. So Césaire was not being original when he claimed that the non-technicity of blacks was not a defect but a virtue, that it is the obverse of an essential responsiveness unknown to Europe, that the West has nothing to teach the rest of the world in the essential human qualities of brotherhood, openness to experience, and rootedness.

Césaire himself was perfectly aware of this. Like his friend Senghor, he was almost as happy to invoke the authority of Malinowski, Herskovits and other functionalists as that of Frobenius. It is therefore true to say that nationalism in the colonies has never involved a total rejection of the colonizer's culture; rather, it has always consisted in choosing from the many currents of that culture those which are most favourable to the Third World. An initial stage of spontaneous revolt and unreflective self-assertion has been followed by a second stage, involving the discovery of favourable currents in violent contrast to colonial practice as it was experienced.

Thus there has arisen what can truly be called a complicity between Third World nationalists and 'progressive' Western anthropologists. For years they will assist each other, the former using the latter in support of their cultural claims, the latter using the former to buttress their pluralistic theses.

Culture and politics: culturalist ideology

The hypertrophy of the cultural

I have cited Césaire as an exponent of nationalism. I could just as well have cited Senghor who, of course, has done much more than Césaire, its inventor, to popularize the word 'negritude' and whose endless dissertations have woven around it a whole negro ideology. This garrulous negrism has a very simple explanation: whereas for Césaire the exaltation of black cultures functions merely as a supporting argument in favour of political liberation, in Senghor it works as an alibi for evading the political problem of national liberation. Hypertrophy of cultural nationalism generally serves to compensate for the hypotrophy of political nationalism. This is probably why Césaire spoke so soberly about culture and never mentioned it without explicitly subordinating it to the more fundamental problem of political liberation. This also explains why, in works like *Liberté I*, Senghor, as a good Catholic and disciple of Teilhard de Chardin, emphasizes rather artificial cultural problems, elaborating lengthy definitions of the unique black mode of being and of being-in-the-world, and systematically evades the problem of the struggle against imperialism.

The above-mentioned complicity between the nationalist and the ethnologist is therefore particularly disastrous in the case of the cultural nationalist – that is to say, the nationalist who is inclined to emphasize only the cultural aspect of foreign domination at the expense of other aspects, the economic and political in particular. For want of a more adequate term, we can call this attitude 'culturalism' (by analogy with 'economism' and without reference to the anthropological current usually so named). The characteristic of culturalism in this sense is to distort the political and economic problems, neatly side-stepping them in favour of exclusively cultural problems. Worse still, these cultural problems are themselves strangely simplified as culture is reduced to folklore, its most obvious superficial and flashy aspect. Its deeper life and internal contradictions, the fruitful tensions by which it is animated are all neglected, along with its history, development and revolutions. Culture is petrified in a synchronic picture, flat and strangely simple and univocal, and is then contrasted with other cultures which are also trimmed and schematized for the sake of the comparison.

A deceptive singular

In this way we speak of African civilization as 'traditional' in contrast to Western civilization, as if there could be African civilization, Western civilization, in the singular, and as if civilization were not, by nature, a permanent clash of contradictory cultural forms.

I am not saying, of course, that the use of the word 'civilization' in the singular should be proscribed for ever, but simply that this singularity must be reinterpreted: it should refer not to the imaginary unity of a system of values but to the real empirical unity of a specific geographical area. European civilization is not a closed system of values but a set of irreducible cultural products which have appeared on the European continent; or, at a deeper level, it is the set of these products and of the creative tensions which underlie them, the necessary infinite act of these products and tensions, in the forms they have assumed in the past and in the as yet unpredictable forms they will assume tomorrow in that little strip of the world called Europe. Nor is African civilization a closed system in which we may imprison ourselves (or allow ourselves to be imprisoned). It is the unfinished history of a similar contradictory debate as it has proceeded, and will continue to proceed, in that fraction of the world called Africa. Only in this sense – as an external label rather than an impossible inner description – can we speak of African civilization in the singular, the only real unity being here that of a continent.

However, while the use of the word 'civilization' in the singular may in the last resort be acceptable, the adjective 'traditional', in the phrase 'traditional African civilization', must be banished once and for all because it favours a pernicious misconception. In practice the phrase is used to mean 'pre-colonial African civilization', and there is no real objection to the idea of 'pre-colonial African civilization', but again only in the sense of a purely conventional historical division. But when, instead of this neutral phrase, we use the more vivid phrase 'traditional African civilization', we add a value connotation, and pre-colonial civilization as a whole is being contrasted with so-called 'modern' civilization (that is to say, colonial and post-colonial civilization, with the connotation 'highly Westernized'), as if they were two essentially distinct systems of values. The pre-colonial history of Africa is condensed into a single synchronic picture, whose points exist simultaneously and are uniformly opposed to the points in a different synchronic chart, symmetrical with the first, the two being distinguished in terms of what is taken to be the only important division in the history of the continent, the moment of colonization. We ignore, or pretend to ignore, the fact that African traditions are no more homogeneous than those of any other continent, that cultural traditions are always a complex heritage, contradictory and heterogeneous, an open set of options, some of which will be actualized by any given generation, which by adopting one choice sacrifices all the others. We ignore, or pretend to ignore the fact that cultural traditions can remain alive only if they are exploited anew, under one of their aspects at the expense of all the others, and that the choice of this privileged aspect is itself a matter for struggle today, for an endlessly restless debate whose ever uncertain outcome spells the destiny of society. Above all, we ignore or pretend to ignore the fact that African cultural traditions are not closed, that they did not stop when colonization started but embrace colonial and post-colonial cultural life. So-called modern Africa is just as 'traditional' as pre-colonial Africa in the only acceptable sense of the word 'traditional' – tradition does not exclude but necessarily implies a system of discontinuities.

The culturalist system

All these flaws, real or imaginary, are present in culturalism. They are even organized into a vast ideological (i.e. indirectly political) system. I do say *indirectly political*, for ideology is camouflaged politics. Culturalism is an ideological system because it produces an indirect political effect. It eclipses, first, the problem of effective national liberation and, second, the problem of class struggle.

In the first moment culturalism, in the guise of an exclusively cultural nationalism, drastically simplifies the national culture, schematizes and flattens it in order to contrast it with the colonizer's culture, and then gives this imaginary opposition *precedence* over real political and economic conflicts.

In independent countries culturalism takes the form of a backward-looking cultural nationalism, flattening the national culture and denying its internal pluralism and historical depth, in order to divert the attention of the exploited classes from the real political and economic conflicts which divide them from the ruling classes under the fallacious pretext of their common participation in 'the' national culture.

Césaire is therefore not the typical cultural nationalist because for him culture has always been subordinate to politics. He merely invented the word 'negritude' and crystallized the arguments for revolt around it; but unfortunately these were subsequently taken over by others and degraded into a mystifying ideology.

However, negritude is not the only form of cultural nationalism. There are other phrases – for instance, 'authenticity' or 'the repersonalization of the African', which it has seized upon. The diversity of labels and the importance of local variations should not be allowed to conceal the unity of the structure. The dominant feature of this structure is always what is commonly called traditionalism, understood as the exclusive valorization of a simplified, superficial and imaginary blueprint of cultural tradition.

It is this structure for which I use a very general term, 'culturalism'. I say 'culturalism' and not merely 'cultural nationalism', because this structure is characteristic of Third World nationalists and Western ethnologists: it is the locus of their objective complicity.

Ethnologists too tend to isolate the cultural aspects of society and to stress it at the expense of the economic and political aspects. Even when dealing with politics, ethnologists will generally be concerned with the traditional kind, arbitrarily reduced to its pre-colonial dimension, petrified, ossified and emptied of its internal tensions, discontinuities and confrontations. The political problem of colonial or neo-colonial domination is never posed. Anthropology presents itself as apolitical, even when it specializes in the study of political structures. The numerous works devoted to 'political anthropology' have always attempted to evade the problem of the national liberation of the peoples under study. In some cases, it is true, they felt compelled to describe what they abstractly called the 'colonial situation' (cf. Balandier), thus translating what was in fact a (political) *conflict* into terms of (cultural) *ambiguity*. But in the large majority of cases political anthropologists do not even go as far as this: they prefer to ignore the present political life of dominated peoples and interest themselves exclusively in their so-called traditional (i.e., in fact, pre-colonial) political organization.

Thus the flight from politics permeates even so-called political anthropology. Different anthropologists at various times have always either affirmed the supremacy of the West, presenting it as possessing the only mature civilization while other societies are at best at the early stages of a process which the West has already completed (Lévy-Bruhl and the classical evolutionists), or, conversely, in a gesture of repentance which is still motivated by the same comparative problematic, they have tried to show that European civilization is not unique but that there are others, equally valid. But, of course, these other civilizations are now in contact with Europe and as a result of colonization have been subjected to an involuntary process of Westernization; pluralist anthropologists refuse to consider their present condition, but prefer to try and reconstruct their pre-colonial existence. Moreover, when they investigate this pre-colonial past, they refuse to see the evolution, revolutions and discontinuities that may have affected it, and the precarious balance which has made these civilizations temporarily what they are today. Anthropologists need to play with simple units, univocal cultural totalities without cracks or dissonances.

They need dead cultures, petrified cultures, always identical to themselves in the homogeneous space of an eternal present.

Such are the main features of the culturalist mode of thought, in which the complicity of ethnologists and nationalists takes shape. Such is the all-embracing structure which accommodates the otherwise differing activities of 'progressive' anthropology (functionalist, structuralist, dynamic, etc.) and cultural nationalism. This is the universal structure which has given rise to the common thesis of 'progressive' ethnologist and nationalist: the plurality of cultures. For both groups this thesis functions as a refuge: it enables Western anthropologists to escape from the boredom of their own society and third-world nationalists to escape from the psychological and political rape perpetrated upon them by Western imperialism, by plunging back into their (imaginary) cultural origins.

True pluralism

The false problem of acculturation

Thus a theoretical affirmation of the plurality of cultures invariably serves as a pretext for a conservative cultural practice. Neither the anthropologist nor the nationalist can today be unaware of the fact that the 'exotic' cultures no longer exist in their pure state: that they no longer offer the nostalgic European or the rebellious nationalist an absolute alternative. If they ever did represent *the* difference as such, they can certainly no longer do so, owing to the growth of cultural interpenetration. Both ethnologist and nationalist readily recognize that we are more and more witnessing the irreversible advent of a world civilization. But instead of grasping this phenomenon in all its complexity, they simplify and trivialize it, emptying it of all real content by calling it 'acculturation'.

A young (and 'entirely francophone') anthropologist, Gérard Leclerc, has recently shown in an admirable book how field anthropologists, faced with the impossibility of sweeping the facts of colonialism under the carpet, have introduced it surreptitiously into their discussions under the name of 'acculturation'.[7] Between 1930 and 1950 an enormous literature was devoted to this theme, but learned discussions of the 'changing native', 'culture clash' and 'culture contact' or 'social change', etc., were all founded on the same pervasive ideological assumption: in a non-Western culture, change can only come from outside.

Gérard Leclerc draws attention to the mechanistic vocabulary that is invariably used in all these analyses. But what he fails to point out (and has possibly not noticed)[8] is that this vocabulary, far from 'driving out speculation and ideology', actually expresses the ideological conception that non-Western cultures are dead, petrified, reified, eternally self-replicating and lacking any internal capacity for negation or transcendence. But Gérard Leclerc has not sustained his critique to the point of finally abandoning the (epistemologically indefensible) ideological prejudice which makes anthropology an autonomous discipline and has chosen instead to try to resurrect ethnology in the form of a 'critical anthropology', and this is why he fails to make the all-important point that we must stress: that a culture is always active and creative; it is a contradictory debate between people chained to the same destiny and anxious to make the best of it. What we must understand is that never in any society does everyone agree with everyone else. One of the most perverse myths invented by ethnology, whose effects in return contribute to the survival of ethnology itself, is the myth of primitive unanimity, the myth that non-Western societies are 'simple' and homogeneous at every level, including the level of ideology and belief. What we must recognize today is that pluralism does not come to any society from outside but is inherent in every society. The alleged acculturation, the alleged 'encounter' of African civilization with European civilization, is really just another mutation produced from within African civilizations, the successor to many earlier ones about which our knowledge is very incomplete, and, no doubt, the precursor of many future mutations, which may be more radical still. The decisive encounter is not between Africa as a whole and Europe as a whole: it is the continuing encounter between Africa and itself. Pluralism in the true sense did not stem from the intrusion of Western civilization into our continent; it did not come from outside to a previously unanimous civilization. It is an internal pluralism, born of perpetual confrontations and occasional conflicts between Africans themselves.

A dangerous polarization

Far from having come to Africa with colonization, it is highly probable that cultural pluralism was checked and impoverished by its advent, which artificially reduced it to a confrontation between two poles, one dominant and the other dominated. All the profit that might have accrued to our cultures from free exchange with European cultures, and the extraordinary enrichment our internal debate might have known if it had been able to supplement its own terms through the assimilation of terms derived from abroad (as European art, for instance, was able to broaden its range by adopting a style known as 'African art'), all these fine hopes were betrayed and dashed because no genuine exchange has ever been possible in a climate of violence. Colonialism has thus arrested African cultures by reducing their internal pluralism, diminishing the discords and weakening the tensions from which they derived their vitality, leaving Africans with an artificial choice between cultural 'alienation' (which is supposedly connected with political betrayal) and cultural nationalism (the obverse of political nationalism and often a pathetic substitute for it).

What we must now realize is that this polarization has been disastrous and that its destruction is one of the first and most important conditions of our cultural renaissance. African culture must return to itself, to its internal pluralism and to its essential openness. We must therefore, as individuals, liberate ourselves psychologically and develop a free relationship both with African cultural tradition and with the cultural traditions of other continents. This will not be a process either of Westernization or of acculturation: it will simply be creative freedom, enriching the African tradition itself as an open system of options.

World civilization

There remains the well-known problem of world civilization. According to some, mankind is moving with great strides towards a sort of supra-culture, which will synthesize all regional cultures and smooth over their differences. But if we look at it carefully, we can see that this conception too is an over-simplification, since it treats regional cultures as complete and closed systems which are only now beginning to open up and exchange values with each other. This apparently dynamic conception of world civilization, as usually stated, is actually based on a static conception of regional cultures.

On the other hand, if we acknowledge the internal dynamism of these cultures and accept that they exist as cultures only in the form of contradictory debates taking place in particular societies, in specific geographical areas, then the reality of world civilization will be conceived no longer as a system of universally accepted values but rather as an extension of the debate to a world scale, which will give rise to new ideological, artistic and scientific conflicts that straddle various societies. In its present state world civilization is not a synthesis; it is an intensification of cultural conflicts which have always existed within every society and an awareness that these conflicts are ultimately the same in every society.

The situation on the cultural plane is thus analogous to the situation on the political plane. The late lamented Kwame Nkrumah was fond of repeating in his later works that the struggle against imperialism today is in fact an international class war, and that therefore the real opposition is no longer between an exploited nation and its colonial or neo-colonial metropolitan power but between the exploited classes in the neo-colonies and the bourgeoisies of these same neo-colonies, allied and subordinated to the bourgeoisies of the great imperialist powers.

No doubt it is impossible to reduce cultural conflicts entirely to political ones. Things are certainly much more complicated, and the cultural pluralism within each society will be infinitely richer than its class pluralism, which can always be reduced to the duality between an exploiting and an exploited class. Moreover, cultural conflict is certainly not as dramatic as political conflict. On the whole, it is less ruthless and venomous, since essentially it is not a clash between classes but a confrontation between people or groups who may belong to the same class and are united in a common search for truth.

But while cultural and political conflicts differ, they are nevertheless analogous. Just as the class struggle knows no frontiers and takes precedence over the conflicts between nations or ethnic groups, cultural debates now straddle the old boundaries and create new international solidarities between people and groups fighting for the same ideals and the same kinds of culture.

The role of the universities

Let us conclude with a few words on the role of universities. In the first place, it must be said that many African universities practise what may be called the Africanist ideology, which is another name for cultural nationalism on our continent. These universities deserve credit for having at last tackled the problems of the Africanization of their courses, after years of slavish imitation of the courses offered in the metropolitan countries, all offered in the name of cultural 'assimilation'. But Africanization often takes the form of a rabid particularism, which is extremely dangerous for our scientific culture.

The 'human sciences' are the most vulnerable of all disciplines to this danger. We no longer study sociology but 'African sociology' or even 'ethnology'; no longer history, but African history; instead of geography, African geography; instead of linguistics, African linguistics. This is no doubt a praiseworthy reaction to the false universalism of colonial culture, a legitimate attempt to explore the environment, natural and human. But it also carries a serious risk of theoretical imprisonment and, still worse, of hollow affirmations of the specificity of the phenomena under study, without any term of comparison.[9]

Perhaps the time has come to recognize that the most important thing today is not to study African cultures but to *live* them, not to exhibit them to ourselves or dissect them with scrupulous scientific objectivity but to practise them, not to digest them passively but to transform them.

In this respect the teaching of African languages, for instance, should give way to teaching *in* the African languages. Instead of using French or English to discuss the structures of Yoruba or Fon, we would do better to use Yoruba or Fon to discuss the structures of French or English and, more generally, to use African languages in advanced work in the various sciences: mathematics, physics, chemistry, biology, history, linguistics, etc. Rather than treat our languages as objects of science, we should practise them as vehicles for it – though they may need to be enriched and transformed if we are to raise them to the level of complexity necessary for modern scientific knowledge. This will obviously require an enormous amount of preparatory work, which only the universities can undertake.

What is needed, and what must be staged, is no less than a complete revolution. I hesitate to call it 'Copernican', for I am neither Kant nor Césaire. But Césaire was saying something very like this in his remarkable *Lettre à Maurice Thorez*,[10] which is still pertinent. In the matter of culture, we have got into the habit of exhibiting ourselves to ourselves and so looking at ourselves through the eyes of others. We ought now to restore a dimension of real experience to this display and revive the internal dramas and heartbreaks which are precisely what make it a culture; we must rouse the internal pluralism of our original culture, beneath which lies the false plurality of cultures, and we must now take sides within that culture, while putting to good use all the information acquired through contact with other traditions. We must look beyond the limited horizons imposed upon us by anthropologists, liberate the collective initiative of our peoples and thereby set our own creativity free.

Postscript

I

At a time when the gap between oppressors and oppressed is widening throughout our continent and political differences are becoming more radical, the ethnophilosopher claims that we have always been, still are and always will be unanimous. On every side we can see terror tightening its stranglehold on us, knocking the breath out of us and parching our throats; every word spoken spells danger and exposes us to untold brutality or may even cost us our lives; insolent neo-colonial state apparatuses parade in triumph, leaving a trail of intimidation, arbitrary arrest, torture and legal assassination and poisoning genuine thought at its source. And the official ideologue smiles, content, and declares: 'Alleluia, our ancestors have thought!'[1]

On one side, there is force – a brute, blind, savage force, a direct heir to colonial violence – trying to dictate to the minds and hearts of all; on the other, there are the bare hands of men and women so exploited and mystified that they make themselves active accomplices of their executioners: this is as close as you can get to a true description of the real face of contemporary Africa, behind the ideological folklore and the carnival variety of political 'colours', of official labels, and the divisive 'options' which nearly always turn out to be no more than superficial verbalisms.

It is against this political background that ethnophilosophical discourse is to be understood. If this discourse strikes us as futile, it is not only because of its utter unreality, its crass indifference to the daily tragedies of our increasingly Fascistic countries (for any scientific discourse is, in a sense, unreal), it is also and above all because in this context ethnophilosophy has a positive function to fulfil as a powerful opiate, as one of the mainsprings of the huge machine that is mounted against our consciences.

There was probably a time when this reminder served a useful purpose, when what we badly needed, in the face of colonial power and its positive attempts to depersonalize us, was the restoration of self-confidence and the reaffirmation of our creativity. In those circumstances ethnophilosophy could appear, among all the inventions of Western culture, as a form of discourse that could be profitably taken over and developed by colonial peoples for their liberation.

But today that discourse has lost its critical charge, its *truth*. Yesterday it was the language of the oppressed, today it is a discourse of power. Formerly a romantic protest against European pride, it is now an ideological placebo. The function of ethnophilosophy has changed: it is no longer a possible means of demystification but a powerful means of mystification in the hands of all those who have a vested interest in discouraging intellectual initiative because it prompts not living thought in our peoples but simply pious rumination on the past.

I have tried to show in this book the ambiguities and theoretical inadequacies which have led to this reversal: the reasons for it lie not in accidental historical circumstances but in the fact that this discourse was in principle vitiated from the outset, because its entire logic consists in playing on a homonymy, in developing *ad absurdum* the ambiguity of the word 'philosophy' in ordinary language. It is precisely for this reason that a purely political criticism of ethnophilosophy is insufficient. It is also necessary to mount a theoretical critique of it and to attack not only its contingent practical effects as an ideological discourse but also the concepts on which they are founded – concepts whose ambiguity explains, in the last analysis, the reversibility of these effects.

II

This is the kind of critique I have attempted in this book, whose oldest chapter dates (need I remind the reader?) from 1969. In the course of the book I have cited other critiques pointing in the same direction, particularly Marcien Towa's *Essai sur la problématique philosophique dans l'Afrique actuelle*.[2] I am in fundamental agreement with the main argument developed in this brief but concentrated piece of work. Its greatest merit is to have explored the political terrain in which the discourse of African ethnophilosophers unfolds, to have shown the necessity of recognizing there has been a change of line and an alteration in the political stakes and that these should produce 'a new philosophical orientation in Africa'. We should read and reread the marvellous passages in which Towa – while recognizing the 'underlying dialectic' which at the climax of classical imperialism gave rise to the 'project of a Bantu philosophy . . . born precisely of a revolt against the assertion of the essential and exclusive Westernness of philosophy'[3] – manages nevertheless to show why and how this project is now a thing of the past, why and how, with the accession of most of our countries to independence, it is now necessary to replace 'the quest for originality and difference as a certificate of humanity . . . by a quest for ways and means of achieving power as an inevitable condition for the affirmation of both our humanity and our freedom'.[4]

On the one hand, originality; on the other, power. This change of perspective profoundly modifies our relation with our own cultural past: we can now regard it coolly, critically, without complacency or self-satisfaction, and try to discover not our unrecognized greatness or nobility but the secret of our defeat by the West. What Towa proposes is nothing less than 'revolutionary iconoclasm', a 'destruction of traditional idols' which will enable us to 'welcome and assimilate the spirit of Europe, the secret of her power and of her victory over us'.[5] Rather than pitting our culture against that of Europe, we must, for the sake of our own real liberation, take up European science and technology; and to attain this goal, we must begin by putting to work the European concept of philosophy that goes hand in hand with this science and technology and by developing free and critical thinking on the subject of our present realities.

The main interest of Towa's analysis lies in the emphasis that he places on science as a principle of power and on its relationship with philosophy, in the courage with which he affirms the 'necessity of freedom of thought and freedom in general for the development of science and therefore also indirectly of power'.[6]

III

However, Towa's book has its limitations. We noted above that when he thought he was criticizing ethnophilosophy in general he was in fact criticizing only *African* ethnophilosophy. This has at least two consequences: (1) ethnophilosophy in general is treated as a by-product, 'a late aspect of the negritude movement',[7] whereas in fact it antedates that movement and extends well beyond the African continent; (2) whereas the discourse of African philosophers is subjected to searching criticism, European ethnophilosophy gets off more or less scot-free. Thus Tempels gets a prize because, soon after Masson-Oursel, he had the courage to challenge the alleged Western monopoly of reason from within European culture.[8] So Towa overlooks the limitations of Tempels' initiative and is silent also on the ambiguities of Tempels' positive project, except for a brief footnote reference to Eboussi-Boulaga's criticism at the beginning of the second chapter. Nor does Towa mention the wide methodological gulf separating the attitude of Masson-Oursel, who starts from an analysis of the *history of thought*, from the attitude of the Belgian missionary, which is actually based on a rejection of that history.

There is a further flaw in Towa's work. Through this polemical concept of ethnophilosophy Towa wishes to attack only the *method* of the philosophers of negritude, not their *object*. His reproach is that they confuse the procedures of ethnology with those of philosophy and slide surreptitiously from one to the other. The philosophers of negritude begin by describing objectively, with the scientific detachment that (according to Towa) befits the ethnologist, the facts of African cultural life – beliefs, myths, rituals, etc. – but then they suddenly drop this descriptive approach and begin to defend these values, without making an attempt at justifying their commitment to them, as philosophers would have done. It is this hybrid method, 'neither purely philosophical nor purely ethnological', that Towa stigmatizes under the name of ethnophilosophy. But he hardly questions the actual status of the object to which this equivocal approach has been addressed, namely, philosophy as a collective system of beliefs which secures the unanimity of all members of a society. And yet Towa's methodological critique of ethnophilosophy brings him to the brink of this more radical critique. He recognizes, indeed, that ethnophilosophers habitually project their own ideas and values on to the African tradition and then claim that they simply found them as objects. But it requires only a little careful reflection on this process of projection (or retrojection, as Towa prefers to call it) to see that it is not just one of several possible ethnophilosophical procedures; it is the only possible method for the philosopher of negritude, the basic gesture of ethnophilosophy in general (and not only African ethnophilosophy) as a mystified discourse and a dreamlike description of a collective thought that exists only in the inventor's head.

Failing to pursue his critique to this conclusion, Towa is unaware of the remnants of ethnophilosophy which cling to a work like *Consciencism*, a book which he admires enormously, even proposing it as a model for the new orientation of philosophy in Africa.[9] He fails to see that this book, although far removed from classical ethnophilosophy, is still a complete vehicle for the belief in unanimism which is the real cornerstone of ethnophilosophy.

A word now on the new role assigned by Towa to philosophy in Africa. Let us say straightaway that this problem envelops another, the problem of the specificity of philosophy in general in relation to other forms of discourse – that is to say, whether philosophy has a distinct object, like every science, or whether it is defined only by its method, as being, for instance, a critical reflection or ceaseless questioning. On this difficult problem all I can do now is to propose one or two tentative hypotheses. But what is certain is that those offered by Towa elicit serious reservations. To say that the task of philosophy is 'the investigation of our deepest aims and of the direction that should be given to our existence',[10] or again 'the definition. . .of what we should be, of our basic and still unrealized capacity to change',[11] or 'the conceptual elucidation of our future selves in a world we must bring into being in the place of this one'[12] is to reduce philosophy to the role of an ideological comment on a fundamentally political project. For it is *politics* and nothing else, politics in the deepest sense of the word, that requires us to abandon the cult of difference in favour of material power. It is *politics* and nothing else that requires us to open ourselves to others and particularly to take possession of European culture, philosophy and science in order to assimilate and master them. It is therefore *politics* that commands us to leave the well-worn paths of ethnophilosophy and adopt a critical attitude towards our cultural past. *Politics*: our vision of the destiny of our people and, in this context, the project of our real and effective liberation. But if this is so, it is difficult to see what philosophy has to do with it: it can do no more than repeat, in pointlessly scholarly language, a completely self-sufficient political discourse – unless, of course, it has something else to say, something *different* from this political discourse, in which case the relationship between the two discourses becomes infinitely problematic. According to the first hypothesis philosophy is tautological; according to the second, it is a tissue of arbitrary assertions. It is here that my critique of *Consciencism* finds its proper application. It is no accident that Towa takes this book as a model, for he shares Nkrumah's belief in what we have called the metaphysical illusion, the belief in a metaphysical dimension to politics. This belief inevitably leads people to put forward all sorts of unprovable theological (or indeed anti-theological) ideas on behalf of political positions which may well, nevertheless, be perfectly correct.

For my part, I affirm the autonomy of the political, and I ask that it be granted its own consistency. Metaphysical stances have too often served as alibis while distracting attention from real political problems. Ideological purring, even when it is revolutionary, often does nothing except conceal the most abject and indefensible actions, a lesson which we are only now beginning to learn.

So, if philosophy is to have a meaning, it cannot be a tautological redundancy. Although it is itself determined in the last instance by a political project, it cannot be reduced to a mere commentary on it. It must place itself on the terrain of science itself, as the ultimate source of the power that we seek, and it must contribute in some way to its progress. The prime problem of philosophy in present-day Africa is therefore how far it can contribute to the development of science. This is an immense problem, calling for inquiries into the history of the sciences and of philosophy, a definition of their actual relations in the past and their possible relations now. Such an orientation would mean that our philosophy courses would concentrate not on the sort of existential meditation on 'what we should be' advocated by Towa but on instruction in those philosophical disciplines most likely to foster the development of scientific thought in Africa: logic, the history of the sciences, epistemology, the history of technology, etc. – and, of course, the indispensable study of the history of philosophy.

The position here defended is neither scientistic nor positivistic. On the contrary, it tries to lure philosophers away from their fantasies and daydreams and destroys the naïve positivism of those half-baked scientists who are too inclined to see only the results of their science and to forget the long, uncertain and winding paths that led up to them. On the other hand, the refusal to absorb philosophy into politics by no means excludes the possibility of a philosophical theory of the political. On the contrary, it is precisely the total politicization of philosophical discourse that constitutes the most serious obstacle to any theory of the political, since one of the tasks of such a theory would be to analyse the real functioning of ideologies and to identify the forms, the modalities and the multiple sources of political mystification. The theory of politics as a theory of ideological discourses is thus indirectly linked with the theory of science, which is the analysis of another particular form of discourse. The theory of politics is not a political theory any more than the theory of science is, although in the last analysis, like every other discipline, its motivation derives from a political project.

A final difference between Towa's position and my own: the very title of his *Essay . . .* betrays embarrassment. I do not believe that present-day Africa simply has a 'philosophical problematic', but there is, without the slightest doubt, an African *philosophy*, a set of *discourses*, a *literature* conveying this 'philosophical problematic' – an alienated literature no doubt, since it conveys an essentially alienated problematic, but a materially real literature, inscribed, for better or no doubt for worse, in the cultural history of our peoples. Thus we begin where Towa leaves off, with a clear affirmation of something which he suggests only as a tentative hypothesis at the end of his discussion: the real existence of African philosophical works. The basis of this affirmation is the recognition of the irreducible material reality of texts and an emphasis on explicit discourse as distinct from allegedly implicit thoughts, whatever the inadequacies of that text or discourse may be. Our position on this point is materialist: philosophy is above all a cultural fact with an objective social existence, and it must be approached empirically rather than postulated, like the sedative power of opium, as the conclusion of a process of induction.

IV

Having recognized the existence of African philosophical texts, it is possible to evaluate them and, in the first place, to investigate their concept of themselves and of philosophy. This is what has been attempted in the first part of this book, through a critique of the ethnological conception of philosophy and a re-examination of the concept of philosophy as it has always functioned in the history of Western philosophy. The second part of the book consists essentially of a fairly arbitrary set of case studies within this already abundant literature. It is obviously incomplete, but its main aim is to illustrate, and possibly to begin to realize, the ambitious project of a history of African philosophy. The discussion of cultural pluralism in the last chapter is part of this same project and is complementary to our critique of unanimism. No doubt the discussion is inadequate and needs to be taken further, but it was necessary to include it in order to forestall certain objections by exposing some of the theoretical assumptions behind the popular but highly ambiguous notions of Westernness, Africanness, Europeanness, etc. – in short all the notions which tend to link, explicitly or implicitly, certain systems of values to certain regions of the globe or geographical areas. For it is imperative to go that far, to investigate the limits of such seemingly simple and self-evident ideas, if we are to produce a complete critique of ethnophilosophy.

I start from the assumption that values are no one's property, that no intrinsic necessity lies behind their distribution across various civilizations or their changing relative importance; for instance, if science is today more spectacularly developed in Europe than in Africa, this is due not to the specific and unique qualities of the white race but to a particularly favourable set of circumstances. This historical accident does not make science an essentially European value – any more than syphilis, introduced into Amerindian societies by the first visitors from the Old World, is an essentially European disease. Cultural values are like venereal diseases: they flourish here and there, develop in one place rather than another according to whether the environment is more or less favourable; but this purely historical accident cannot justify any claim to ownership or, for that matter, to immunity.

It is possible that it is not immediately obvious what is at stake in this critique. From the present point of view, the effect of the critique is to relativize our ideas of Africanness, Westernness, etc., by making them purely formal concepts whose content cannot be fixed once and for all but is essentially open, plurivocal and contradictory. We wish, in fact, to extend the process of demythologization (with apologies for this barbaric term!) from the concept of Africa to the concepts of other continents, by showing that they can be defined only as empirical, geographical concepts, not at all as moral or metaphysical ideas. This completely destroys the European claim to a monopoly of logical reason, science and technology as cultural phenomena and also undermines such terms as 'Europeanization', 'Westernization', 'acculturation', 'cultural borrowing', etc., and especially 'cultural alienation', all of them used to characterize some of the changes that are taking place in the contemporary history of African cultures. In short, it exposes all the subtle ruses of the cult of Difference. This relativization of historical cultures provides the justification for a 'revolutionary iconoclasm', a thorough subversion of our cultural heritage in terms of our present projects, our *politics*.

And yet. . .! the reader might say. And yet. . . . Civilizations exist; the cultural heritage cannot be ignored. It is first and foremost through that heritage that a people defines itself in relation to others and acquires an identity. Agreed, agreed. But I would just add that such a heritage is never univocal, and that we must learn to recognize it as plurivocal and contradictory and to discover behind the frozen appearances the internal principle of transformation and renewal.

This applies, of course, to African thought too. When one observes the daily life in our cities and countryside and tries to investigate certain practices, rituals and behaviours, one cannot help feeling that they are really institutionalized manifestations of collective codes of conduct, patterns of thought which, viewed as a whole, can constitute what might be called a practical ideology. Moreover, as we have said, quite apart from this practical ideology there exists a considerable body of oral literature, esoteric or exoteric, the importance of which we are only beginning to suspect. We must have the patience to study it, analyse it, investigate its logic, its function and its limits.

So let there be no mistake about it: I have never for a moment in this essay argued that pre-colonial Africa was an intellectual *tabula rasa*. On the contrary, my view is that every society in the world possesses practico-theoretical codes or 'practical ideologies' on the one hand and, on the other, written or oral texts, transmitted from generation to generation.

But this admission is different from, and indeed totally opposed to, the project of ethnophilosophy. Ethnophilosophy *misses* the true nature of practical ideology; it cannot see it as it really is, in its essence, as a set of schemes each with its own history and its own logic, like the backyard of the do-it-yourself man; it cannot understand the patchwork quality of this makeshift arrangement of bits and pieces, nor the very particular coherence of its residual 'logic', because it always assumes that this field of practical ideology must contain a single, coherent system with a clear theoretical logic. This totally obscures the obvious question of the differential histories of the various elements of the patchwork and the history of their coming together, their reciprocal transformations, their possible future. More serious still is the fact that what appears at first sight to be the clear, practical ideology (in the singular) of a group is never anything more than its *dominant* practical ideology. Careful observers will refuse to accept the dominant ideology at face value or to assume that it can be attributed to all members of the group. Nor will they try to extract from it a philosophical theory that is supposed to command the assent of the community as a whole. They will try to discover what is masked by this apparent unanimity, the whole spectrum of non-dominant ideologies or at least the diverse differential relations to the dominant ideology.

Like practical ideology, oral literature is utterly distorted by its treatment in ethnophilosophical discourse. Ethnophilosophers seize hold of religious, historical, poetical and moral texts, etc., and extract violently from them what they take to be their 'substantific marrow': a philosophy. In the process the original flavour of these texts, their sap, their meaning and, in the end, their theoretical significance itself are lost. Worse still, this conceals their historical relativity as texts produced at a given time by an individual or a group of individuals motivated by specific interests which might have placed him or them in conflict with other individuals or groups of individuals in the same community. In his interesting study of Dahomey in the eighteenth century Georg Elwert has shown how the same facts were differently interpreted in 'popular tradition' and 'court tradition'.[13] And this can only mean that what we commonly call *oral tradition* in the singular is an artificial yoking of distinct traditions, which may be concordant or discordant but which we must learn to recognize as such. Ethnophilosophers neglect this plurality, this irreducible polysemy of discourses. They impoverish African literature by reducing all the genres to one and by giving its infinite variety a single metaphysical common denominator.

In short, we have not been trying to deny the existence of African thought. Our contention is that it deserves to be taken far more seriously than it is by the ethnophilosophers and that instead of reducing it to a closed and dogmatic system, we must exploit its richness, its contradictions, its life.

V

I would like to conclude by returning to Nkrumah. The two chapters about him in this book were written more than three years ago, with an eye on the current political and ideological situation in the particular corner of the world where history has deposited me. The rightist myth of 'Nkrumaism', as well as Nkrumah's own determination, at one stage in his career, to distance himself from Marxism, seemed at the time to be one of the subtler effects of the cult of Difference which was then ravaging my own country.

Today I would still maintain the main lines of this critique. But it needs to be reviewed, completed and, on some points, clarified to take account of a changed situation.

To mention one example, I would no longer use in such a cut-and-dried way the phrases 'rightist or leftist readings', 'rightist or leftist critique', etc., although the phrases do retain their value within the limits of those studies on Nkrumah. I certainly still believe that it is politically disastrous to shut up an author in a closed system, to flatten a work by stripping it of its tensions, of its evolution, by abstracting it from its historical context and the concrete problems it strove to solve. This applies not only to Nkrumah but also, even more, to the great revolutionary thinkers like Marx, Engels, Lenin, Mao. To be a Marxist today is not to be content with a few stereotyped phrases from the first part of the *German Ideology*, or Stalin's *Dialectical and Historical Materialism*, or Politzer's *Elementary Principles of Philosophy*. To be a Marxist one must actually *read* Marx and his followers, identify the problematic behind the phrases and understand its genesis and evolution; one must assimilate the doctrine so that one can *think Marx* and *use his theory in analysing actual historical situations* with a view to their being called in question and their revolutionary transformation.

I also continue to regard as suspect a critique which, in order to discredit a work, seeks to discredit its author. This expedient was adopted by many of the critics of Nkrumah after his fall. Bereft of *political* arguments, they relied on a purely psychological portrait of Nkrumah as maniac, megalomaniac, paranoiac and so on. Psychologism in political analysis is a sure sign of lack of political arguments: it is no wonder that it should be the favourite mode of argument for petty thinkers and all those who have literally nothing to say about politics.

Finally, I continue to believe that it is no accident that the word 'Nkrumaism' was invented by the rightists in the CPP in order to mask the socialist content of the party programme and of Nkrumah's thought.

Yes, but in attempting to express these theoretical and political oppositions in terms of rightist or leftist readings or critiques, I may have given the impression of trying to divide the world into two halves. These cut-and-dried antitheses are uncomfortably reminiscent of the notorious Stalinist distinction between bourgeois and proletarian science. Taken literally, they may lead to an attempt to batten scientific life mechanically to political life so as to make the former an immediate reflection of the latter, thus emptying it of its richness, of its essential open-endedness.

But the most serious matter is that the notions of right and left have once again become very confused in Africa. It is no longer possible to define them simply in terms of imperialism (campaigning for liberation on the one hand, submitting to imperialism on the other) or even of Marxism (verbal loyalty on the one hand, visceral hostility on the other). For we now know that it is one thing to proclaim oneself an anti-imperialist or a Marxist-Leninist and quite another thing to be one. It is not language but practice that determines whether a person or a regime is objectively on the right or on the left. And we are beginning to realize that practice can follow very different principles from those officially proclaimed – indeed, that such a gap is the rule rather than the exception and can lead to terrible tragedies. The most revolutionary ideology can be put to an objectively reactionary use, and individuals or regimes which claim to belong to the left do not necessarily do so. In every case we must look beneath the internal and external propaganda, beneath official statements at international congresses, and analyse the nature of the relations between the state and the people, the degree of real mass participation in public affairs and the people's real capacity to *control* the power machine and not merely *applaud* it.

In an excellent Marxist critique of the Nkrumah regime[14] Bob Fitch and Mary Oppenheimer have shown the wide gap that existed between the international reputation of the regime, universally regarded as one of the most left-wing in Africa, and its political and economic practice. I would almost say that the same sort of study is imperative today in all those African states that call themselves revolutionary. We would then be able to see why these regimes are so often judged differently according to whether they are seen from outside, through their official propaganda and international declarations, or from inside, through the weight and concrete methods of their oppressive and repressive apparatuses.

The Nkrumah regime is particularly interesting because of its archetypal character. We have paid it so much attention both because of the immense optimism it initially inspired and subsequently disappointed and because it is strikingly similar to many present-day regimes. We need to meditate today upon these dashed hopes, analyse the reasons for failure and draw lessons for the future from the experience.

The reader may wonder why we called consciencism 'a

philosophy in the image of the CPP'. The reason why we criticized Nkrumah's movement is that it always wanted to be a mass organization without a *vanguard* party and therefore had no way of acquiring the homogeneous social base it needed in order to tackle the economic and social objectives of the 'second revolution'. The weakness of *Consciencism*, however, appears to be exactly the reverse: it tried to create philosophical unanimity among CPP militants and throughout African revolution in general, and it also tried to elicit from them all a sincere commitment to a single philosophical doctrine. Thus we are confronted with basic social heterogeneity at the base on the one hand and a demand for theoretical homogeneity on the other. This situation seems contradictory, and one does not readily see how the one could reflect the other.

But the truth is that from the first gesture to the second there is a remarkable consistency between the two attitudes. The demand for unanimity becomes all the stronger and more urgent as real unity becomes more precarious. There was an illusion that metaphysical unanimity could counterbalance conflicts of interest at the base. Conversely, metaphysical unity would not have seemed necessary if there had been a real group solidarity, founded on an identity or convergence of material interests. Thus the project of *Consciencism* is indeed in the image of the CPP, but not a direct image, an inverted one. Nkrumah's ambitious philosophical synthesis, which is supposed to win everybody's agreement, makes sense only as an imaginary antidote to intractable material conflict. However, when there is a real community of political options, directly or indirectly based on a community of economic interests, then a diversity of opinion on such-and-such a political problem and, *a fortiori*, on such-and-such a philosophical or scientific problem will not be regarded as evil; and, more generally, open criticism, frank and loyal disagreement, will be experienced as a source of richness and an essential ingredient of progress.

Thus our critique of ethnophilosophy leads us to question unanimism in all its forms. Conversely, it highlights the need to promote in our countries a philosophical and scientific tradition of the highest quality, made up of a plurality of conflicting researches. Force will never bring unity of thought to our peoples. What is needed is the recognition of everyone's right to self-expression, criticism and even error.

I shall add a last word: if we wish to put an end to the ideological confusion now raging in our countries and to discover the true face of Marxist theory and ideology beneath all the corrupt distortions, then it will not be enough to denounce particular abuses and confusions as and when they arise. We must promote positively a *Marxist theoretical tradition* in our countries – a contradictory scientific debate around the work of Marx and his followers. For let us not forget this: Marxism itself is a *tradition*, a plural debate based on the theoretical foundations laid by Marx. There have been plenty of disagreements within this tradition, but the progress of Marxist thought has been possible thanks to public debates between Lenin and Rosa Luxemburg or between Lenin and his fellow countrymen Pleckhanov, Bukharin, Bazarov, Trotsky, etc., and thanks to the theoretical individuality of thinkers like Gramsci or Mao, to cite only the greatest among hundreds.

There is still a vacuum in Africa. We learned our Marxism from popular works and, having swallowed it in little pills, we used to enjoy whispering about it in tightly closed circles. I do not wish to minimize the scale of the work accomplished, even in those conditions. After all, it would have been difficult to do anything else at a time when our elders and betters had to find their own way to Marxism, at their own risk and in semi-clandestine circumstances – at a time, moreover, when Stalinism was still dominant, stifling all authentic research and dogmatizing at the expense of Marx and Lenin. We must therefore be grateful to them for having realized, in these difficult circumstances, that Marxism was not as the bourgeois university system wanted to show it. But on the whole the record is meagre. We have failed to develop this heritage, and now we are powerless to prevent it from being taken over shamelessly by completely cynical and reactionary political groups, aided and abetted, it is true, by those of us for whom dialectics is a subtle way of justifying their own impatience and thirst for power. There is a danger that the time may soon come when, in the name of Marxism, we will be forbidden to read Marx.

The only solution is that here and now, in the semi-silence in which we are compelled to work, we should set about broadening our knowledge of Marx and the rich tradition he inaugurated and thus stamp out once and for all our unanimist and dogmatic prejudices: we must restore to theory its birthright. In that way our *politics* will become clearer and, in spite of current difficulties, more effective in the long term.

Notes and references

Introduction

1 Cf. Robert July, *The Origins of Modern African Thought* (Faber 1968).
2 Peter Bodunrin, 'The Problems of, and Prescriptions for, an Action Philosophy in Africa', paper delivered at the Colloquium on the Place and Role of the Humanities in Africa Today, University of Ghana, Legon, April 1975, p. 5.
3 Lucien Lévy-Bruhl, *Les fonctions mentales dans les sociétés inférieures* (Paris 1910).
4 Lucien Lévy-Bruhl, *La mentalité primitive* (Paris 1922; 4th ed., Paris 1960). See also Jean Cazeneuve, *La mentalité archaïque* (Paris 1961).
5 Lévy-Bruhl, *Les fonctions mentales*, pp. 505–6. (My translation.)
6 Lucien Lévy-Bruhl, *Carnets* (Paris 1939).
7 See his article, 'Native self-government', in *Foreign Affairs*, 1944.
8 Marcel Griaule, *Dieu d'eau* (Paris: Editions du Chêne 1948); Germaine Dieterlen, *Essai sur la religion bambara* (Paris 1951).
9 This current is represented in the British school of anthropology by the work of Evans-Pritchard and Darryl-Forde.
10 Placide Tempels, *Bantu Philosophy*, English translation (Paris: Présence Africaine 1959), p. 16.
11 ibid., p. 23.
12 ibid., p. 35.
13 ibid., p. 121.
14 Gérard Leclerc, *Anthropologie et colonialisme* (Paris 1972), p. 170.
15 Léopold Sédar Senghor, *Les Fondements de l'africanité* (Paris 1967).
16 Léopold Sédar Senghor, *Liberté I* (Paris: Seuil 1964).
17 Bergson's *Les deux sources de la morale et de la religion* and *L'Evolution créatrice* probably exerted the greatest influence on Senghor's thinking.
18 Janheinz Jahn, in his *Muntu*, published in an English translation (1961), has helped to popularize Kagamé's system.
19 In addition to *Nations nègres et culture* (Paris: Présence Africaine 1954), Diop's other major publications are: *L'Afrique noire précoloniale* (Paris), *L'Unité culturelle de l'Afrique noire* (Paris 1959) and *Antériorité des civilisations nègres* (Paris 1967).

20 See, in particular, his paper entitled 'Existe-t-il une philosophie africaine?' in Claude Sumner (ed.) *African Philosophy* – *Philosophie Africaine* (Addis-Ababa 1980).

21 Frantz Fanon, *Les Damnés de la terre* (Paris 1961), p. 164. (My translation.)

22 Stanislas Adotevi, *Négritude et négrologues* (Paris).

23 Marcien Towa, *Essai sur la problématique philosophique dans l'Afrique actuelle* (Yaoundé: Editions Clé 1971), pp. 51–2.

24 ibid., p. 41.

25 Towa, *L'Idée d'une philosophie négro-africaine* (Yaoundé: Editions Clé 1979), p. 112.

26 See Claude Lévi-Strauss, *Le Totémisme aujourd'hui* (Paris 1962) and *La Pensée sauvage* (Paris 1962).

27 The points summarized here are taken principally from the following: Pathé Diagne, *L'Euro-philosophie et la pensée négro-africaine* (Dakar 1981); Niamey Koffi, 'L'impensé de Towa et de Hountondji', in Claude Sumner, *African Philosophy*; Olabiyi Yai, 'Théorie et pratique en philosophie africaine: misère de la philosophie spéculative', *Présence Africaine*, no. 108 (1978). An abridged English version of the last-named article had earlier been published in *Second Order*, University of Ife, vol. II, no. 2 (1977).

28 See Peter Bodunrin, 'The question of African philosophy', *Philosophy*, no. 56 (1981); Henry Oruka, 'Four trends in current African philosophy', Kwasi Wiredu, 'What is African philosophy?', both papers presented at the conference referred to in note 2 above; for Wiredu, see also *Philosophy and an African Culture* (Cambridge 1980), especially the first four chapters.

29 Paulin Hountondji, 'Occidentalisme, élitisme: réponse à deux critiques', *Recherche, Pédagogie et Culture*, Paris, no. 56 (January–March 1982).

1 An alienated literature

1 Here is a minimal bibliography: W. Abraham, *The Mind of Africa* (Weidenfeld & Nicolson 1962); Jean-Calvin Bahoken, *Clairières métaphysiques africaines* (Paris: Présence Africaine 1967); Aimé Césaire, *Discours sur le colonialisme* (Paris: Editions Réclame 1950; Several reprints by Présence Africaine); Alioune Diop, 'Niam M'Paya ou de la fin que dévorent les moyens', preface to P. Tempels, *La Philosophie bantoue* (Paris: Présence Africaine 1949); Fabien Eboussi-Boulaga, 'Le Bantou problématique', *Présence Africaine*, no. 66 (1968); Frantz Fanon, *Peau noire, masques blancs* (Paris: Seuil 1952); Frantz Fanon, *Les Damnés de la terre* (Paris: Maspero 1968); Basile-Juleat Fouda, 'La Philosophie négro-africaine de l'existence' (unpublished doctoral

thesis, Lille, Faculté des Lettres, 1967); Alexis Kagamé, *La Philo-sophie bantou-rwandaise de l'être* (Brussels 1956); François-Marie Lufuluabo, *Vers une théodicée bantoue* (Tournai: Casterman 1962); François-Marie Lufuluabo, *La Notion luba–bantoue de l'être* (Tournai: Casterman 1964); Vincent Mulago, *Un visage africain du christianisme* (Paris: Présence Africaine 1965); A. Makarakiza, *La Dialectique des Barundi* (Brussels 1959); Alassane N'Daw, 'Peut-on parler d'une pensée africaine?', *Présence Africaine*, no. 58 (1966); Kwame Nkrumah, *Consciencism* (Heinemann 1964); Léopold Sédar Senghor, *Nation et voie africaine du socialisme* (Paris: Présence Africaine 1961); Léopold Sédar Senghor, *Liberté I. Négritude et humanisme* (Paris: Seuil 1964).

The reader may also wish to include the present book and some earlier articles of mine: 'Charabia et Mauvaise Conscience: psycho-logie du langage chez les intellectuels colonisés', *Présence Africaine*, no. 61 (1967); 'Pourquoi la théorie?', *Bulletin de liaison de la Commis-sion Inter-africaine de Philosophie*, Société Africaine de Culture, no. 3 (Paris: Présence Africaine 1969); 'Le Problème actuel de la philo-sophie africaine', in *Contemporary Philosophy. A Survey*, ed. Raymond Klibansky, vol. IV (Florence: La Nuova Italia Editrice 1971).

I have cited only African authors, in accordance with my definition of African philosophy. Non-African Africanists are not included. It is for the readers to judge whether I am justified after they have read the book.

But I have included West Indians like Aimé Césaire and Frantz Fanon. They are African of the Diaspora, and although they are not, and do not claim to be, philosophers, they afford us the means of conducting a fruitful political criticism of a certain form of philosophy.

To be complete the list should also include all the doctoral theses and other similar works by African students and researchers in philosophy, even if they bear on the most classical European authors, for they are works of philosophy by Africans. Our 'naïve' definition of African philosophy as a set of texts enables us to see the internal discords of that literature, torn between a tragic renunciation of African allegiances on the one hand and imprisonment within an 'Africanist' ideology, itself of non-African origin, on the other. The only reason, therefore, for not citing texts in this category is that I have not been able to make an exhaustive inventory of it or even a representative choice.

Finally, North-African literature is omitted for material reasons alone. It is, of course, an integral part of African literature in general, although it constitutes a comparatively autonomous subset, no less than the black African literature on which we focus here. One day it would be useful to investigate systematically the problem of the real unity which underlies the obvious differences between these two literatures.

2   Rev. Father Placide Tempels, *La Philosophie bantoue*, translated from the Dutch by A. Rubbens (Paris: Présence Africaine 1949). A first translation had been published in 1945 by Editions Lovania, Elisabethville (now Lubumbashi). Présence Africaine has recently printed its third edition, which says a good deal! References are to the 1961 edition.

3   Cf. Tempels, *La Philosophie bantoue*:

> A better understanding of the field of Bantu thought is equally necessary for all those who are called upon to live among the natives. Therefore this first concerns colonials, but more especially those who are charged with the administration and justice of the Blacks, all those who wish to see a fruitful development of clan law, in short all those who want to civilize, educate, raise the Bantus. But if this concerns all colonials of good will, it is addressed more particularly to missionaries. (p. 17)

4   In the last resort, this is perhaps the basic vice of ethnology in general (and not only of ethnophilosophy). Lévy-Bruhl's work at least had the merit of displaying, in a naïve and clumsy way, how ethnological discourse has always depended on an ethnocentric attitude itself dictated by a concrete historical situation ('primitive' societies were in fact always societies dominated by imperialism). From this point of view, Lévy-Bruhl's belated self-criticism in his *Carnets* is far from being as radical as is sometimes supposed, for it retains the central notion of 'primitivity' and fails to explain the reasons for his earlier misconceptions.

   Many recent ethnologists have tried to practise a neutral ethnology, free of value judgements and of racism and ethnocentrism. This intention may be praiseworthy in itself, but it does not prevent ethnology, as a type of discourse, from resting, as much as ever, on an ideological foundation. Ethnology (or anthropology, or whatever we care to call it) always assumes what it wants to prove, i.e. a real distinction between its object and that of sociology in general, the essential difference between 'primitive' (or perhaps 'archaic') societies and other societies. On the other hand, it also attempts to abstract from the real power relationship between these societies and the others – in other words, imperialism. In any case, it is clear that the societies selected for study by anthropology are in fact always dominated societies and that the scholarly discourse of the anthropologist has meaning only in a scientific debate originating elsewhere (in the dominant classes of the dominating societies) and in which these peoples do not participate. More detailed analysis is, of course, necessary here.

5   Tempels, *La Philosophie bantoue*, pp. 35–6.

6   ibid., p. 45.

7   *Discours sur le colonialisme*, 4th ed. (Paris: Présence Africaine 1962), p. 44.

8   This applies, of course, to only one of the currents of African philosophy. A glance at the bibliography above will show that it has always provoked contestations within African philosophy itself (within African *philosophical literature*) and that it coexists with other currents, though these are relatively insignificant.

9   Kagamé, *La Philosophie bantou–rwandaise de l'être*, p. 8.

10   ibid., pp. 17, 23.

11   Kagamé presents his analysis as a reflection on the particular structures of the Kinyarwanda language. These structures are seen as delineating a kind of articulation of reality, a sort of grid through which the Rwandais perceives the world. Hence the idea of constructing a table of Bantu ontological categories, doing for Kinyarwanda what Aristotle, according to Kagamé, did for Greek. The results of the inquiry are by no means unattractive. Kagamé proposes four Bantu metaphysical categories, which he aligns with Aristotle's in the following table:

1 *Umuntu* (pl. *abantu*): man, being endowed with intelligence	
2 *Ikuntu* (pl. *ibintu*): thing, being without intelligence	1 Substance
3 Ahantu: time–place	2 Time
	3 Place
	4 Quantity
	5 Quality
	6 Relation
4 *Ukuntu*: modality	7 Action
	8 Passion
	9 Position
	10 Possession

This table calls for a number of remarks:

(1)   The first two categories fracture the unity of the Aristotelian concept of substance and make it appear irremediably ambiguous. Man and things are not part of the same genus but constitute two radically different genera. More accurately, man is the originary category in relation to which things are thinkable. These, by definition, are non-man, *ibintu*, beings without intelligence (a category which includes, let us not forget, minerals and vegetables as well as animals).

(2)   The originary concept of man can only be defined in tautological terms. Man is the sole species of a unique genus. This is why Kagamé can write:

Some Europeans have taken great pleasure in the 'naiveté' of the Bantus, when asked '*Umuntu ni iki?*' ('What is man?'). Called upon to give a definition of the being endowed with intelligence, our Bantus, after much embarrassment, ended up by answering: '*Umuntu, ni umuntu nyine!*' ('Man!'), precisely, is which meant something like this: 'By formulating the question, you have yourself given the answer, and it is impossible to explain further! You have stated the genus and the unique species! What would you answer if you were asked: 'What is the rational animal (i.e. man)?' (ibid., p. 118)

We may ask ourselves, however, to what extent the Bantus' embarrassment described here is not due rather to the intrinsic difficulty of the question asked (the most difficult of all questions, after all). The average European would certainly have been equally embarrassed and would have answered no less 'naïvely' than the Bantu, even though European languages enable the concept of man to be divided into simpler categories.

But perhaps the most serious difficulty concerns the interpretation given by Kagamé of Aristotle's project (which inspired him). No doubt Aristotle's ontology was connected with the structures of the Greek language, but this should not lead us, surely, to underestimate the originality of his project, which was intended not so much to explore the actual structures of the Greek language as to transcend all such contingencies by grounding language in a universal and necessary order.

12 ibid., p. 39.
13 ibid., p. 27.
14 ibid., particularly pp. 64–70.
15 ibid., pp. 121–2.
16 The reader may have recognized here the title of a book by Paul Ricoeur, *Le Conflit des interprétations* (Paris: Seuil 1969). Without any doubt, the problem of African 'philosophy' refers us back to the problem of hermeneutics. The discourse of ethnophilosophers, be they European or African, offers us the baffling spectacle of an imaginary interpretation with no textual support, of a genuinely 'free' interpretation, inebriated and entirely at the mercy of the interpreter, a dizzy and unconscious freedom which takes itself to be *translating* a text which does not actually exist and which is therefore unaware of its own *creativity*. By this action the interpreter disqualifies himself from reaching any *truth* whatsoever, since truth requires that freedom be limited, that it bow to an order that is not purely imaginary and that it be aware both of this order *and* of its own margin of creativity. Truth is attainable only if the interpreter's freedom is based on the nature of the text to be interpreted; it presupposes that the text *and* the interpreter's discourse remain rigorously within the same category, i.e. the same univocal field. Aristotle's doctrine of the 'genera of being' means just this.

17   Cf. Kagamé's other works, particularly: *La Poésie dynastique au Rwanda* (Brussels 1951); *Le Code des institutions politiques du Rwanda précolonial* (Brussels 1952); *Les Organisations socio-familiales de l'ancien Rwanda* (Brussels 1954).

18   European ethnophilosophy is still going strong. No wonder, if one remembers the praise lavished by a philosopher of Bachelard's rank (followed in this by Albert Camus, Louis Lavelle, Gabriel Marcel, Chombard de Lauwe, Jean Wahl, etc.) on a book as equivocal as *Bantu Philosophy* (cf. 'Témoignages sur *La Philosophie bantoue* du Père Tempels', *Présence Africaine*, no. 7, 1949). So, if we want to break out of the vicious circle of ethnocentric prejudice, must we indiscriminately praise any work, whatever its quality, which attempts, equivocally, a problematic rehabilitation of the black? The most serious aspect of the matter, in the case of the European *philosophers* (I mean the genuine ones), is that they flagrantly flouted the theoretical implications of their own philosophical practice, which obviously rested on responsible thinking, on theoretical efforts on the part of the individual subject, and so excluded the reduction of philosophy to a collective system of thought.

 The healthiest European reaction to Tempels' enterprise remains, as far as I know, that of Franz Crahay's 'Le Décollage conceptuel, condition d'une philosophie bantoue' (Conceptual take-off: a precondition for a Bantu philosophy), *Diogène* no. 52 (1965). We shall return to this and explain its limitations.

 But more complete, more systematic and of exemplary lucidity, in my view, is the remarkable critique by the Camerounian Fabien Eboussi-Boulaga, 'Le Bantou problématique', *Présence Africaine*, no. 66 (1968).

 It may be worth adding that my criticism of Tempels, and also the article by Eboussi, is aimed in no way at the man but at his work, or rather at a particular idea of philosophy which has unfortunately become dominant since his time and which, if it is not destroyed once and for all, is likely to stifle any potential African creativity. All I want to do, therefore, is to clear the ground for a philosophical practice worthy of the name, based on rigorous scientific practice, and at the same time to provide a new reading of existing African philosophical literature and, by ridding it of its ethnophilosophical illusions, to show that this theoretical practice has actually already begun and needs only to liberate itself and to recognize its autonomy and its possible functions in a new Africa.

19   It would be an entirely different matter, of course, if Kagamé had succeeded in providing philosophical *texts* by African sages or in *transcribing* their words. His interpretation would then have been founded on actual philosophical discourses, universally accessible and verifiable.

This perhaps indicates an urgent task for present African philosophers: the systematic transcription of everything that can be recorded of the discourses of our ancestors, sages and scholars who are still alive.

But here again, one must distinguish. The thought of an African sage, even if he purports to be the spokesman for a group, is not necessarily that of all the individuals in that group, and still less that of all Africans in general. Also, if such discourses are to be transcribed, it should not be only for the sake of advertising them for the possible admiration of a non-African public but, first and foremost, so that they can be scrutinized by all contemporary Africans. In any case we can be grateful to Marcel Griaule for having so faithfully recorded the words of an Ogotemmeli (cf. Marcel Griaule, *Dieu d'eau. Entretiens avec Ogotemmeli*, Paris: Editions du Chêne 1948). A transcript of this kind by a European ethnologist is infinitely more valuable than all the arbitrary fabrications by other 'Africanist' Europeans about the African soul or the Bantu world-view and all those impressionistic sketches of 'Dogon wisdom', 'Diola philosophy', etc.

At present I confine my discussion to the Bantu area, for the simple reason that it seems to have produced the most abundant philosophical or ethnophilosophical literature of *African* origin; and it is in this kind of *explicit discourse* that African philosophy must be sought: elsewhere we shall find nothing but the mirages of our desires, the fantasies of our regrets and nostalgias.

20   *La Philosophie bantou–rwandaise de l'être* pp. 37, 180, 187 and *passim*.

21   The reader will have immediately understood the discriminative (i.e. conceptual) use I make of the following terms: philosophy (without quotation marks) in the proper sense – a set of explicit texts and discourses, a literature intended as philosophy; 'philosophy' in an improper sense, as indicated by the quotation marks – the collective, hypothetical world-view of a given people; ethnophilosophy – a research resting, in whole or in part, on the hypothesis of such a world-view and the attempt to reconstruct a supposed collective 'philosophy'.

22   These, of course, are not at issue. Some of the authors mentioned are extremely instructive, and Africans will gain by reading them. My critique, I repeat, is not negative; but it is natural to demand more of those who have already given because we know they could do better.

23   This is the real meaning of Lévy-Bruhl's work. Cf. *La Mentalité primitive* and other texts of the kind; cf. also all the ideological discourses collected by Césaire in that inspired anthology of follies, the *Discours sur le colonialisme*.

24   F. Eboussi-Boulaga, 'Le Bantou problématique', *Présence Africaine*, no. 66 (1968).

25   The phrases *rendez-vous du donner et du recevoir, civilisation de l'universel*, etc., are, of course, favourite expressions of Senghor.

26   Here lies the inadequacy of the analysis offered in Franz Crahay's 'Le Décollage conceptuel, condition d'une philosophie bantoue'. The 'take-off' has already taken place. All people think conceptually, under all skies, in all civilizations, even if their discourse incorporates mythological sequences (like that of Parmenides, Plato, Confucius, Hegel, Nietzsche, Kagamé, etc.) and even if it rests *wholly* (as is nearly always the case) on fragile ideological foundations, from which, of course, it must be liberated by critical vigilance. In this respect, there is nothing exceptional about African civilizations.

But Crahay ignores the real problem, which is the *choice of interlocutor* and the *destination of the discourse*. Mythical or scientific, ideological or critical, language is always forced by social discussion to improve itself and to pass by successive leaps through all the levels of consistency and rigour. The main task in Africa is to subject language to social discussion and to allow it to develop its own history through writing and its necessary complement, political democracy.

27   We are, of course, considering science not in terms of its *results* (as a system of constituted truths) but as a *process*, as an actual search, as a project which takes shape within a society and which is always greater than its provisional findings.

2   History of a myth

1   *Supplément d'âme* is a phrase of Bergson's that is particularly apt for this kind of spiritualistic project.

2   The word is, of course, meant ironically: beneath the apparent spontaneity of this myopic reading, the theoretical semi-blindness which prevents the African public from noticing the most obvious thing in a book, we can see the results of long intellectual conditioning and the psychological effects of colonization.

3   *African* ethnophilosophy can be traced back to 1956, the year when Kagamé's book appeared. However, certain texts by Senghor dated the problem to as early as 1939, as we shall see below.

4   Much might be said about the implacable dialectic which under certain conditions produces the spectacular transformation of a given theoretical position into its opposite. Thus on the one hand the desperate particularism which passionately affirms the irreducible and omnilateral specificity of African cultures ('Bantu philosophy', 'authenticity', 'negritude', denunciations of 'foreign ideologies', etc.) and, on the other, the abstract universalism which cheerfully subjects entire populations to intensive brainwashing in the name of the universal value of a certain wilfully caricatured 'scientific' ideology, unknown to

the very people who claim to teach it and simply functioning as an alibi, a mere pretext. Both depend, despite appearances, on the persistence, in two different modalities, of the same conformism, the same refusal to think, the same incapacity to carry out 'the concrete analysis of concrete situations', as required by one of the greatest founders of an ideology whose claim to scientificity was never more than meta-phorical.

3 African philosophy, myth and reality

1 P. Tempels, *La Philosophie Bantoue* (Paris: Présence Africaine 1949) (AS 601). The letters AS, followed by a number, refer to the 'biblio-graphy of African thought' published by the Rev. Father Alphonse Smet, in *Cahiers philosophiques africains* no. 2 (July–December 1972), Lubumbashi. This 'bibliography', despite the fact that it lumps together philosophical and non-philosophical (i.e. sociological, ethno-logical, even literary) texts, is nevertheless a useful instrument for any research on African literature or Western literature concerning Africa. The number following the letters AS indicates the number of the text in Smet's 'Bibliography'.

2 F. Eboussi-Boulaga, 'Le Bantou problématique', *Présence Africaine*, no. 66 (1968).

3 Aimé Césaire, *Discours sur le colonialisme* (Paris: Editions Réclame 1950) (AS 95), p. 45.

4 Comparisons between the 'world-view' of Third World peoples and European philosophy involve stripping the latter also of its history, its internal diversity and its richness and reducing the multiplicity of its works and doctrines to a 'lowest common denominator'. This common stock-in-trade of European philosophy is represented in Tempels by a vague system of thought made up of Aristotle, Christian theology and horse sense.

5 AS 214.

6 M. Griaule and G. Dieterlen, *Le Renard pâle* (Paris: Publications of the Institute of Ethnology 1965) (AS 220).

7 Dominique Zahan, *Sociétés d'initiation bambara: le n'domo, le koré*, (Paris/The Hague: Mouton 1963 (AS 718); *La Dialectique du verbe chez les Bambara* (Paris–The Hague: Mouton 1963) (AS 713); *La Viande et la Graine, mythologie dogon* (Paris: Présence Africaine 1968) (AS 719); *Religion, spiritualité et pensée africaines* (Paris: Payot 1970) (AS 716). See my review of this last book in *Les Etudes philosophiques*, no. 3 (1971).

8 Louis-Vincent Thomas, *Les Diola. Essai d'analyse fonctionnelle sur une population de Basse-Casamance*, vols. I and II (Dakar: Mémoires de l'Institut Français d'Afrique Noire 1959) (not mentioned in AS);

'Brève esquisse sur la pensée cosmologique du Diola', *African Systems of Thought*, prefaced by M. Fortes and G. Dieterlen (OUP 1965) (AS 620); 'Un Système philosophique sénégalais: la cosmologie des Diola', *Présence Africaine*, nos. 32–3 (1960) (AS 638); *Cinq Essais sur la mort africaine*, Publications de la Faculté des Lettres et Sciences humaines (Philosophie et Sciences sociales) Dakar no. 3 (1969) (AS 621); 'La Mort et la sagesse africaine. Esquisse d'une anthropologie philosophique', *Psychopathologie Africaine*, no. 3 (1967). See also other texts by the same author, cited in AS 617–39.

9   AS 294. See also, by the same author, 'L'Ethnologie des Bantu', *Contemporary Philosophy. A Survey*, ed. Raymond Klibansky, vol. IV (Florence 1971) (AS 754).

10 AS 347.

11 Mongameli Antoine Mabona, 'Philosophie africaine', *Présence Africaine*, no. 30 (1960) (AS 342); 'The Depths of African Philosophy', *Personnalité africaine et Catholicisme* (Paris: Présence Africaine 1963) (AS 343); 'La Spiritualité africaine', *Présence Africaine* no. 52 (1964) (AS 344).

12 A. Rahajarizafy, 'Sagesse malgache et théologie chrétienne', *Personnalité africaine et Catholicisme* (Paris: Présence Africaine 1963) (AS 504).

13 Respectively, AS 341; 'La Conception bantoue face au christianisme', *Personnalité africaine et Catholicisme* (Paris: Présence Africaine 1963); AS 339.

14 AS 414. The chapter in question is the eighth, entitled 'Philosophical outline'; 'Dialectique existentielle des Bantous et sacramentalisme', *Aspects de la culture noire* (Paris 1958) (AS 410).

15 Jean-Calvin Bahoken, *Clairières métaphysiques africaines* (Paris: Présence Africaine 1967) (AS 46).

16 John Mbiti, *African Religions and Philosophy* (Heinemann 1969) (AS 372); *Concepts of God in Africa* (New York: Praeger 1970) (AS 375); *New Testament Eschatology in an African Background. A Study of the encounter between New Testament theology and African traditional concepts* (OUP 1971).

17 See in particular the texts (written between 1937 and 1963) collected in *Liberté I. Négritude et humanisme*. As a theory of 'negritude', the Senghorian ethnology was always, above all, an ethnopsychology concerned essentially with defining the 'Negro soul', where sociology (usually idyllic descriptions of 'Negro society') and aesthetic analyses (commentaries, many of them excellent, on various works of art) are used mainly to reinforce this fantasy psychology. However, *ethnopsychology* always betrays the ambition to become an *ethnophilosophy* by accounting for the black 'conception of the world' as well as for the psychological characteristics. The project is clearly formulated in the

celebrated 1939 article 'Ce que l'homme noir apporte' ('The black man's contribution') in which the black 'conception of the world', however, still appears as a psychological quality: an animism, or rather, according to Senghor, an anthropopsychism. This is no longer so in the 1956 text 'The Black African aesthetic' and the 1959 text on the 'Constitutive elements of a civilization of Black African inspiration' *Liberté I*, pp. 202–17 and 252–86: apart from a few alterations, these are reprints of Senghor's reports to the First International Congress of Black Writers and Artists, Paris 1956, and to the Second Congress, Rome 1959. Explicitly referring to Tempels, but still wishing to *explain* the black's 'metaphysics' in terms of black 'psychophysiology', Senghor defines it rather as a system of ideas, an 'existential ontology' (ibid., pp. 203–4, 264–8).

The reader will therefore readily understand that I should feel reluctant to situate ethnophilosophy 'in the wake of negritude' or to treat it as a '(late) aspect of the negritude movement', as Marcien Towa does in *Essai sur la problématique philosophique dans l'Afrique actuelle* (Yaoundé: Editions Clé 1971), pp. 23, 25. If *African* ethnophilosophers are undoubtedly part of the negritude movement, they owe the philosophical pretensions of their nationalist discourse rather to the ethnophilosophy of *European* Africanists.

18 A. Adesanya, 'Yoruba metaphysical thinking', *Odu*, no. 5 (1958) (AS 15).
19 W. Abraham, *The Mind of Africa* (Chicago: University of Chicago Press and Weidenfeld & Nicolson 1962) (AS 5).
20 AS 436 and 438. This book will be discussed below, chapters 6 and 7.
21 Alassane N'Daw, 'Peut-on parler d'une pensée africaine?', *Présence Africaine* no. 58 (1966) (AS 420); 'Pensée africaine et développement', *Problèmes sociaux congolais* (Kinshasa: CEP SI Publications 1966–7) (AS 419).
22 This unpublished thesis is mentioned here mainly because it is discussed at length by Marcien Towa in his critique of ethnophilosophy (Towa, *Essai sur la problématique philosophique* pp. 23–33) (AS 646).
23 Subtitled 'A phenomenological approach' and prefaced by Philippe Laburthe-Tolra (Berne: Herbert Lang 1970) (AS 325).
24 The article was published in *Présence Africaine*, no. 73 (1970) (AS 39).
25 For instance, G. de Souza, *La Conception de 'Vie' chez les Fon* (Cotonou: Editions du Bénin 1975); a doctoral thesis defended in 1972.
26 Henry Oruka Odera, 'Mythologies as African philosophy', *East Africa Journal*, vol. IX, no. 10 (October 1972) (not mentioned in AS).
27 See, on this point, Ola Balogun, 'Ethnology and its ideologies', *Consequence*, no. 1 (1974). See also my article on 'Le Mythe de la philosophie spontanée', *Cahiers Philosophiques Africains*, no. 1 (1972), and Chapter 8 below.

28   That is, 'Language gone mad'. I have borrowed this phrase from the
     Zaïrois V. Y. Mudimbe, whose book *L'Autre Face du royaume. Une
     introduction à la critique des langages en folie* (Lausanne: L'Age
     d'homme 1973) ranks among the finest works written to this day *on*
     (not *of*) ethnology.

29   How revealing that this work was published in France 'with the help of
     the Centre National de la Recherche Scientifique'.

30   For an interpretation of the qualifications added to the 1970 edition of
     Consciencism and for an appreciation of the ideological limitations of
     the work, see Chapters 6 and 7 below.

31   I have mentioned this article as the most vigorous and complete
     critique of Tempels to date for its rigorous analysis of the contra-
     dictions in his work. Eboussi-Balaga shows that these can ultimately be
     reduced to

     an interplay of value and counter-value. . .which characterizes the colonizer's
     judgements on the colonized. Bantuism is partly admirable and partly abomin-
     able. It is valuable when the colonized wish to forsake it for equality: then they
     are reminded that they are losing their 'souls'. But Bantuism becomes a vile
     hotchpotch of degenerate magical practices when the colonizer wishes to affirm
     his pre-eminence and legitimize his power. ('Le Bantou problématique',
     p. 32)

     However, Eboussi does not totally reject the idea of an 'ethnological
     philosophy', a philosophy which would abandon the search for an
     'ontological substratum for social reality', would deal with the
     'mythical discourse of "native theorists" ', instead of bypassing it with
     scorn (ibid., p. 9). On this point I believe a more radical view should be
     taken. Later (particularly in chapter 4) we shall see why.

32   Towa, *Essai sur la problématique philosophique*; *Léopold Sédar Seng-
     hor: négritude ou servitude?* (Yaoundé: Editions Clé 1971) (AS 647).

33   Odera, 'Mythologies as African philosophy'.

34   S. A. Adotevi, *Négritude et négrologues* (Paris: Union Générale
     d'Editions, Coll. 10/18 1972) (not mentioned in AS).

35   J. E. Wiredu, 'Kant's synthetic *a priori* in geometry and the rise of
     non-Euclidean geometries', *Kantstudien*, Heft 1, Bonn (1970) (not in
     AS); 'Material implication and "if. . . . then" ', *International Logic
     Review*, no. 6, Bologna (1972) (not in AS); 'Truth as opinion', *Univer-
     sitas*, vol. 2, no. 3 (new series), University of Ghana (1973) (not in AS);
     'On an African orientation in philosophy', *Second Order*, vol. 1, no. 2,
     University of Ife (1972) (not in AS).

36   H. Odera, 'The meaning of liberty', *Cahiers Philosophiques Africains*,
     no. 1, Lubumbashi (1972) (not in AS); D. E. Idoniboye, 'Freewill, the
     linguistic philosopher's dilemma', *Cahiers Philosophiques Africains*,
     no. 2, Lubumbashi (1972) (not in AS).

37   E. P. Elungu, *Etendue et connaissance dans la philosophie de Male-branche* (Paris: Vrin 1973) (not in AS). One may also mention the unpublished thesis defended in Paris in 1971 by the Senegalese A. R. N'Diaye, 'L'Ordre dans la philosophie de Malebranche'.

38   T. Tshibangu, *Théologie positive et théologie spéculative* (Louvain/Paris: Béatrice-Nauwelaerts 1965) (not in AS).

39   E. N'joh Mouellé, *Jalons: recherche d'une mentalité neuve* (Yaoundé: Editions Clé 1970) (AS 775); *De la médiocrité à l'excellence. Essai sur la signification humaine du développement* (Yaoundé: Editions Clé 1970) (AS 432).

40   On Amo, see below, Chapter 5.

41   More generally, this new definition of African philosophy opens up the possibility of a history of African philosophy, whereas the very notion of such a history was unthinkable in the ideological context of ethnophilosophy. If African philosophy is seen not as an implicit world-view but as the set of philosophical writings produced by Africans, we can at last undertake to reconstruct their chequered history, including those of Afro-Arab authors like Ibn Khaldun, Al Ghazali, etc., whatever may be the historical and theoretical distance between these texts.

42   On the gross simplification of 'primitive' societies by Western anthropologists and the need to recognize the internal diversity of African culture by 'demythologizing' the concept of Africa itself, see below, chapter 8.

43   For a consideration of these questions and some representative answers, see: L. Althusser, *For Marx* (1965), trans. B. Brewster (Allen Lane 1969); L. Althusser, *et al.*, *Reading Capital* (New Left Books 1970); G. Bachelard, *La Formation de l'esprit scientifique* (1947) (Paris: Vrin 1969); *Le Nouvel Esprit scientifique* (1934), 9th ed. (Paris: PUF 1966); G. Canguilhem, *Etudes d'histoire et de philosophie des sciences* (Paris: Vrin 1968); M. Foucault, *The Birth of the Clinic* (1972), trans. A. M. Sheridan Smith (Tavistock 1973); *The Order of Things* (1966), (Tavistock 1970); *The Archaeology of Knowledge* (1969), trans. A. M. Sheridan Smith (Tavistock 1972).

44   It is worth mentioning here the part that can be played in promoting this new type of dialogue by the departments of philosophy in African universities and the philosophical associations (e.g. the Inter-African Council for Philosophy) and their respective journals.

4   Philosophy and its revolutions

1   In *The Greater Hippias* Socrates' interlocutor, a brilliant rhetorician and occasional itinerant ambassador for his country, congratulates himself on having made more money out of his art than any other

known sophist and on having conquered even the public of Sparta, where, however, it was unfortunately illegal to remunerate members of his profession. When Socrates asks what are the topics of his successful speeches, Hippias replies: neither astronomy, nor geometry, nor arithmetic, nor grammar, but 'the genealogies of heroes and of men and stories of the foundation of cities in olden times, and, to put it briefly, all forms of antiquarian law'. Socrates quickly gives vent to his irony: 'I am sorry, I quite forgot about your mnemonic art. Now I understand how naturally the Lacedaemonians enjoy your multifarious knowledge and make use of you as children do of old women, *to tell them agreeable stories*' (*Greater Hippias*, 285d–286a, Jowett translation).

The remainder of the text clarifies this by emphasizing the contrast between Hippias' science of erudition and memory and Socratic reflection on essences. To the question 'What is beauty?' Hippias replies by offering *examples of beautiful things*: a beautiful virgin, a beautiful mare, a beautiful lyre, a beautiful pot, gold and, to end up with, the fact of 'being rich, in good health, honoured by the Greeks; to reach ripe old age, to bury one's parents with dignity, to be oneself buried with dignity and magnificence by one's children'. But all these examples leave the question entirely unanswered. Hippias the brilliant 'international lecturer', as he might be called today, remains incapable throughout of seeing the difference between beauty and beautiful things, between meaning and fact, between reflection on essences and empirical examples. Throughout the dialogue he goes on 'telling stories' without ever managing to raise himself to the level of ontology.

Mutatis mutandis, it might be said that the many modern authors who insist on defining 'African philosophy' without first determining the general meaning of the word 'philosophy' or considering its *essence*, its *conditions of possibility* and its *articulations* as a theoretical activity are simply 'telling stories' and fastening on an example, and a hopelessly inadequate one at that, and thus depriving themselves of the universal concept which alone might have guaranteed its representativeness.

2 *Theaetetus*, 201c and e, ibid., p. 908.
3 It may perhaps be useful here to remind the reader of the reasons adduced by Socrates in the dialogue for his final rejection of this definition. The weightiest stem from an examination of the possible meanings of the word *logos*.

(a) *Logos* may mean simply the expression of opinion in discourse; but then the second part of the proposed definition is superfluous, for anybody who has an opinion can express it unless he is deaf and dumb by birth, and so 'there will be no place left anywhere for a correct notion that is apart from knowledge' (*Theaetetus*, 206d–e).

(b)   *Logos* can mean the enumeration of the elements of a whole; but then even a complete catalogue of the elements does not guarantee that one will be able to recognize these elements in another whole (for instance, it is possible to write the first syllable of 'Theaetetus' correctly, with the letters th and e, and yet be mistaken about the first syllable of 'Theodore' if we write t and e). The definition proposed is therefore again inadequate, for 'there is such a thing as right belief, together with a *logos* account, which is not yet entitled to be called knowledge' (208b).

(c)   Finally, *logos* may mean 'some mark by which the thing one is asked about differs from everything else' (208c); but this is still a 'vicious circle', for 'correct belief together with knowledge of a difference' is the same as 'adding an account' to 'correct belief' (210a).

Whether it is complete or tautological, the definition of knowledge as 'correct belief with an account' seems to Socrates unacceptable in all three cases. It is, however, for the reader to judge whether the reasons adduced are really decisive or whether it is possible to get round them one way or another.

4   If the *Theaetetus* rejects the definition of knowledge as 'correct belief together with an account' ($\dot{\eta}\ \mu\epsilon\tau\grave{\alpha}\ \lambda\acute{o}\gamma o\upsilon\ \dot{\alpha}\gamma\eta\vartheta\dot{\eta}\varsigma\ \delta\acute{o}\xi\alpha$) there remains the fact that Plato, in an earlier dialogue, the *Meno*, had proposed a definition that was very close to this one. Right opinion, Socrates tells his interlocutor, is like the statues of Daedalus: 'if no one ties them down, they run away and escape'. In the case of right opinion, the tethering is done by 'working out the reason' ($\alpha\dot{\iota}\tau\acute{\iota}\alpha\varsigma\ \lambda o\gamma\iota\sigma\mu\tilde{\omega}$). Hence, knowledge ($\dot{\epsilon}\pi\iota\sigma\tau\acute{\eta}\mu\eta$) is something more valuable than right opinion: what distinguishes them is the tether (*Meno*, 97d–98a).

This 'working out of the reason', Socrates also says, is nothing else but recollection ($\dot{\alpha}\nu\acute{\alpha}\mu\nu\eta\sigma\iota\varsigma$). It is clear at any rate that from the moment we accept that right opinion does not suffice but must be tethered to other 'right opinions' by 'working out the reason', i.e. through a discursive chain of causes, we acknowledge the historical dimension of science as an essentially open process, an endless quest, the project of a system which will never be completed.

5   As is well known, in Hegel's case this recognition, far from being tacit, affords the work its major theme: dialectic. Indeed, one of the most difficult problems raised by Hegelianism is the reconciliation of this theme with the apparently antithetical one of Absolute Knowledge.

6   This was the theme of the Third Seminar of the International African Institute, which met at the University College of Rhodesia and Nyasaland in December 1960. Papers and discussions were published in 1965 under the title *African Systems of Thought*, Preface by Meyer Fortes and Germaine Dieterlen (OUP 1965).

7   E. Husserl, *Logical Investigations*, trans. J. N. Findlay, Routledge & Kegan Paul 1970).

8   Cf. 'Témoignages sur *La Philosophie bantoue* du R. P. Tempels', *Présence Africaine*, no. 7 (1949).

9   P. Radin, *Primitive Man as Philosopher* (New York: D. Appleton & Co. 1927; new, revised and enlarged edition, New York: Dover Publications Inc. 1947).

10   Radin added an exceptionally interesting Foreword to the 1957 edition entitled 'Methods of Approach', in which he defined his method and situated his work in relation to the more recent work of Tempels and Griaule. The former is criticized for the subjectivity of his approach: however attractive his reconstruction of 'Bantu philosophy', says Radin, it tells us not what that philosophy is but what he, Tempels, thinks about it. The illustrious missionary's formulations, whatever their value and legitimacy, 'must not in any circumstances be regarded as primary sources. . . . They can be demonstrated only by actual texts from philosophically minded aboriginal philosophers' (p. xxx).

But Tempels is not the only one to practise this method: in fact, most anthropologists resort to it when writing about the thought of 'primitives'. So Radin also tilts at S. F. Nadel, whose book *Nupe Religion* (1954) claimed to speak in the name and place of the 'primitives'. Radin's preference is rather for the 'Method of Question and Answer' practised, for instance, by J. R. Walker, 'Oglala Sun Dance', *Anthropological Papers of the American Museum of Natural History*, vol. XVI (1917) and even for the method by which the investigator tries to stay 'in the background and let the native philosopher expound his ideas with as few interruptions as possible'. It is this last method, which he credits to Griaule, which Radin claims to have followed himself, but with particular attention to the transcription of 'the great collections of native texts', so as to avoid even 'this minimal type of pressure' exercised on the interlocutor by the anthropologist's request.

11   M. Griaule, *Dieu d'eau*, (Paris: Editions du Chêne 1948; reissued by Fayard 1966). Reference is made in the Preface to Tempels' book, the essential thesis of which Griaule takes to be confirmed by his own discussion.

12   Griaule, *Dieu d'eau*, p. 5.

13   There has always existed a tacit assumption that there is but one true version of a myth, one true version of a rite. Where deviations or variants were present, this was to be ascribed to errors due either to forgetfulness or ignorance, or to general inert degeneration. . . . We are justified then in insisting that part of the uniformity postulated of a rite or a myth is due to the utter inadequacy of the ethnological record and that this, in turn, is due not always or predominantly to unfortunate circumstances but to tacit or expressed assumptions of the investigator. The most cursory glance suffices to show that we are indeed not here

dealing with an inert degeneration but with the free play of participants and story-tellers. (pp. 47–8)

14 Only a cursory perusal of these proverbs is necessary to convince even the most sceptical that we are dealing here not with any vague group activity or folkway – that last refuge of the tired sociologist and ethnologist – but with the personal envisaging of life by those individuals who in any group are concerned with and interested in formulating their attitude towards God, towards man, and towards society – the philosophers, the sages, and the moralists. (p. 169)

15 ibid., p. 35.

16 ibid., p. 37.

17 ibid., p. 42.

18 ibid., p. 43.

19 ibid., p. 59.

20 This phrase was inspired by Pathé Diagne who, in an unpublished *Anthology of Wolof Literature*, distinguishes between 'literature of imagination' and 'literature of knowledge'. We prefer 'thought' to 'knowledge' as being less restrictive.

21 Radin, *Primitive Man as Philosopher*, p. 103.

22 ibid., p. 143.

23 ibid., p. 178 and *passim*.

24 I realize that in a strong sense there is a 'history' of theories of art, a history of aesthetics, in the sense of Ovid's *Ars Poetica* or Boileau's *Art poétique*, or of Romantic, of Surrealist, etc., aesthetics. All of these involve questioning and answering between authors and between generations. However, this is not a history *of* art in the direct sense of the term; it is not a history of aesthetic forms themselves but a history of theories, inquiries, debates, discussions etc., which take these forms as their object, a history of discourse about art. In the sense in which we must now use the concept, history is always the history of a discourse, so that art, which is not a discourse, cannot have a history. The 'verbal arts' (poems, songs, novels, short stories, etc.) are no exception to this rule, at least inasmuch as they are arts, i.e. regulated procedures designed to produce the specific effect which we call beauty, and to the extent that they invite the reader or listener to rise above discursive content (whether semantic, theoretical, or intellectual) to the realm of pure form where artistic value resides.

25 I. Kant, *Critique of Pure Reason*, trans. Norman Kemp Smith (Macmillan 1963), p. 57.

26 ibid., p. 30.

27 I. Kant, *Prolegomena to any future Metaphysics which will be able to come forth as Science* (1783): 'I openly confess my recollection of David Hume was the very thing which many years ago first interrupted my dogmatic slumber and gave my investigations in the field of speculative philosophy a quite new direction.' (The Mahaffy-Carus translation

202 Notes and references

extensively revised, with an introduction by L. W. Beck, Indianapolis and New York: Library of Liberal Arts, H. W. Sams, 1950, p. 8).

28 The title of the final chapter of the *Critique of Pure Reason*.

29 ibid., p. 607.

30 Our age is, in especial degree, the age of criticism, and to criticism everything must submit. Religion through its sanctity, and law-giving through its majesty, may seek to exempt themselves from it. But they then awake just suspicions, and cannot claim the sincere respect which reason accords only to that which has been able to sustain the test of free and open examination. (ibid., Preface to 1st edition, 1781, p. 9)

31 See 'What is enlightenment?' (1784) in I. Kant, *On History*, ed. L. W. Beck (Indianapolis and New York: Library of the Liberal Arts, Bobbs-Merrill 1963), p. 3.

32 Edmund Husserl, 'Philosophy as rigorous science', in *Phenomenology and the Crisis of Philosophy*, trans. Lauer (New York: Harper & Row), pp. 71–147, 146.

33 Bachelard, *Le Nouvel Esprit scientifique*, p. 58.

34 L. Althusser, 'Lenin and philosophy' (1968), in *Lenin and Philosophy and Other Essays* (New Left Books 1971), p. 32.

35 K. Marx and F. Engels, *The German Ideology* (1846) (Lawrence and Wishart 1965), p. 27.

36 ibid., pp. 37–8. Our emphasis.

37 See L. Althusser, *For Marx* (1965), trans. B. Brewster (Allen Lane 1969) especially the essays 'Contradiction and determination', and 'On the materialist dialectic'; 'The object of *Capital*', in *Reading Capital* (New Left Books 1970), especially Section 4: 'The errors of classical economics: an outline for a concept of historical time', and Section 5: 'Marxism is not a historicism'.

    See also E. Balibar, 'The basic concepts of historical materialism', translated in *Reading Capital*, especially pp. 201–8.

38 For a good statement of the problem, see Balibar, 'The basic concepts of historical materialism', pp. 273–308.

39 Althusser, *Lenin and Philosophy*, p. 44.

40 This is how Althusser originally tried to explain the historical 'backwardness' of Marxist philosophy (dialectical materialism) in relation to Marxist science (historical materialism). Later, however, he returned to the notion of 'backwardness' and corrected it in the light of Lenin's conception of the struggle between philosophical tendencies and the need to 'take sides' in philosophy. If philosophy is a battlefield where idealism and materialism perpetually contend (as Engels had already said), and if its history is just a continual repetition of this confrontation, then the idea of philosophical 'backwardness' can make no sense and there can never really be a history *of* philosophy but only history *in*

philosophy, a history of the displacement of the demarcation lines by which philosophy separates the ideological from the scientific within the discourse of the sciences. But then philosophy can be defined no longer solely in terms of its relation to the sciences but by its dual relation both to the sciences and to politics, as a representation of politics in the theoretical field attached to the sciences, and conversely representing scientificity in politics.

I shall not enter into the debate over these later theses of Althusser, which appear to be faithful to the spirit of Lenin's great philosophical texts and to have a manifest effect in the *Reply to John Lewis* and the *Essays in Self-Criticism* (1974), trans. G. Locke (New Left Books 1976). For our purposes it will suffice to say that this theoretical annihilation of the history of philosophy, which reduces it to the repetition of a single move, the inversion of the terms of a single categorial dichotomy (matter/spirit), does not alter the fact that this move is made in words and is, properly speaking, the activity of philosophical doctrines themselves, the practical effect of their theoretical order or of the differences between their theoretical orders and therefore the practical effect of their theoretical history. The displacement of the demarcation line, which Althusser sees only as history *in* philosophy, is in fact the history *of* philosophy itself and necessarily refers to that history as its condition of possibility.

41   See, for instance, Alain Badiou, *Le Concept de modèle* (Paris: Maspero 1969) and especially Pierre Raymond, *Le Passage au matérialisme* (Paris: Maspero 1973).

42   T. Obenga, *L'Afrique dans l'Antiquité* (Paris: Présence Africaine 1973).

43   Cheikh Anta Diop, *Nations nègres et culture* (Paris: Présence Africaine 1955); *L'Afrique noire précoloniale* (1960); *L'Unité culturelle de L'Afrique noire* (1960); *Antériorité des civilisations nègres: mythe ou verité historique?* (1967).

44   This is now so widely accepted that the phrase 'African philosophical literature' appears to some tautological and pointless. It recalls an epic discussion in the Department of Philosophy at the National University of Zaïre in 1972. Courses were being reorganized for the following session and the issue was the title to be given to a course on 'African philosophy'. The phrases 'African philosophical literature' and 'African philosophical texts' were fiercely opposed because of their tautological character. But the most remarkable thing is that this tautology (for which I have long sought recognition) was opposed most vociferously by representatives of the most extreme ethnological tendency, who refused, in fact, to draw the theoretical and pedagogical consequences and who believed that a teachable 'philosophy' could be extracted from a 'phenomenological description' of African religious beliefs and customs.

45   J. Derrida, *Of Grammatology* (1967), English translation (Baltimore: Johns Hopkins University Press 1976).

46   See G. Charbonnier, *Entretiens avec Lévi-Strauss* (Paris: Union Générale d'Editions 1961).

5   An African philosopher in Germany in the eighteenth century: Anton-Wilhelm Amo

1   Present-day Ghana, of course, dates from 1957.

2   See below, Chapter 6.

3   There is a copy of this book in the Bibliothèque Nationale in Paris (reference Z 2027). The translation of the complete title is: *On the literature of the Negroes, or an investigation into their intellectual faculties, their moral qualities and their literature, followed by Notices on the life and works of Negroes who have distinguished themselves in the sciences and the arts*.

One cannot help smiling at the notion that it should have been thought necessary, at that time, to prove that blacks could sometimes be as intelligent, moral and artistic as whites; that it should have been thought possible to destroy racial prejudice with pious philanthropic sermons. But it is also necessary to put Grégoire's work into its historical context, and to understand how it may have been progressive in its time.

This example can at least serve in a negative way: I shall not use Amo's philosophical works to try to persuade people that blacks can be good philosophers too. That is a meaningless exercise. It is completely absurd for blacks to try to win certificates of humanity from whites or to display the splendours of past African civilizations to them. One cannot plead for respect, and neither can dignity be a gift: both are won in practical confrontations and struggles. If it is worth going into the splendours of our history, then it should be primarily for our own benefit, for the African peoples, so that we can gain the necessary courage and knowledge to build our future according to our own plans.

More generally, if theoretical discourse is to be meaningful in modern Africa, it must promote within African society itself a theoretical debate of its own that is capable of developing its themes and problems autonomously instead of remaining a remote appendix to European theoretical and scientific debates. We shall see below how Amo's career forces this problem on us.

4   On the other hand, Michaud's *Biographie universelle* makes no mention of Amo.

5   In 1910 a 'Ghanaian' pastor, Attoh Ahuma, published a book entitled *West African Celebrities: 1700–1850*, a chapter of which was devoted to Amo. In Germany Professor Wolfram Suchier, Librarian of the

University of Halle, rediscovered Amo's story at the beginning of the century and published two articles on the subject: 'A. W. Amo, Ein Mohr als Student und Privatdozent der Philosophie in Halle, Wittenberg und Iena, 1727–1740', *Akademische Rundschau*, Leipzig (1916); 'Weiteres über den Mohren Amo', *Altsachen Zeitschrift des Altsachenbundes für Heimatschutz und Heimatkunde*, Holminden, nos. 1–2 (1981).

Since then, further efforts have been made to reconstruct as accurately as possible the different stages of Amo's life and career. To my knowledge, the most recent are: Norbert Lochner, 'Anton-Wilhelm Amo', *Ubersee Rundschau*, Hamburg (July 1958); reprinted in *Transactions of the Historical Society of Ghana*, vol. III (1958); William Abraham, 'The life and times of Anton-Wilhelm Amo', *Transactions of the Historical Society of Ghana*, vol. VII (1964).

6 See Abraham, 'The life and times of Anton-Wilhelm Amo', p. 61. It is surprising that this very substantial article does not mention the confusion of Axim and Axum by Amo's earliest biographers.

7 This curious personage is credited with several works, including *Fifty Reasons why the Catholic and Roman Religion is to be Preferred to all the Sects*. It must have been quite successful, as it was translated into English in 1798. Grégoire mentions it, favourably of course. The author was himself converted to Catholicism in 1710, shortly after the publication of this work.

8 Abraham is therefore mistaken when he writes that 'Christian Wolff had been expelled from Halle just a month before Amo's arrival' (p. 71). Nor is it true to say that he then went to Leipzig. He moved to Marburg, where he stayed until 1740, the year of his return to Halle on the invitation of the new king, Frederick II.

9 The British Museum in London also had a copy, mentioned in its Catalogue, but it was destroyed as a result of German bombing during the last war.

10 It should be noted that Grégoire says not that Amo stayed in Berlin but only that he received the title of State Counsellor.

11 *De humanae mentis apatheia*, chapter II, thesis I, 2nd proof, remark I.

12 ibid., remark II.

13 This does not mean that it is impossible to construct a psychology of knowledge in general, taking account of the sensory element. But sensation cannot be the immediate theme of such a psychology of knowledge. It can only figure indirectly, as a bodily function which is the object of a different science (the *physiology* of sensation), reflected in the mind through the operation which Amo calls *ideas*. The psychology of (human) knowledge is a science of *re-presentation*, not of presentation, i.e. of affect, although it presupposes such a science, namely physiology. We shall return to this problem later.

14   Ch. I, member III, para. 2.

15   The reader will have noticed the inverted nature of our reading, which begins at the end of Amo's text and finishes at the beginning. This is because it is necessary to begin by defining the aim of the work, which is revealed only in the second of the two chapters, in order to understand the initial discussion and the development of the work as a whole.

Having said this, I must add that the plan of the work is simple. The first chapter, entitled 'Definition of the concepts contained in the Statement of the thesis', is intended to define the various concepts involved in the 'Statement': the spirit in general, the human mind in particular, sensation, the faculty of sensation, insensibility as the absence of sensation, insensibility as the absence of the faculty of sensation, and finally, by way of synthesis, the insensibility of the human mind. The second chapter, entitled 'Application of the foregoing analyses', contains the argument proper. It begins with a *Status Controversiae*, in which Amo defines his own position by reference to other authors and goes on to develop the three aforementioned theses.

16   Ch. I, member I, para I, development II.

17   ibid., remark.

18   ibid.

19   The contrast between intellectual fictions and real entities was to play an important part in the *Treatise on the Art of Philosophizing with Sobriety and Accuracy*, where it serves in particular to differentiate human and divine thought in terms of their effects.

20   Ch. I, member I, para I, development II, remark.

21   Cf. I. Kant, *Critique of Pure Reason*, Preface to 2nd ed. (1787). Here Kant contrasts metaphysical dogmatism, which the *Critique* was designed to destroy, with the *dogmatic procedure* inherent in any science, 'for (science) must always be dogmatic, that is, yield strict proof from sure principles *a priori*' (p. 32). Further on Kant adds:

In the execution of the plan prescribed by the critique, that is, in the future system of metaphysics, we have therefore to follow the strict method of the celebrated Wolff, the greatest of all the dogmatic philosophers. He was the first to show by example (and by his example he awakened that spirit of thoroughness which is not extinct in Germany) how the secure progress of a science is to be attained only through the orderly establishment of principles, the clear determination of concepts, insistence upon strictness of proof and the avoidance of venturesome, non-consecutive steps in our inferences. (pp. 32–3)

6   The end of 'Nkrumaism' and the (re)birth of Nkrumah

1   The *Autobiography* is, of course, our main source of information on Nkrumah's youth, training and early political struggles. For an assessment of Nkrumah's political achievement, *Mission to Ghana* (Benin

City: Ethiope Editions) by the Nigerian writer Samuel Ikoku is recommended as providing an exceptionally lucid analysis. For present purposes a few biographical landmarks will suffice.

Kwame Nkrumah (or Francis, as he was baptized in the Roman Catholic Church) was born into a blacksmith's family around 1909 at Nkroful on the 'Gold Coast'. After graduating from the Achimota Teachers' Training College, he studied in the USA from 1935 to 1945, obtaining a BA and an MSc in education at Lincoln University in Pennsylvania and an MA in philosophy at the University of Pennsylvania. He had begun work on a doctoral thesis when he left the United States for London in 1945, but it was never completed. With George Padmore he was an assistant secretary to the Fifth Pan-African Congress held in Manchester in October 1945 under the chairmanship of W. E. B. Du Bois. Then he became secretary of the West African National Secretariat which was founded in London shortly after the Congress, inspired by a semi-clandestine group, the Circle, of which he was the leader. In 1947, he accepted an invitation from several political friends to return to the Gold Coast and act as Secretary-General to the recently formed United Gold Coast Convention (UGCC); but he soon left this organization and founded the Convention People's Party (CPP), through which he led the struggle which culminated in the declaration of independence on 6 March 1957. In June 1951 he had received an honorary doctorate from Lincoln University.

He was the first Prime Minister of independent Ghana (with the Queen of England still as Head of State) and President of the Republic following the constitutional amendment of 1960. With the support of the CPP he struggled during the period to gain real economic independence for his country while encouraging national liberation movements throughout Africa. Though admired by all African patriots as the architect of Pan-Africanism, Nkrumah eventually succumbed to conflicts within his own party, which had become a bureaucratized battlefield of rival factions. Hence the easy success of the *coup* of 24 February 1966, which was organized by police and army officers during Nkrumah's official visit to Peking. Nkrumah then moved to Conakry, where his counterpart Sekou Touré gave him the title of co-President of the Republic of Guinea. Eventually, in failing health, he went to Romania, where he died on 27 April 1972.

2 The authenticity of the work was contested mainly, of course, in the wake of Nkrumah's fall from power in 1966, when the accusation of literary fraud became one of the favourite themes of the 'National Council of Liberation' which sprang up after the *coup*. In assessing this propaganda, the following points should be borne in mind.

Nkrumah himself had always been the first to acknowledge, where appropriate, his debts to his collaborators. For instance, at the beginning of his *Autobiography* he expressly thanks his personal secretary, Erica Powell, 'to whom I *dictated* (emphasis mine) most of this book. . . . Without her patience and industry the book would never have been completed for publication in so short a time.' Also he explicitly dedicated *Consciencism* 'to the members of the Philosophical Club, without whose encouragement and help this book would not have been written'. Now, everyone in Ghana at the time was aware of the important part played in this Club by the Ghanaian philosopher William Abraham, then Head of the Department of Philosophy at the University of Ghana, and by the Senegalese Habib Niang, the President's adviser for francophone Africa. More generally, Nkrumah never sought to conceal his attempts to surround himself with a veritable international 'brains trust', comprising all the most brilliant intellectuals he could find, whether Ghanaian, African or even non-African.

To my knowledge, no member of this 'brains trust' has ever claimed the authorship of works attributed to Nkrumah, and it can be assumed that they knew more about the matter than the officers of the 'National Council of Liberation'. So all that can be said, pending more accurate information, is that even granted the most unfavourable hypothesis (i.e. that Nkrumah's books were sometimes *drafted* by others), the fact remains that the inspiration and the main lines and structure of the arguments were always his, as therefore was the entire moral and intellectual responsibility for them (for better or worse). This is confirmed by the Ghanaian writer Peter Omari in his highly critical and objectively *rightist* book on Nkrumah, *Kwame Nkrumah, the Anatomy of an African dictatorship* (Accra: Moxon Paperbacks 1970): 'He [Nkrumah] may have sought help for the drafting of these books, but he went over each manuscript line by line with those who helped him; and the views expressed in them were undoubtedly his' (p. 142).

3   This bibliography is placed in the text rather than in a footnote or appendix because it is the primary aim of this article to show that the works *exist* and cannot be ignored, whoever their author may be.

4   In addition to the works cited above, it is worth recording two important posthumous collections published by Panaf.

The Struggle Continues (1973, 83 pages) reproduces the short 1949 pamphlet *What I Mean by Positive Action* and texts from five other pamphlets written in Conakry between 1966 and 1968: *The Struggle Continues*, *The Way Out*, *The Spectre of Black Power*, *The Big Lie* and *Two Myths*.

Revolutionary Path (1973), a bulky collection (532 pages), gathers into one volume some basic texts of which a number had not been previously published. It is in three parts: (1) the struggle for national liberation (texts dated from 1945 to 1957); (2) the construction of socialism and the struggle for the liberation and unification of Africa (1957–66); (3) the class struggle and the armed stage in African revolution (1966–70). The introductions to the different texts are said to have been written by Nkrumah himself and the conclusion dictated by him in a Bucharest clinic in October 1971.

As for works on Nkrumah, Ikoku's *Mission to Ghana* and Omari's *Kwame Nkrumah* have already been cited. At the end of the latter volume the author provides a 'Select Bibliography' which is more complete than the present one as regards Nkrumah's political work but obviously obsolete as regards his theoretical work. The following texts may also be consulted: Dennis Austin, *Politics in Ghana (1945–1960)* (OUP 1964); Timothy Bankole, *Kwame Nkrumah: His Rise to Power* (Allen & Unwin 1957); Stephan Dzirasa, *The Political Thought of Dr Kwame Nkrumah* (Accra: Guinea Press 1962); Bob Fitch and Mary Oppenheimer, 'Ghana: end of an illusion', *Monthly Review*, vol. XVIII, no. 3, Special Issue (July–August 1966); Roger Genoud, *Nationalism and Economic Development in Ghana* (New York: Praeger 1969); *Hommage à Kwame Nkrumah* (Conakry: Imprimerie Nationale Patrice-Lumumba 1972), a collection of the speeches made on the occasion of the funeral of Kwame Nkrumah, co-President of the Republic of Guinea, on 13 and 14 May 1972; *Hommage à Kwame Nkrumah – Homage to Kwame Nkrumah* (Paris: Présence Africaine 1973), a special issue of the journal *Présence Africaine*; John Philipp, *Kwame Nkrumah and the Future of Africa* (Faber & Faber 1960); Alex Quaison-Sackey, *Africa Unbound: Reflections on an African Statesman* (New York: Praeger 1963); *Some Essential Features of Nkrumaism*, compiled by the editors of the *Spark* (Lawrence & Wishart 1964, and Panaf 1970).

5   The 'Convention' referred to in this title is the UGCC, of which the new party was initially intended as a branch. In his *Autobiography* (ch. 8), Nkrumah explains how the rank and file of the UGCC gathered around him on 12 June 1949 and, in opposition to their leaders, expressed a wish to call the new party the Ghana People's Party. It was only at the end of the meeting, and at Nkrumah's own suggestion, that it was decided to retain the word 'Convention', on the grounds that Nkrumah's name was popularly associated with the Convention. Subsequent unsuccessful negotiations with the other leaders of the UGCC led to Nkrumah's resignation on 1 August 1949, which shows that Nkrumah was not opposed *a priori* to the possibility of the new party's remaining a branch of the UGCC, the latter being not a party but a national movement.

6   *Consciencism*, p. 74.

7   *Neo-colonialism, the Last Stage of Imperialism*, pp. 255–6.

8   *Two Myths*, p. 8.

9   *Handbook of Revolutionary Warfare*, pp. 56–67.

7   The idea of philosophy in Nkrumah's *Consciencism*

1   On the question of the authenticity of Nkrumah's work, see chapter 6, n. 2.

2   Samuel Ikoku, *Mission to Ghana* (Benin City: Ethiope Editions).

3   Jacques Berque argues that the English neologism *consciencism* 'is based on the French word rather than on the English word, and that this was intentional on Nkrumah's part' (Jacques Berque, 'L'Elan fracassé', in *L'Ouest second*, Paris: Gallimard, and *Présence Africaine*, no. 85, 1973). But it is hard to see why Nkrumah should have chosen the French word. It seems more reasonable to suppose that the neologism was simply coined from the English word *conscience*, designating the subjective sense of right and wrong, as opposed to *consciousness*, which denotes the ability to feel, perceive and think. Thus the term *consciencism* is intended to suggest that the new collective consciousness envisaged by Nkrumah would be not only cognitive but also practical, consciousness in the most political sense of the term, as well as the definition of a new cultural identity.

4   *Consciencism* (Heinemann 1964, 4th ed. 1966); (5th rev. ed. Panaf 1970), p. vii.

5   V. I. Lenin, *Imperialism, the Highest Stage of Capitalism* (Central Books 1978).

6   On this point, however, there is still some hesitation in Nkrumah's later works. At times, he interprets the class struggle in Africa as an *extension* of the class struggle in the West, arguing that prior to colonization African society had a communal and egalitarian organization which was only just entering a phase of degeneration. This was the position suggested in *Neo-colonialism* (Nelson 1965), and it was to be clearly reaffirmed in *Class Struggle in Africa* (Paris: Panaf 1970). On other occasions, however, he took a far more radical position and showed that colonialism, far from having introduced exploitation from the outside, merely complicated existing conflicts in a society which had long known such exploitation. This attempt to 'demythologize' the African past can be seen, for example, in the 1966 article 'African socialism revisited'.

7   See, for instance, *Neo-colonialism*, p. 258.

8   In his analysis of the *coup* by which he was overthrown on 24 February 1966 Nkrumah stressed the decisive part played by pro-imperialist elements in the army and police, allied to the local bourgeoisie and supported by some imperialist powers worried by the progress towards socialism and economic independence. The CIA and the State Department are named as being involved (*Dark Days in Ghana*, New York:

International Publishers 1968), pp. 49–50, 95–6 and *passim*). Nkrumah fails to mention, however, the purely internal factors, which were largely due to his own political mistakes and which, of course, his right-wing critics emphasize. See, for instance, Omari, *Kwame Nkrumah, the Anatomy of an African Dictatorship* (Accra: Moxon Paperbacks 1970), and Kweku Folson, 'An African tragedy: Kwame Nkrumah and Mr Bing', *Encounter*, vol. XXXIII, no. 1 (July 1969), pp. 35–43. (Let us take this opportunity to complete our definition of the right: in contemporary Africa, it is characterized by a deliberate neglect of the fact of imperialism even going so far as an outright denial of its existence. This in turn causes the right systematically to avoid all political discussion and to resort instead to psychological and moral arguments designed to *denigrate* – rather than to *refute* – people who place the fact of imperialism at the centre of their analysis.) For a lucid critique of Nkrumah's actions, the reader is referred to the very balanced analysis in Ikoku, *Mission to Ghana*.

Whatever the truth of this matter, Nkrumah has a clear tendency to interpret all subsequent *coups* in Africa on the model of the one by which he was overthrown, i.e. as results of imperialist plots (cf. *Dark Days in Ghana*, ch. 3; *Handbook of Revolutionary Warfare*, New York: International Publishers 1969, pp. 11, 52, 54 and *passim*; *Class Struggle in Africa*, ch. 8, etc.). The truth is probably more complex, but it must still be correct to say that every military coup should be seen in terms of the social composition of the army and the class allegiance of the fraction which carries out the *coup* (cf. *Class Struggle in Africa*, ch. 7).

9   *Consciencism* (1964), p. 74.
10 *Consciencism* (1970), p. 74.
11 Quoted by Dennis Austin, *Politics in Ghana, 1946–1960* (OUP 1964), p. 162. (Cf. Charles Martin, 'Nkrumah's strategy of de-colonization: originality and classicism', *Présence Africaine*, no. 85 (1973), p. 79, n. 15). However, the concrete definition of the economic tasks arising from this socialist choice was elaborated only in the programme approved by the party at Kumasi in 1962 and in the Septennial Plan (1963–70) (cf. Martin, 'Nkrumah's strategy of de-colonization'). On the real meaning of the word 'socialist' in the vocabulary of Nkrumah and the CPP, where it tends to denote a sort of state capitalism, see Ikoku, *Mission to Ghana*, esp. chs. 2, 9 and 10, and Martin, 'Nkrumah's strategy of de-colonization'.
12 Cf. 'The myth of the "Third World" '. The criticism of the notion of 'Third World' goes hand in hand with that of non-alignment, neutralism, etc. Nkrumah criticizes these concepts as 'anachronistic': they may have had some meaning at the time of the cold war (when non-aligned countries could interpose themselves between the two Great

Powers, impose *détente* and thus prevent the outbreak of a third world war); today they function as myths which tend to conceal the real inseparability of the struggle for socialism and the anti-imperialist struggle. Thus Nkrumah does not hesitate to write:

Non-alignment is an anachronism. . . . There are . . . two worlds only, the revolutionary and the counter-revolutionary world – the socialist world trending towards communism, and the capitalist world with its extensions of imperialism, colonialism and neo-colonialism.

We shall never know, alas, whether Nkrumah would still have maintained this position in the celebrated debate which was to take place at the Conference of Non-Aligned Countries in Algiers in 1973.

13   This subtitle is abridged in the last edition to *Philosophy and Ideology for Decolonization*.
14   *Consciencism* (1970), p. 56.
15   ibid.
16   On writing systems in pre-colonial Africa, see the interesting discussion in Théophile Obenga, *L'Afrique dans l'Antiquité* (Paris: Présence Africaine 1973), ch. X, p. 355: 'Systèmes graphiques africains'.
17   *Consciencism* (1970), p. 59.
18   On the illegitimacy of such simplifications, see below, chapter 8.
19   'If we fail to do this (i.e. if we do not regard the other two currents as experiences of African society), our society will be racked by the most malignant schizophrenia' (*Consciencism*, 1970, p. 78).
20   ibid., pp. 69–70.
21   ibid., p. 68.
22   ibid.
23   Cf. Martin, 'Nkrumah's strategy of de-colonization', p. 92.
24   The reader will find an excellent account of this process in Ikoku, *Mission to Ghana*, chs. 3, 4, 5 and 6.
25   *Consciencism* (1970), p. 66. This interpretation of philosophy is, of course, extremely reassuring: by enclosing philosophy within ideology, we reduce it to a repetitive discourse, forever reproducing the same figures in various forms. In addition, we avoid the need to consider the history and essential incompleteness of philosophy as a theoretical discourse articulated within a scientific one and evolving with it.
26   For an internal analysis of this content, see e.g. M. Towa, 'Consciencisme', *Présence Africaine*, no. 85 (1973), pp. 148–77.
27   The doctrine is expounded in *Consciencism*, ch. 4.
28   *Consciencism* (1970), p. 84.
29   But even if it is not contradictory to assert the material origin of mind, it is impossible to derive God from matter without abandoning the usual concept of God, which implies, among other essential attributes,

infinity and absolute priority. But if the concept is altered, why keep the word? Obviously, Nkrumah is trying to have it both ways, and his attempt at synthesis results in eclecticism.

30 'The great moral principle of consciencism is to treat each human being as an end in itself and not as a simple means' (*Consciencism*, 1970, p. 95). It is easy to recognize in this 'great principle' an echo of Kant's celebrated formula in the *Groundwork of the Metaphysic of Morals*: 'Act in such a way that you always treat humanity, whether in your own person or in the person of any other, never simply as a means, but always at the same time as an end' (*The Moral Law*, trans. H. J. Paton, Hutchinson 1948, p. 91).

But this is not the only formula in *Consciencism* that is reminiscent of Kant. The well-known sentence with which chapter 4 opens: 'Practice without theory is blind; theory without practice is empty' (p. 78) obviously refers to Kant's celebrated formula: 'Concepts without intuitions are empty; intuitions without concepts are blind.'

31 This theme is developed in an earlier work: *I Speak of Freedom: a Statement of African Ideology* (1961). Note that the subtitle uses the phrase 'African Ideology' in the singular: it was 1961, and the use of the singular could still be justified (as could, at another level, the heterogeneous composition of the CPP as a mass organization). African ideology, in the singular, was the ideology of Africa in revolt, of Africa united against foreign domination. It was simply the common aspiration to freedom and dignity, which was rendered overpowering at the height of colonial oppression. But as we have tried to show, the 'African ideology', which was forged in the struggle against oppression, tended to survive the period in which it was historically justified, so as to become a second-order ideology: the ideology *of* African Ideology in the singular, the demand for complete unanimity on all theoretical problems and the premature closure of philosophical and scientific discourse for the sake of a supposedly collective and final system of thought.

32 The theme was developed in official documents of the CPP as early as 1949 (see above, n. 11) and later in the *Autobiography* (1957) and *Africa Must Unite* (1963; see especially ch. 14), etc.

33 *Consciencism* (1970), p. 75.

34 ibid., p. 52.

35 This does not mean, of course, that they are self-determining. We are firmly convinced that they are always determined in the last instance by the class to which we belong. The autonomy at stake here is that of a certain *type of discourse* (political discourse) in relation to another *type of discourse* (metaphysical discourse), whatever their respective *origins* may be, even if we accept that these origins partly coincide and that metaphysical discourse is also conditioned by class membership.

36 For a more extended treatment of this topic, see my article 'The myth of spontaneous philosophy', *Cahiers philosophiques africains*, no. 1, Lubumbashi (1972). I owe the idea of philosophy as the theory of science, or the theory of theoretical practice, principally to Louis Althusser (though he would probably now deprecate the use I make of it). Cf. L. Althusser, *For Marx*: 'From *Capital* to Marx's Philosophy' and 'The Object of *Capital*' in *Reading Capital* (New Left Books 1970). Unfortunately, one of the most remarkable texts in this field remains unpublished: the Fifth Lecture of the *Philosophy Course for Scientists* organized by Althusser and a few other comrades at the Ecole Normale Supérieure in 1967–8. The book later published, *Philosophie et philosophie spontanée des savants* (Paris: Maspero 1974), contains only a partial record of this lesson – and for obvious reasons! Recently Althusser has laid more emphasis on politics (largely because of his great familiarity with the works of Lenin), so that he now defines philosophy as the 'class struggle in the realm of theory'. Cf. 'Lenin and Philosophy' (1968), in *Lenin and Philosophy and Other Essays* (New Left Books 1971) and especially *Essays in Self-Criticism* (1974) (New Left Books 1976). He now regards his previous definitions (as well as his previous use and abuse of the word 'epistemology') as fraught with 'theoreticism', and 'speculative rationalism'.

This will be sweet music to the ears of modish ideologues on this side of the Mediterranean. Even Althusser, they will say, has recognized his error; so why should *we* waste time on this obsolete definition? But this is too precipitate: first, we do not need to *follow* Althusser, in the way our official ideologues *follow* the regime in power, sinking to the level of servile and irresponsible puppets. Secondly, we cannot regard the development of an author as pure anecdote. We must understand and assess the reasons for the development (and these are very strong in Althusser), as well as the *problems* which elicited this adjustment of concepts and what remains of the original positions after the revision. For present purposes it should suffice to say that if indeed philosophy is class struggle, it is specifically class struggle *in theory*. With all due respect to our official ideologues, philosophy does not merge with ideology any more than algebra or linguistics do, although any discourse within such a discipline is bound to convey some ideology. Philosophy can no more be reduced to a tissue of slogans or to pedantic propaganda than can mathematics or physics. It is a specific kind of *labour*, comparable with any other discipline. And, like them, it demands training and methodological rigour, which unfortunately tend to be scorned by our ideologues.

8 True and false pluralism

1 I am adopting the conventional landmark of the publication of Malinowski's classic work *Argonauts of the Western Pacific* in London in 1922. But in fact the idea of a plurality of cultures is really much older than this, and was widely debated, for instance, in 1911 at the first Universal Congress of Races in London (cf. Gérard Leclerc, *Anthropologie et colonialisme*, Paris 1972, p. 83).

2 Bronislaw Malinowski, 'The rationalization of anthropology and administration', *Africa* (journal of the International Institute of African Languages and Culture), vol. 3, no. 4 (1930), pp. 405–30. The quotation is on pp. 405–6.

3 See in particular G. Charbonnier, *Entretiens avec Lévi-Strauss* (Paris 1961), pp. 51–65.

4 Aimé Césaire, *Cahier d'un retour au pays natal* (Paris: Présence Africaine 1956), pp. 71–2.

5 It is common to credit Senghor with the invention of the word 'negritude'. But he himself is ready to deny it. Cf. the Introduction of *Liberté I. Négritude et humanisme* (Paris: Seuil 1964): 'We merely studied it [negro-African civilization] and gave it the name of negritude. I say "we", but I must not forget to render unto Césaire that which is Césaire's. It was he who invented the word in the years 1932–1934' (p. 8).

   The stanza quoted is in fact the second place where the word 'negritude' occurs in the *Cahier*. However, the earlier use of the word is not very enlightening. It is in a stanza in which, in the course of summarizing his historical heritage, Césaire mentions 'Haiti where negritude stood on its own feet for the first time' (p. 44). The word seems to be used simply to denote the black race, without any evaluative overtones. However, in the long stanza I have quoted, it is clearly used to designate a set of virtues connected with blacks.

6 The poem was first published in the twentieth and last number of a review entitled *Volontés*, Paris (August 1939). It later appeared in a bilingual edition, with a Spanish translation, in Cuba in 1944. It was prefaced by André Breton ('Martinique, charmeuse de serpents') in a new edition by Bordas (Paris 1947), and reissued by Editions Présence Africaine.

7 Leclerc, *Anthropologie et colonialisme*.

8 Leclerc attempts a sort of defence of this 'mechanistic vocabulary which may perhaps be a mockery of rigour and "science", but which was at least intended to reduce speculation and ideology' (p. 89).

9 See my own short work entitled *Libertés; contribution à la révolution dahoméenne* (Cotonou: Editions Renaissance 1973), esp. pp. 41–52, 'Science et révolution'.

10   Aimé Césaire, *Lettre à Maurice Thorez* (Paris: Présence Africaine 1956). This is Césaire's letter of resignation from the French Communist Party.

As for the 'Copernican' revolution, this was, of course, Kant's word for the inversion of the natural hypothesis according to which the human mind acquires knowledge by adjusting itself to the order of things. Kant himself argued that in fact things accommodate themselves to the *a priori* structure of the human mind and therefore cannot be known except as phenomena. There was an analogy between this inversion and the Copernican revolution in astronomy, i.e. the replacement of the classic geocentric hypothesis by the heliocentric hypothesis. Césaire was calling for an analogous revolution in politics. I hope I will be excused a further long quotation:

> I hope I have said enough to make it clear that I am abandoning neither Marxism nor communism but only the use which some people have made of them, which I deplore. I wish to see Marxism and communism serving the black peoples, not the black peoples serving Marxism and communism. The doctrine and the movement should exist for the sake of the people, not the people for the good of the doctrine and the movement. And, of course, this principle does not apply only to communists. And if I were a Christian or a Muslim, I would say the same thing: every doctrine is worthless unless it is rethought by and for us and adapted to our own needs. . . . This is why we must insist upon a veritable Copernican revolution in order to break the European habit, which is deeply rooted in every party and group from extreme right to extreme left, of acting on our behalf – of deciding for us, thinking for us and, in short, denying us the right of initiative which I have already mentioned – the right, in fact, to personality.

Postscript

1   The problem is substantially the same when these 'ancestors' are replaced by Marx or Lenin, who then function as mere alibis too.

2   M. Towa, *Essai sur la problématique philosophique dans l'Afrique actuelle* (Yaoundé: Editions Clé 1971).

3   ibid., p. 23.

4   ibid., p. 53.

5   ibid., p. 52.

6   ibid., p. 59.

7   ibid., p. 35.

8   ibid., pp. 9–10.

9   ibid., p. 53.

10   ibid.

11   ibid., p. 55.

12   ibid., p. 75.

13   G. Elwert, *Wirtschaft und Herrschaft von 'Dâxome' (Dahomey) im 18.*

Jahrhundert (Economy and Domination in Dahomey in the 18th Century) (Munich: Kommissionsverlag Klaus Renner 1973).

14　B. Fitch and M. Oppenheimer, 'Ghana: end of an illusion', *Monthly Review*, vol. XVIII, no. 3, Special Issue (July–August 1966).

Index

Abraham, William, 44, 59, 115, 117
acculturation, 164–5, 166
Adotevi, Stanislas Spero, 24, 65
African philosophy: as ethnophilosophy, 38, 52–3, 75–6; as Europe directed, 45, 48, 50, 67; bibliography, 185n; definition, 8, 33, 62–6, 101, 103, 105, 176; French speaking versus English speaking, 29; inseparable from science, 98, 106; myth of, 44, 51, 56; writing and, 106
African unity, problem of in Nkrumah, 138
Africanization, 167–8
Althusser, Louis, 28, 91, 94–5, 97, 202–3n, 214n
Amo, Anton-Wilhelm, 66, 111–30
Aristotle, 39, 41, 88, 119, 189n
Ayer, A. J., 30

Bachelard, Gaston, 76, 78, 90, 96, 100
Bantu philosophy, 16–17, 34–44 *passim*, 49; *see also* Tempels
Bodunrin, Peter, 11, 29

Césaire, Aimé, 37, 57, 158–9, 162, 168, 216n; *see also* negritude
class struggle *see* Nkrumah
colonialism, 17, 134, 135, 143, 150, 163

consciencism, 134, 142–55, 182; *see also* Nkrumah
critical reflection, 104–6
cultural relativity, 177; in anthropology, 14, 163; in philosophy, 20
culturalism, 160, 162–4

Derrida, Jacques, 102–3, 149
Descartes, Réné, 30, 89, 90, 126, 153
Dieterlen, Germaine, 15, 58
Diop, Cheik Anta, 21–3, 100

Eboussi-Boulaga, Fabien, 45, 57, 65, 105, 173, 190n
Elwert, Georg, 179
Engels, Friedrich, 91–5, 180
ethnology, 61, 148, 163, 165, 173, 187n; complicity with nationalism, 160, 164
ethnophilosophy, 42, 45, 48, 61, 178; critique of, 21, 25, 27, 53, 57, 62, 79, 171–2, 176, 182; definition, 34; examples, 58–9
European ethnocentrism, 11, 12, 156; break with, 17, 22

Fanon, Frantz, 23–4
Fitch, Bob, 181

Gandhi, Mahatma, 135, 146
Gödel, Kurt, 75
Griaule, Marcel, 15, 58, 77, 78, 81

Hegel, G. W. F., 11, 73, 74, 90, 93, 94, 96, 97
Herskovits, Melville, 14, 159
history, 71–2, 84, 94–7; Marxist, 96; of philosophy, 86–97
Hountondji, Paulin, 25, 26; criticism of, 27–30
Hume, David, 86–7, 126
Husserl, Edmund, 75, 84, 89

ideology, 92, 148–9, 175; colonial, 11, 14, 17, 24, 37; practical, 177–8
Ikoku, Samuel, 133, 141
imperialism, 135, 164, 172, 181

Kagamé, Alexis, 20, 39–43, 48, 58, 62, 188n; relation to Tempels, 39–42, 51
Kant, Immanuel, 62, 65, 84–90, 128, 153

Leclerc, Gérald, 17, 164–5
Lenin, V. I., 142, 180
Lévi-Strauss, Claude, 15, 104, 156, 157
Lévy-Bruhl, Lucien, 18, 34, 43, 77, 80, 156, 157, 163; ethnocentrism of, 12–15
Locke, John, 88

Malinowski, Bronislaw, 157, 159
Marx, Karl, 52, 84, 91–6, 136, 148, 149, 156, 180, 183
Marxism, 69, 92–3, 141, 179, 181, 183
materialism, 152–3, 176
Mulago, Vincent, 44, 48, 58

negritude, 18–19, 20, 24, 59, 65, 128, 158, 162, 172, 194n, 215n; *see also* Césaire, Senghor
Nkrumah, Kwame, 59, 64, 112, 131–40, 141–55 *passim*, 167, 174, 179–89; class struggle in, 135–8,

143, 147, 150, 152; communalism, 136, 144–5; consciencism, 134, 142–55, 182; historical reading of, 133, 141; life, 207n; philosophy and ideology in, 147–9; socialism of, 133, 134, 136, 144–5, 153; system of, 134–9; violence in, 135, 137
Nkrumaism, 133–40, 179; rightish nature of, 133, 141, 180
Nyerere, Julius, 137

Obenga, Theophile, 100
Odera, Henry Oruka, 65, 105
Ogotemmeli, 77–8, 81, 83; *see also* Griaule
Oppenheimer, Mary, 181

philosophical revolutions, 84–90; and scientific revolutions, 98–100
philosophy, 7–8, 106, 171, 191n; as history, 71–3, 83–4; as politics, 26, 174–5; collective, 38, 39, 43, 44, 55, 60, 76, 77, 103, 149; definition, 47, 60, 66, 174–5; distinguished from poetry, 82–3; in Nkrumah, 148–9
Plato, 7, 52, 72, 73, 88, 198–9n
pluralism, 18, 149, 151, 155, 156, 164–6, 168
politics, 26, 33, 46, 167, 174, 183
primitive mentality, 12–13, 77; attack on, 15, 34; positive sense of, 19; *see also* Lévy-Bruhl
primitive unanimity, 60–1, 154, 165, 170, 176

Radin, Paul, 76, 79–81
Ricoeur, Paul, 189n

science, 54, 67, 73, 97, 155, 172; philosophy as, 47, 67, 175
scientific revolutions, 98–100

Senghor, Léopold Sédar, 18–19, 23, 59, 137, 159–60; critics, 21, 24; *see also* negritude

socialism, 133, 134, 136, 144–5, 153; *see also* Nkrumah

Socrates, 106, 198n

Spencer, Herbert, 12

Spinoza, 73, 74

system, 71–5; in Nkrumah, 134–9

Tempels, Placide, 15–17, 19, 20, 34–7, 48–9, 56–7, 62, 76, 77, 105, 173; criticism by Césaire, 37; relation to Kagamé, 39–42, 51

Towa, Marcien, 25, 65, 105, 171–4

truth, 72–3, 74

unanimism, 62, 174, 182; *see also* ethnophilosophy; primitive unanimity

universities, 167

violence: in Fanon, 24; in Nkrumah, 135–7

Wiredu, Kwasi, 29, 65

Wolff, Christian, 89, 116–18 *passim*

writing, 101, 102–5

PAULIN J. HOUNTONDJI

is Professor of Philosophy at the National University of Benin, Cotonou. His works include numerous articles on philosophy, the anthropology of knowledge, the politics of science, and African politics. He is also editor of and contributor to *Philosophical Research in Africa: A Bibliographic Survey* (1987 and 1988) and *Endogenous Knowledge: Research Trails* (1994). Hountondji is former Minister of Culture and Communication and Special Adviser to the Head of the State of Benin.